The
Writing Requirements
for Graduate Degrees

Prentice-Hall International, Inc., *London*
Prentice-Hall of Australia, Pty., *Sydney*
Prentice-Hall of Canada, Ltd., *Toronto*
Prentice-Hall France, S.A.R.L., *Paris*
Prentice-Hall of India (Private) Limited, *New Delhi*
Prentice-Hall of Japan, Inc., *Tokyo*
Prentice-Hall De Mexico, S.A., *Mexico City*

The
Writing Requirements
for Graduate Degrees

PAUL E. KOEFOD
University of Florida

PRENTICE-HALL, INC., *Englewood Cliffs, N. J.*

To Janey

Any man who has the genuine impulse of the teacher will be more anxious to survive in his books than in the flesh.

BERTRAND RUSSELL

My role, I know, is not to transform the world, nor man: for that I have not virtue enough, nor clear-sightedness. But it consists, perhaps, in serving, where I can, those few values without which a world, even transformed, is not worth living in, without which a man, even new, would not be worthy of respect.

ALBERT CAMUS

The mission [of American teachers and scholars] is the same as that of scholars anywhere . . . to keep the tradition of disinterested learning alive; to add to the knowledge possessed by the race; to keep some solid, just, and circumspect record of the past; and to use what knowledge, skill, and critical intelligence exists for the improvement of the human estate.

CHARLES FRANKEL

Foreword

During the present century undergraduate student enrollments have increased 15 fold (238,000 to 3,600,000) but the number of graduate students has been multiplied by 50 (6,000 to 300,000). Despite the fact that the graduate school population has expanded three and one-third times faster than the undergraduates, the gap between the supply and the demand for advanced degrees is wider than ever before.

This paradoxical situation derives from (1) the population explosion which, combined with other factors, doubled in 20 years the number of college students to be taught; (2) the swelling tide of interest in science and technology, which have captured the imaginations of men since the discovery of atomic fission and the excursions into outer space; and (3) the overwhelming and unprecedented faith of business, industry, and government in research as a means of progress which, since Sputnik I, has involved considerations of national defense.

These three new and basic factors account for the incredible demand for advanced graduate work. Both the universities and the general public have been caught off guard. This has resulted in great concern, both inside and outside university circles, over the effectiveness of graduate schools. This has led to a probing of all aspects of graduate education. Why is the attrition rate in graduate schools so high? Why does it require on the average seven to twelve years to reach the doctorate after securing the bachelor's degree? Why is there not better articulation between undergraduate and graduate work? Why is the graduate school, the most important segment of the university, presided over by a dean who has no authority and manned by a part-time teaching staff? Why is there such great uncertainty and inconsistency within graduate schools in the matter of requirements? What is meant by the pathology of graduate education? When professors of good standing describe some graduate school practices as "disgraceful," why are these practices not corrected? These and many other questions have been raised and will probably continue to be raised until some basic reforms are effected.

The vast literature on graduate education—brochures, papers, articles, and books—and the great variety of conferences, symposia, and debates concerned with the subject attest the wide public interest and deep concern of laymen as well as educators. This may raise the question whether another volume is needed.

One has only to read a single chapter of Professor Koefod's *The Writing Requirements for Graduate Degrees* to see that his focus is different from that of other authors and speakers on the subject. He has discovered a gap in the literature and discussions and proceeds to fill it in. He does not attempt to analyze and comment on the global problems of graduate deans, graduate faculties, graduate schools, articulation of graduate and undergraduate programs, recruitment, etc. His concern is about the graduate student who, after all, is the central figure of the graduate education enterprise. His welfare and progress constitute the measure of the success of that enterprise.

The author believes that a chief obstacle to the graduate student's success is his lack of understanding of the nature of the written work required whether it be a report, an essay, a thesis or a dissertation. A second handicap is that he has little or no knowledge of the standard of performance expected or required of him. Frequently, the faculty adviser himself is not clear on either of these points and hence cannot be an effective mentor. These two problems are effectively dealt with at length in Part I. In Part II he describes the environment and climate of the graduate academe.

In Part I Professor Koefod emphasizes three points: (1) some intellectual achievement is a prerequisite to effective writing; (2) graduate students must be capable of independent intellectual effort and must exercise that talent if they are to succeed; and (3) knowledge of the difference between the nature and purpose of the thesis and dissertation is essential to an effective performance whatever the form of the writing may be. Since the writing requirements are the chief stumbling block to achieving the degree, the nature and signifi- cance of these requirements are fundamental to success.

The thorough discussion of these matters in Part I should prove a most valuable guide to graduate students. It serves as an orientation, a frame of reference, a perspective, in the consideration of the nature and meaning of the writing requirements. It should be useful to the adviser as well as to the student. Frequently professors do not visu- alize clearly the distinction between the thesis and the dissertation and therefore fail to give proper guidance. Professor Koefod's discus- sion of these matters should at least provide a common basis of think- ing for the student and his counselor. It should relieve the counselor of much routine guidance work.

In Part II Professor Koefod essays a delicate task, that of inform- ing the student of some of the shortcomings of graduate academe without discouraging him too much. He believes that some knowledge of faculty foibles and some understanding of possible pitfalls along the path to the Ph.D. would be helpful to the novice in finding his way to his goal. While the author is impatient with the needless un- certainties accompanying the pursuit of the Ph.D., he believes the student, who is the victim, should know "the facts of life" in order that he might the better cope with them. It is conceivable that it will save many students from frustration. It is also possible that the pro- fessor who has read *The Writing Requirements* might be influenced to "cease and desist" from those unwarranted practices which are de- scribed so vividly in this volume.

In conclusion it may be useful to comment on the author's edu- cational philosophy and the rationale of the volume. Such comments, though necessarily brief, may make clearer the significance of his concerns and the importance of his suggestions made to graduate stu- dents and faculties, designed to improve both the environment and the products of graduate schools.

The motivation behind this volume is the conviction that the basic functions of graduate education are enhancement of intellectual capital and improvement of human capacity for creativity, and that bad pedagogy and adverse academic conditions often militate against the achievement of optimum results. The lag between the B.A. and Ph.D., the attrition rate, absence or inadequacy of recruitment prac- tices, and the laissez-faire attitude of faculties are live issues. He laments that "more thought seems to be given to monetary subsidization of academic boondoggling than to eradication of basic academic difficulties."

Studies of graduate education have overlooked the interests and difficulties of graduate students and their supervisory committees. Professor Koefod considers it a major fault of graduate councils and deans and a disadvantage to graduate education, that supervisory committees often are forced to make policies because they are not made elsewhere. This underlies the indefiniteness of requirements and inconsistency as to performance standards and treatment of graduate candidates. It represents a built-in negation of a solution.

Declining faculty-student ratios are functions of growing enrollments and the paucity of Ph.D. recipients. This condition calls for simplification of student guidance procedures and facilitation of student independence. Growth of graduate supervisory committee loads will require improvement of student capacity to work alone. Increasingly it will require committee concentration on evaluation of student theses and dissertations. Supervisory committees will have to be emancipated from miscellany and graduate students from academic uncertainties if individual and social interests are to be served effectively by graduate schools.

It becomes increasingly clear that identification of talent must be made early, that the idea of university scholarship including independent study, research, and writing should be introduced at the junior year and that the upper two years of undergraduate work should be truly preparatory to research and graduate education which, in many universities, is not true today. The experiment of combining the upper two years of college with the first year of graduate work in what is styled A Three-Year Master's Program is now in progress in 30 odd institutions. This may offer some help in the solution of a variety of graduate education problems. If the floundering normally characteristic of the first year of graduate work could be experienced in the upper two years of college, it would be a great gain. This is reported to have taken place in some of the institutions now participating in the new Three-Year Plan.

Oliver C. Carmichael

Preface

Free in mind must be he who desires to have understanding.
RHETICUS

Reason never has failed men.
WILLIAM ALLEN WHITE

This book is an outgrowth of attempts to help graduate students understand the writing requirements for advanced degrees. Its evolution and development have been in response to their questions and expressed needs. Its roots lie in their problems and their point of view. It has been designed with their aid to meet their needs.

Graduate students confront a dearth of written guidance as to the essential nature, substance, and value of the kind of writing they must do in fulfillment of degree requirements. They need to know far more about theses and dissertations than most college catalogues tell them.

The purpose of this book is to make clear the concepts of thesis and dissertation as essays based on intellectual achievements in criticism, inquiry, and understanding. The thesis and dissertational essays suitably fulfill the writing requirements for all fields of learning. Whether they must do so is a policy question which lies outside the scope of this book. The premise that they can do so is sufficient for it. Subject matter may be delimited by fields, but learned argument is not. This book takes the classical, liberal, and ideal points of view, which simplifies somewhat the problem of attaining clarity. Without judging other means of fulfilling writing requirements, it is concerned with what theses and dissertations ideally and properly are.

Two aspects of the writing requirements for graduate degrees are treated in order to provide students with all-around help for their intellectual tasks. The first part of the book attempts substantive clarification of the writing requirements which are listed in most graduate school catalogues. The second part describes and attempts to explain the general academic environment in which these requirements normally are met. Part I is didactic, and Part II is an informational complement to it. Appendices at the end of the book supplement both parts.

Besides providing something of value for students, it is hoped that this book may prove useful to graduate faculties by relieving advisers of their burden of repetitious guidance detail. Student use of it could conserve faculty energy and time for more interesting professorial concerns. By aiding both faculty and students, it is hoped that this book may make some modest contribution to the enhancement of graduate education.

This book is only in part a function of my own experiences and observations of graduate teaching in two universities. The study has been far broader than that, both spatially and in time. Ideas and manuscript drafts have been discussed with graduate faculty members and graduate students of a dozen institutions in the eastern half of the United States. Visiting foreign faculty and graduate students have contributed their criticisms and ideas to it. Perhaps in the course of time, additional readers will be kind enough to contribute their thoughts on the topics covered and on the examples employed to illustrate them. Suggestions for model theses and dissertations will be especially appreciated.

This book is the outcome of a part-time labor of love which has reached fulfillment slowly. Its five-year fruitional process has provided many opportunities for discussion of its topics. My thanks are due the many graduate students, colleagues, and academic friends who have given me the benefit of their questions, views, ideas, and encouragement. Because of limitations of space, only three of these shall be specified.

My especial gratitude is due Dr. Oliver C. Carmichael, former President of the Carnegie Foundation for the Advancement of Teaching, for his foreword to this volume, and for his generous interest in and encouragement concerning it. Special thanks also are due Professor Maurice A. Unger, now of the University of Colorado, and Mr. Peter Fannon, of Prentice-Hall, for their help and suggestions respecting matters of style and organization.

These and all other friendly contributors should not be repaid for their generosity by being held in any way responsible for such errors of fact or interpretation as may appear. Responsibility for my formulations must rest with me.

P. E. K.
July, 1963

Table of Contents

PART ONE

The Writing Requirements

Overture to
the Writing Requirements

*The longer you are in the presence of a difficulty, the less
likely you are to solve it.*

NICOLLE

Think like a man of action and act like a man of thought.

HENRY BERGSON

Too many attempts to fulfill writing requirements for graduate degrees begin in bewilderment, and too few in hope. It seems useful, therefore, to try to provide a means whereby graduate candidates may begin their thesis and dissertational essay projects in hope and consummate them with success.

American graduate education is basically good education. This has been well established on the basis of both direct and comparative studies of the subject. The point is well taken, however, that graduate education is better in some institutions and fields than in others. It is often better in coursework requirements than it is with respect to the writing requirements for graduate degrees.

Studies of graduate education have tended to focus on classroom, laboratory, and library facilities, on curricula, on teaching, or on student success and career achievements. Study of the writing requirements for graduate degrees has been far less diligently pursued. As graduate schools have increased in number and size, and as their curricula have proliferated, the state of the writing requirements has become increasingly confused.

The purposes and functions of many graduate schools are unclear and at issue. Competition of conflicting ideas about their roles and goals must be expected to continue for some time. As long as this contest of interests lasts, graduate students will have to cope with confusion of educational ideas. Knowing the reasons for this academic uncertainty can help students attain at least approximate poise for their endeavors. Navigational aids are more important for sailing stormy seas than calm ones.

Graduate students face present realities, not future possibilities. Their interest and immediate task, frequently in a climate of uncertainty, is to qualify for one or another advanced degree. They can do this by fulfilling two distinct but usually interrelated sets of requirements, which normally are dealt with in succession. Upon completion of the first requirement, most graduate students are cut more or less adrift academically and must fulfill the second on their own.

The first requirement to be met is generally familiar and readily understood. It is the satisfactory completion of a certain amount of specified coursework. Once a student's curricular program has been decided upon, completion becomes largely a matter of time. For most graduate students, their prescribed coursework is complete, or nearly so, before they attempt fulfillment of their second requirement.

The second requirement for a graduate degree differs in kind from the first. It consists of a project of more or less independent inquiry and related research, together with a derivative in the form of an essay. The former is a vital prerequisite to the latter, which may be a thesis or a dissertation. The fact that a thesis or dissertation is named as the requirement apparently obscures for many unperceptive students the need for an original intellectual achievement on which to base it. Candidates are certified for their degrees when their writing requirements have been satisfactorily met.

These terminal requirements are new and unfamiliar to most beginning graduate students. Few have had previous experience with them. Some of the better liberal arts colleges require senior theses or dissertations, but most undergraduate schools do not. Although the thesis or dissertational essay requirement is stated in graduate catalogues and by graduate faculty advisors, it seldom is further clarified or defined. Herein lies the beginning of academic difficulty for many graduate students. Their capstone degree requirement is neither familiar to them nor made readily understandable.

Throughout the years, graduate schools of the Western world have established the custom that, as a test of intellectual and professional competence, a candidate for a graduate degree must submit an original essay based on his own inquiry and research. When completed, this must be defended before a group of professors representing the university. Some schools require that the writing and content be "publishable," or "of publishable quality." This writing, as traditionally and explicitly required, has been in the form of theses or dissertations.

When universities and their faculties were few and their curricula limited, the traditional forms of these required essays were determining. But the old academic certainty has been undone by the failure of thinking about the writing requirements to keep pace with the changes resulting from proliferation of curricula and graduate schools.

Especially since World War I, professions and quasi-professions, technical services and vocations have gained access to graduate schooling. Fundamental learning and basic science have represented decreasing proportions of graduate studies at least during the last fifty years. Meanwhile, graduate degrees have become increasingly available for applied studies as graduate schooling has grown as a basis for professional, technical, and vocational careers.

Together with these changes, a growing variety of work has been submitted under the thesis and dissertation labels to meet writing requirements. Various kinds of writing are openly offered or furtively insinuated under these distinguished labels by those who have found ways to get around explicit graduate school requirements. Many of the professionally-oriented faculty assert that research reports satisfy writing requirements; especially do some chemists and physicists who lean toward industrial research. Even within the liberal arts college, opinion is divided. In the humanities some suggest that a published novel, play, biography, or symphony will do.

This diversity of opinion frequently has produced situations in which the willfulness of some professors has been abetted by the carelessness or indifference of others to the point where even simple reporting has been permitted to satisfy writing requirements. When this has occurred, it has worked to the disadvantage of student scholarship and permitted many unqualified candidates to obtain advanced degrees. The practice is intellectually and morally false and academically unsound. It works against the important graduate school functions of locating and enhancing intellectual capital, and of criticizing and extending knowledge.

Graduate schools decide for themselves what requirements must be met for the degrees they award. This individualistic practice is subject to some restraint because of periodic review of school standards by accrediting agencies. But there are many ways of fulfilling and testing the fulfillment of intellectual commitments; and the basic need is not to confuse tests of artistic or technical ability with those of intellectual competence. Writing requirements can take any appropriate form relevant to a candidate's field of study or career expectancies. In some instances they may be omitted; many schools allow additional coursework plus short research reports to meet Master's degree requirements. The faculty advisory committees in various disciplines occasionally approve a novel or play, an historical sketch, a bibliography, an empirical report, or even a statement of completion of certain types of scientific experiments.[1] Such actions may be contrary to graduate school policy but advisors sometimes can make them stand. The problem of confusion of types of academic tests has been stated. Another problem in this connection is that of finding and applying meaningful performance standards and evaluative criteria so that all students may be treated with fairness and with at least approximately relative equality.

Questions of the proper selection and use of kinds of writing cannot be answered until decisions have been made as to what graduate education and its writing requirements are for. If graduate education is to include artistic and technical training as well as education for intellectual work, the several means of fulfilling writing requirements may have to be carefully segregated along these different lines. Unresolved issues of this nature are bound to appear in so far-flung an educational apparatus characterized by rapid change and growth.[2] Nevertheless, graduate students must be kept in mind. Many

---

[1] For an opinion on descriptions and art works as alternatives to thesis and dissertational essays—and one of the problems involved, expressed at the Ninth Annual Deans' and Directors' Pinebrook Conference, September, 1959, see Preston E. James, "The Dissertation Requirement," *School and Society,* LXXXVIII, No. 2171 (March 26, 1960), 147-48. This question is treated in Chapter Eight.

[2] Students interested in background materials for understanding and insight may wish to read, among other books: Richard J. Storr, *The Beginnings of Graduate Education in America* (Chicago: The University of Chicago Press, 1953); Frederic W. Ness and Benjamin D. James, *Graduate Study in the Liberal Arts College* (Washington, D. C.: Association of American Colleges, 1962), which includes extensive bibliography on this subject and other appendices of value; and James D. Koerner, *The Miseducation of American Teachers* (Boston: Houghton Mifflin Co., 1963), esp. Chap. vi, "Masters and Doctors of Education."

of them are bewildered. Some even are misguided and misled.[3]

It is no help to a student that the terms thesis and dissertation have degenerated to ambiguous labels for vague and uncertain requirements. It is no help to him that all sorts of writing have been lumped under thesis or dissertation labels depending upon degree levels. Confusion of terms has gone so far, since the sprawling growth of graduate education, that in many schools it is customary to say that anything which finds acceptance at the Master's degree level is a thesis; and at the Doctor's a dissertation.

Such changes in usage might be less disadvantageous to students had the relevant concepts of intellectual work, of inquiry and discoursive writing remained clear. They also might have been less harmful had the several kinds of education which have attained graduate status been kept at least conceptually separate. Then intellectual achievements in inquiry could be demonstrated and validated in one or the other sort of academic essay. But the practice of unofficial substitution of other kinds of writing for the thesis and dissertational essays has obscured both their nature and the kind of work which must underlie and precede them. This difficulty could have been avoided if the appropriate terms had been used to name and define the non-essay forms of writing which have gained acceptance in some disciplines and in some graduate schools. The thesis and dissertation differ; but they are definite, traditional types of essays. As long as graduate schools affirm in their catalogues— which are their official publications—their intention actually to require theses and dissertations, students should comply by furnishing such essays. In view of what has been happening to the writing requirements, unless a student is fortunate enough to have a wise advisor he may find himself on his own in a maze of confusion.

What a candidate's written work ultimately is called need not be too confusing for him, however, if the generic kinds of writing are distinguished for him when he begins graduate study. If it is administratively useful to blanket both types of essays and other

---

[3] Cf. James, "The Dissertation Requirement," p. 148: "It is important to keep the candidate himself in mind. Some candidates are treated so harshly that, for them, research study in later years is something carefully to be avoided. . . . It is of major importance that the candidate's efforts to identify a problem, to plan and carry out the research, to present the results, and to defend his results among his older professional colleagues should constitute a 'success experience,' and not a passage through purgatory."

kinds of writing by the term thesis at the Master's degree level, and by the term dissertation at the Doctor's level, as a matter of policy, that will be done. But then catalogues, student handbooks, and academic advisors must make clear what kinds of investigative projects are requisite or permitted as means of meeting degree requirements along academic lines and for each degree level. They also would have to say where essays will be required, and where and under what conditions other forms of writing may serve under their proper titles in fulfillment of degree requirements. The various approaches to knowledge, especially as they vary by fields, disciplines, and interests, can be clarified and taught. It might be found helpful, as well, to recognize different kinds of academic achievement with a set of degrees which are more systematically differentiating than the ones now in use.

Perhaps the root problem is to find ways to deal with the nature of investigative projects at intellectual levels of scholarship. Intellectual work takes place in the mind. Its products are researchable hypotheses and validated ideas which may be stated as theories and theorems. Much will be said of this in the chapters which follow. If projects of inquiry and research are significantly selected and well handled, long steps have been taken toward the essays which eventuate from having something important to say.

The differentiation made between theses and dissertations in this book is undertaken to clarify these academic requirements on the basis of their different concepts and functions. One objective is to differentiate between the investigative projects which underlie the thesis and dissertational essays and the essays themselves. Another objective is to differentiate the wide variety of approaches to knowledge, the variety of methods which may be used in these ventures, and the different sorts of results which may be obtained. In particular, it has seemed vital to differentiate between theses and dissertations in order to clarify them as essays which require and involve different orders of intellectual purpose and achievement.

This should not be taken to imply mere insistence on word usage. Concept usage is involved because of the variety of kinds of learning which has emerged at the graduate level. Words change in use, but surely it is not vital for policy purposes to call both academic essays theses at one level and dissertations at another. It may be true that the human mind rebels at accuracy, but clear conceptual and functional understanding calls for reasonable word usage. Casual misuse of proper names can influence the naïve and unwary where underlying concepts are not well understood. Because lax academic usage has reduced the established names of the academic essays to ambiguity in many quarters, footnotes and quotations in this text are provided to show what established thinking on theses and dissertations is. Representative model theses and dissertations are listed in Appendices G and H.

The kinds of ideation and writing called for by graduate schools can and should be the same for a given level of attainment in all academic fields. As qualitative concepts, they should be the same for all graduate schools. Intellectual scholarship is what it is no matter where encountered. It is a duty and a responsibility of graduate students and faculty alike to consider carefully and thoughtfully what intellectual scholarship is and implies, and to work according to the standards it imposes. Its quality needs to be reflected in the essays submitted to fulfill writing requirements wherever they are met. This is the meaning of "a community of scholars."

The responsibility of making the writing requirements conceptually clear to graduate students is not easy to fulfill. The nature of these requirements is an unresolved issue; and graduate faculties themselves are not in general agreement either as to what they are or what they are for. Few faculty members can remember, and fewer seem to have been taught, the reasons for and the functional significance of the thesis and dissertational essays. The depth of this difficulty is emphasized by the facts that the historic role of graduate schools is education for intellectual work, and that thesis and dissertational essays provide tests for and demonstrations of intellectual capacity. Tests of technical proficiency or of artistic creativity do not serve these particular purposes.

Much hinges on the understanding of the writing requirements. Students who are clear about them go ahead effectively. They attain their degrees and begin their careers more or less expeditiously. Meanwhile, they relieve their faculty advisors of much burdensome guidance detail, thus conserving the latters' time and energy for more significant matters.

Investigation of the writing requirement controversy reveals that the nature and functions of the writing requirements have received relatively little direct or systematic study and thought. Such recent writing as there is on the subject is mainly casual, taking the form of a sentence here and there. Writing requirement guidance for students turns on mechanics rather than on substance. It describes procedures for data collection and card notation, and techniques of putting results on paper. Curiously enough, it says little or nothing about the general methods of scholarship or science, and still less about the essay and good writing style. Yet the recognized proper function of a graduate school is education for intellectual work; and studies at any sub-intellectual level of scholarship are not properly graduate studies. The thesis and dissertational essay concepts and their intellectual significance need to be supplied. Until they are, there will be much error and more vagueness than reality about the writing requirements.

This is not said to carp or cavil against the system of graduate education. The system is basically sound and attaining excellence. It will not be undone because the nature of a degree requirement is at issue. This is a temporary problem which is capable of rational resolution. But students need to understand why, in so many places and respects, once clear requirements have become so indefinite. They are entitled to know the reasons for their problems of performance under conditions of uncertainty.

There is no intention here to overdraw the matter. Neither does this statement presage a plea for reform. However, it does recognize that the time may have come to assert the students' interest and their point of view. It recognizes also that administrators and faculty councils, who long have had their say on policy, are beginning to take hard looks at reasons for writing requirements as they are related to educational purposes and goals. They are beginning to recognize that clean-cut direction is not easily provided students by faculty advisory groups which are unagreed and undecided as to what the writing requirements are or are about. Students need more definite and explicit guidance than most of them have been receiving. The good work done on these counts in some schools and departments could advantageously be generalized to include the rest.

More has been written and said on the purposes served by the academic essay requirements than on their definition; nevertheless, discussion of purposes has been so general, platitudinous, and offhand as to be quite unhelpful. Such as it is, it has in the main reflected the policy problems of deans rather than the qualification problems of graduate students. The gap between the policy and qualification levels suggests that the distinction reflects the "P's and

Q's" of a hard moral matter. Academic public relations might well give place to academic human relations.

Adequate theses and dissertations reflect a certain competence in the intellectual work of inquiry and problem-solving, and in the technical work of research. Moreover, they reflect a certain competence in the intellectual skill of logical argument or discourse, and in the technical skill of putting ideas on paper. Artistry also is involved in the expression of ideas which is called style. Importantly also, the academic essays provide graduate students the opportunity, and a push if need be, to rise on their own above the empirical levels of scholarship to those of intellectual scholarship.[4]

Graduate students must rise above the world of the directly observable to the realm of the indirectly, or mentally, perceivable if they are to become learned. Here is where the problems of pure science are analyzed and solved. This is what Einstein did as a young man, and Newton before him. To establish his own claim to intellectual competence, a graduate student must, in an essay, validate by means of logical argument an intellectual achievement of his own. Such achievement may be a solution to a problem, the answer to a penetrating question, the resolution of a significant issue, eradication of a basic doubt, or a meaningful criticism or refinement. An effective thesis or dissertation is evidence of intellectual and professional maturity. It also serves the faculty as a test of a student's level of attainment in these respects.

One of the better statements on this subject has been made by Dean Blegen of the University of Minnesota Graduate School. He credits the doctoral essay with three distinctive educational benefits:

1. It provides training in the organization and correlation of significant facts and ideas;
2. It gives the student a broad experience in writing as an example

---

[4] Ralph Waldo Emerson referred to the empirical and intellectual modes of knowing in his Phi Beta Kappa lecture at Harvard University in 1837. He affirmed that the latter counts for more than the former. This subject is treated more extensively in Chapter Two. Meanwhile, cf. note 48, p. 41. Emerson's Phi Beta Kappa lecture was published under the title, "The American Scholar," but in England as "Man Thinking." Cf. *Man Thinking: Representative Phi Beta Kappa Orations 1915-1959*, ed. William T. Hastings (Ithaca, N. Y.: Cornell University Press, 1962).

of a type of communication essential to effective college teaching;
3. It represents a unique experience in independent investigation
under the mastery of the student himself without arbitrary limitations of time.[5]

These educational benefits are available to the Master's degree
candidate as much as to the Doctor's. Rightly administered, the
writing requirements provide consummate training not only in the
empirical and inductive but especially in the abstract, conceptual,
model-building, analytical, deductive, and synthetic aspects of learning and scientific investigation. Knowledge is derived and clarified
through criticism, inquiry, research, and discussion. Student as well
as faculty opportunities for scholarly conjecture and disputation are
justified by the idea that they yield respect for responsible thought
as a source of knowledge.

This prospect is an important basis of academic freedom. The
way is open at the intellectual level of scholarship for all who attain
it to produce new ideas, to test them, and to validate as many as they
can. The opportunities for intellectual originality and creativity are
legion and growing. They take a variety of forms in all fields of
endeavor. Thinkers who try, and who are permitted to try, can make
good with them.

A graduate candidate's thesis or dissertation usually represents
the sum of his school training for the performance of his career
role. Comprehension of what these essays are and imply is fundamental to production of adequate ones. So is understanding of how
to select and carry through their underlying investigative projects.
Realization of the educational purposes of the writing requirements
contributes to the student's appreciation of their values. His awareness of the nature and significance of the thesis and dissertation aids
their effective completion. If they can be approached in the right
way, they provide him lively challenges and exhilarating intellectual
experiences and, finally, access to interesting career possibilities.

The purpose of Part I of this book is to make clear to graduate

---

[5] *The Preparation of College Teachers,* eds. Theodore C. Blegen and Russell
M. Cooper (Washington, D. C.: American Council on Education, July 1950),
pp. 97-98. Quoted in *A Guide to Graduate Study: Programs Leading to the
Ph.D. Degree,* ed. Frederic W. Ness (2d ed.; Washington, D. C.: Association
of American Colleges, 1960), p. 52.

students the nature and significance of their writing requirements. The importance of this purpose may be judged in two lights. First, the need for qualified people with Master's and Doctor's degrees exceeds the supply and is growing. Second, the ratio of professors who have Doctor's degrees to graduate students is declining. In part, this condition represents a taking up of slack from times when graduate students were relatively few. Nevertheless, mounting student-teacher ratios now threaten academic quality. If graduate students are to succeed, they must learn to stand on their own feet in more respects than they now do. The key to their success increasingly will be a capacity to produce theses and dissertations of appropriate kind and quality on the basis of effective independent work. This requires that their guidelines be clear.

Part I includes four chapters. Chapter Two defines and compares thesis and dissertational essays. It also contrasts the nature and significance of the writing for Master's and Doctor's degrees. Chapter Three explains preparation to write by relating the required essays to projects of intellectual inquiry and relevant research, and to skills in methodology and essay writing. Chapter Four explains the concept of performance standards for graduate essayists. It completes the treatment of appraisal criteria begun in Chapter Three and implied in Chapter Two. Finally, Chapter Four sets the stage for treatment of the graduate student's academic writing environment in Part II.

What follows, therefore, is intended to establish three things:

1. A concept of the characteristics, attributes, structure, and organization of the thesis and dissertational essays together with an understanding of the difference between them;

2. A concept of the kinds and necessary qualities of brainwork and research which underlie theses and dissertations; and

3. A concept of the performance standards which must be attained if theses and dissertations are to have sufficient merit to fulfill degree requirements.

It will be seen that many of the examples used to illustrate concepts and definitions, especially in Chapter Two, are drawn from the natural and physical sciences. This is done because the tendency to substitute research reports for essays has grown strong in these fields. Secondly, the examples chosen provide neat portrayals of the intellectual work involved in essay writing, which can be done in these fields as well as elsewhere. No slight to other fields is intended.

In any case, it would be improper to overemphasize the author's field, economics, and the other social sciences and the humanities. The thesis and dissertational essays have universal applicability.

Furthermore, this is a deliberate book. Although its style is essentially exposition rather than argument, the writing is more or less in the dissertational manner. Wit and humor do indeed oil a machine but they provide it no works. Production of a first-rate thesis or dissertation is an important matter which merits careful treatment. Graduate students are in process of becoming able and purposeful adults. They are becoming serious scholars and scientists to whom it is proper to write up. Proceeding from this postulate, certain foreign words have been used to aid conceptual thinking. In view of the foreign language reading requirements for most graduate degrees, this may provide a source of interest. The many footnotes and citations of books and articles are there to draw readers beyond this book into the wide and wonderful world of learning.

Finally, this book takes the position that the writing requirements represent an important segment of graduate education, one of its most pressing problems, and perhaps the main stumbling-block in the way of academic fulfillment. These requirements are closely related to the problem of student attrition but in ways not precisely known. They also are involved in most overly-long and incomplete attempts at qualification for advanced degrees.[6] This relationship deserves careful exploration and study. Until it has been clarified, generalizations based largely on intuitive assessments will have to serve as grounds for thought. Meanwhile, it seems sure that aid from financial subsidies alone provides a poor way out of difficulties imposed on students by instructions which are vague, incon-

---

[6] Much graduate dissatisfaction centers on the writing requirements. Cf. *The Graduate School Today and Tomorrow*, F. W. Strothmann for the Committee of Fifteen (New York: Fund for the Advancement of Education, Dec. 1955), p. 5: "Too often, dissatisfaction with the graduate program is felt most acutely by those who have recently been exposed to it, while the senior members of the academic guild, occupying the dual role—unique among the professions—of controlling both the training and the hiring of the products of that training, grow complacent, give only lip service to proposals for reform, or even maintain that, at least in their department, everything that should be done is being done." Cf. also Hans Rosenhaupt, assisted by Thomas J. Chinlund, *Graduate Students: Experience at Columbia University, 1940-1956* (New York: Columbia University Press, 1958).

sistent, and often contradictory.[7] Candidates for graduate degrees can pursue their academic objectives effectively only when they know what they must do, and how well they must do it, to attain them.

This book has been written with the aid of graduate students and with a view to providing the kind of information and guidance they need.

---

[7] Financial subsidies permeate academic life. Few graduate students lack them; and in some quarters they are seen as veritable panaceas for all academic ills.

2

Thesis
and Dissertation

The recent remarkable developments of formal logic and the philosophy of language have rightly emphasized the importance of clear and consistent terminology.

STEPHEN KÖRNER

The first duty of a man trying to plot a course for clear thinking is to produce words that really apply to the situation he is trying to describe. . . . Plain English will do quite well enough, but the good old words have to be brought back to life by being used in their original sense for a change.

Only through a fresh approach, maybe through a variety of fresh approaches, can the terms through which we try to understand the events that govern our lives be reminted to the point of ringing true again.

JOHN DOS PASSOS

Graduate students cross a great academic divide when they complete the coursework requirements for their degrees. This is especially marked at the doctoral level by written and oral qualifying examinations which, in some schools, are known as "prelims." Thereafter, graduate students are on their own to undertake investigations of their own selection as bases for their thesis or dissertational essays. They then may fulfill the writing requirements for their degrees without the pressures and arbitrary limitations of time which characterized much of their coursework.

Candidates for advanced degrees at both levels have a choice between theses and dissertations. Different kinds of intellectual interests and achievements in inquiry require different kinds of exercises in explanation and logical substantiation. The thesis essay

16

is available to the student who wishes to present and support his solution to a problem. The dissertational essay is available to one who wishes to discuss some subject in order to establish a point of view, as in criticism, or a refinement.

The true nature and distinctiveness of these essay types have been obscured by the practice of calling the required writing for a Master's degree a thesis, and that for a Doctor's degree a dissertation. Moreover, the attempt is seldom made to define the stipulated types of writing. Graduate Councils apparently expect that traditional establishment and long use of these essays provide sufficient guidance for them to be understood. They have been further confused by statements in graduate school catalogues which usually are given in terms of research investigation and seldom in terms of intellectual inquiry.

The nature of intellectual findings is that they are not obvious from the terms of the investigation, and that therefore they must be explained and substantiated by logical argument. Ideas become knowledge only when caught by minds of creative intellectual power. Theses and dissertations provide measures of the candidates' skill in communicating the nature of their inquiries and the validity of their findings. The importance of these essays is that, when thought and reason have pursued to a conclusion the opportunity revealed by an insight, they provide practice in setting down a logical argument from premises to conclusion, that is, in discoursive writing. Graduate students succeed in attaining their degrees if their investigative and writing achievements equal or exceed the performance standards for Master's and Doctor's levels of study.

The attempt at definitional reminting which follows is designed to clarify the essential nature of the thesis and dissertation. It would be convenient, indeed helpful, if the writing requirements for graduate degrees could be succinctly defined at once. That would set aside the need for a chapter on the matter. However, the task of their conceptual clarification is too complex for that. Their treatment is spelled out, therefore, step by step.

The methodology of definition is itself involved in the didactic reduction of academic roadblocks. Definition that is precise often is too easily grasped for retention, and it may be dismissed as "too pat." A definition that is too pat may be imprecise because it oversimplifies and, therefore, does not reflect reality. Good definition should be simple or complex according to the simplicity or complexity of the subject; and the definer should strive for the right degree of imprecision. To be really useful, definition needs to be sufficiently imprecise to tax a reader's mind enough to force him to become possessor of a concept by means of his own thought about it.[1]

Some opinion, willing to accept definition elsewhere, holds that definitive explanation of the required academic essays, and thereby of the degree requirements, involves arbitrariness and dogmatism. This is not true. To say definitely what *kind* a thing is expresses clarity, not dogmatism. Moreover, generally accepted *generic* definition mitigates individualistic arbitrariness as does a rule of law. Valid generic definition of a *kind* of writing does not restrict the subject of any particular example of it. To accept definition in respect of one set of academic requirements, coursework, and to refuse it for another, the writing requirements, is inconsistent. It is patently unfair to individual students and disadvantageous to their fields of learning when the nature of degree requirements and the levels of performance standards vary among universities, among colleges and departments within universities, and among advisory committees within departments. To require one or another type of essay in fulfillment of the writing requirements for advanced degrees is only to insist, for sound intellectual and educational reasons, that a candidate's writing be logical argument.

Thesis and Dissertation Defined

The thesis and dissertation are different species of the genus essay. The word essay means a try, or an attempt. The literary form is said to have been invented by Montaigne who, having retired in 1571 at age 38, perfected it during the next five years as a means of conveying his thought and the nature of his mind to others.[2] One of his aphorisms: "Knowledge is nothing if the mind is not there."

---

[1] Professor Galbraith has expressed himself similarly on this pedagogical point. See John Kenneth Galbraith, "The Language of Economics," *Fortune*, LXVI, No. 6 (December 1962), 128 ff. This article elicited at least one affirmative letter to the editor, for which see *Fortune*, LXVII, No. 2 (February 1963), 20. Cf. the definition of mentality, below, p. 143.

[2] *The Complete Works of Montaigne*, trans. Donald M. Frame (Stanford, Calif.: Stanford University Press, 1948-1957). Montaigne's 107 essays range from one to 144 pages in length, and are in interesting contrast to Emerson's.

The essay is a literary type which has certain set-form properties without being a true set-form.[3] It is characterized by its typical structure and organization, however, as well as by its discoursive style. Its length may vary considerably, and it may be used to convey one idea or a complex of ideas on any subject. The essay begins with an *introduction* which states the subject and undertaking, and thereby sets the stage for and the tone of the piece. Then follow *presentation* of the argument and the *exposition* of the main elements of the argument. Thereafter come the *development* of the argument and, finally, *recapitulation* and *conclusion*. In its structure, the essay has much in common with the sonata form.

The essay is further characterized by a variety of species and applications. It is the literary form precisely suited to a graduate student's need to supply a written argument as an attempt to substantiate an intellectual achievement of his own. He must begin by saying what his essay is about. His discourse must proceed by logical steps from some meaningful set of premises to his conclusion. The latter must be the logical outcome of his logical argument. Then if his premises are valid and relevant the conclusion probably will be so. As such, it can provide a basis for a rational judgment and a significant decision with respect to some action. Thus the value of the conclusion can be stated.

The thesis and dissertation have been said to be species of the essay. They now can be conceptually and functionally defined. It will emerge that they are similar in form but different in function. They serve different purposes. A thesis is closer to being a set-form than is a dissertation because of its logical formality and its singularity of purpose.

The word thesis means two different things. First, it is defined as an hypothesis, as a position or proposition which is advanced and maintained, if possible, by argument. From this point of view, a

---

[3] A set-form is characterized by invariable structure, organization, and style. The sonnet, whether Petrarchan or Shakespearean, is an example of a literary set-form. It is a poem usually of 14 lines in one of several fixed verse and rhyme schemes, although it is typically in iambic pentameter. A sonnet expresses a single theme or idea. For a statement of the form of an essay, see Richard E. Hughes and P. Albert Duhamel, *Rhetoric: Principles and Usage* (Englewood Cliffs, N. J.: Prentice-Hall, Inc., 1962), p. 11 ff. Cf. Karl Beckson and Arthur Ganz, *A Reader's Guide to Literary Terms: A Dictionary* (New York: The Noonday Press, 1961), pp. 191-92, for the Sestina, a complicated French fixed form of verse.

thesis is a tentative solution to a problem. Second, a thesis is defined as a formal essay whose function is to convey a logical argument upholding a specific point of view, particularly, a solution to a problem. Like the hypothesis it supports, the argument conveyed must be a product of the writer's own mind and be based on his own original inquiry and research. Professors Cole and Bigelow have well stated that:

> The *first* essential is that the thesis begin with a problem; the *second* that an hypothesis be formulated for its solution. If there is no hypothesis, stated or implied, then whatever the product may be it is not a thesis. . . . *Third,* the thesis must possess validity, which simply means that it must be what it purports to be. . . .[4]

The dissertation represents a species of essay different from the thesis. Its function is to provide a systematic discussion of a subject or topic. Its scope usually is broader than that of the thesis, and its style is less rigorously formal. The purpose of the dissertation is to establish a criticism, clarification, or refinement, that is, to establish an arguable view. To dissertate is to discourse, or argue, in a learned manner. In contrast to the formal, scientific logic of the reasoning in the thesis, the dissertator treats his topic or subject more or less didactically.

The thesis and dissertational essays are closely related literary forms. They are so closely related, in fact, that the name of the latter is employed in the definition of the former. A thesis essay may be defined as: "A dissertation which embodies the results of original inquiry and research, and which strictly substantiates a specific view, especially the solution to a problem."[5] Careless interpretation of

----

[4] Arthur H. Cole and Karl W. Bigelow, A *Manual of Thesis Writing for Graduates and Undergraduates* (New York: John Wiley & Sons, Inc., 1935), p. vii. This useful statement unfortunately does not appear in reprintings such as those of 1946 and 1960 (see note 23, p. 64), which also are revisions. Perhaps the authors' problem was that they did not distinguish between thesis and dissertation, the latter of which is not covered by their definition.

[5] This composite definition is drawn from the major dictionaries of this century. None of them differentiate between thesis and dissertational essays by relating them to particular degrees and levels of study, as does current academic abusage. *Webster's Third New International Dictionary of the English Language, Unabridged* (Springfield, Mass.: G. & C. Merriam & Co., 1961), defines a thesis as "a dissertation embodying results of original research and esp. substantiating a specific view," and as "a substantial paper written by a candidate for an aca-

the definition may provide a partial explanation of the erroneous use of the terms thesis and dissertation as alternative names for a single concept. They are not synonymous terms. They name two species of essay which are distinct and discrete on conceptual, functional, qualitative, and substantive grounds. The word dissertation appears in the definition of the thesis because it names the kind of essay which is the model for the thesis. In the definition of the thesis the important words are not "a dissertation." The significant words are "strictly substantiates a specific view." [6]

This differentiation of these two academic essays does not value judge them. Usually, a dissertation is a product of more or less learned scholarship; and a thesis is derived from a significant scientific exercise. Such distinction as is here made between a scholar and a scientist must be approximate and not absolute. Although both do intellectual work and employ scientific methods, they differ as to field, intent, and particular methods. Their writing needs differ because of their different intellectual undertakings and purposes. However, to attempt to distinguish written products of reason and intellect at the doctoral level from the same at the Master's level by calling the former a dissertation and the latter a thesis is absurd.

---

demic degree under the individual direction of a professor." It defines a dissertation as "an extended usu. systematic oral or written treatment of a subject," and as "a substantial paper that is submitted to the faculty of a university by a candidate for an advanced degree that is typically based on independent research and that if acceptable usu. gives evidence of the candidate's mastery both of his own subject and of scholarly method." *Funk & Wagnalls' New Standard Dictionary of the English Language* (New York: Funk & Wagnalls Co., 1962) defines a thesis as: "a position or proposition the truth of which is not evident from the terms, but that requires evidence, explanation, or proof. . . . Hence an essay or treatise on a particular subject," esp. one "presented by a candidate for a degree." It defines a dissertation as an oral or written presentation of a subject "usually extended and argumentative" in the light of the idea that to dissertate is "to discourse in a learned and formal manner."

[6] The dissertation may have been an earlier lineal descendant of the literary essay than was the thesis. Confusion must reign where both terms are in use for a given project. A college of a state university requires its doctoral candidates to: "Write and successfully defend in a final orals [sic] examination a scholarly dissertation. A satisfactory thesis provides objective evidence that the candidate is capable of original and technical research and has acquired the skills of the professional economist." The latter may indeed be true; but if a thesis serves this purpose, why require a dissertation? On the other hand, a dissertational project could reveal more about a candidate's capacity for original critical and analytical thinking than would a thesis. The passage shows that thesis and dissertation have become academic "buzz-words" whose use is not carefully considered. See *Collegiate News and Views*, XIII, No. 3 (March 1960), 31.

This blankets both types of essay with both names.[7] In certain respects, the word dissertation may best be described as an academic status symbol. It seems a strange perversion to attach importance to words on the basis of their length.

Perhaps a digression at this point will advance the discussion. It may aid understanding of the thesis and dissertation concepts to clarify the kinds of writing they are not. This comparative technique is widely used. For example, *The Catholic Encyclopedia* begins clarification of the indulgence concept by saying what indulgences are not. The forms of writing in academic use include other essay species such as the literary essay, the tract, and the polemic. They also include two non-essay forms, the report and the treatise. There are others, of course; but these will suffice for the purpose.

A literary essay is a cursory prose composition, "the brief and light result of experience and profound meditation." It may be analytical, interpretive, or critical. It deals with its subject from a more or less personal point of view.[8] Occasionally such an essay is found as an article in a literary magazine or even as a book review. The "Adventures of the Mind" series in *The Saturday Evening Post* contained excellent examples. The literary essay usually provides a delightful as well as an informative experience.

The tract is an essay of different breed and purpose. It may be defined as a short discourse or dissertation, especially a brief treatment or discussion of some topic of practical religion. A tract usually appears in the form of a pamphlet or leaflet issued for propaganda purposes or religious exhortation.[9] The British pamphleteers of the

---

[7] Reason might have it the other way around, with a dissertation required at the Master's level and a thesis at the Doctor's. Appreciation and extension of knowledge begin with criticism; and a dissertation provides adequately for research training.

[8] For example, see Bertrand Russell, *Unpopular Essays*, twelve adventures in argument by 1950's Nobel Prize winner. Especially valuable at present is José Ortega y Gasset, *Mission of the University*. Compare Karl Jaspers, *The Idea of the University*. See Alfred North Whitehead, *The Aims of Education and Other Essays*, and Howard Mumford Jones, *Ideas in America*. Also stimulating are C. P. Snow, *The Two Cultures and the Scientific Revolution*, Ernest Nagel, *Logic Without Metaphysics and Other Essays in the Philosophy of Science*, and Joan Robinson, *Economic Philosophy*. See also Lionel Trilling, *The Liberal Imagination: Essays on Literature and Society*. This contains Professor Trilling's essay on the Kinsey Report which is especially apropos here.

[9] For example, a series known as "Tracts for the Times" was published at Oxford, England, between 1833 and 1841. The word tract is variously employed. J. M. Keynes' *A Tract on Monetary Reform* may entertain moral concerns but may better be regarded as a dissertation. For a book-length tract, see Robert

eighteenth and nineteenth centuries, who argued all sorts of questions on morals, politics, and economics, often are called tract writers. Tom Paine was a prolific example.[10] An interesting example of a tract on morals is "Man's Rights and Woman's Duties," written by William Marshall, stern and tough old father of famed economist Alfred Marshall. A more recent example of a tract is A. C. Pigou's "The Great Inquest," an examination of Mr. Chamberlain's proposals, in *The Pilot* (London) in 1903. Colm Brogan's *Who are the People?* and *The Democrat at the Supper Table* are book-length tracts on British problems of the mid-1940's.

The skill of certain writers in the practice of disputation and aggressive controversy places them in the class of polemicists. A polemic is a tract-like essay directed against some person or his ideas, or against some condition or set of circumstances. One hears of A's polemic against B. Examples abound in academic debate as well as in political controversy.[11]

A treatise is an expository kind of non-essay. It is a composition, usually of considerable length, in which the known and given principles and ideas of a particular subject are systematically presented and explained. A good treatise is a product of learning and an intellectual level of scholarship. Examples are provided by Werner Heisenberg's *The Physical Principles of the Quantum Theory*, and by Mordecai Ezekiel's *Methods of Correlation Analysis*. In the former, Heisen-

---

Rennie, *A Demonstration of the Necessity and Advantages of a Free Trade to the East Indies* (London: C. Chapple, 1807). Two tracts on science are Anthony Standen, *Science is a Sacred Cow* (New York: E. P. Dutton, 1950), and Martin Gardner, *In the Name of Science* (New York: Dover Publications, 1952). Some may dispute whether the first of these latter is a tract or a polemic, but the second clearly is a study of human gullibility.

[10] See Alfred Owen Aldridge, *Man of Reason, The Life of Thomas Paine* (Philadelphia: J. B. Lippincott & Co., 1959). Here is a biography which might well illustrate an appropriate substitute for a dissertation, should such be permitted—under the name biography, of course, not dissertation. However, when good biography explains its subject penetratingly it takes on many characteristics of a dissertation. It is indeed possible to dissertate on a person's achievements and influence.

[11] For example, *Keynes at Harvard: Economic Deception as a Political Credo*, a Veritas Foundation Staff Study (New York: Veritas Foundation, 1960). Cf. F. R. Leavis, *Two Cultures? The Significance of C. P. Snow* (New York: Pantheon Books, 1963). William F. Buckley, Jr., provided a tirade against many things in his book *Up From Liberalism*. In his shorter essay, *The Anti-Capitalist Mentality*, Ludwig von Mises worked his idea so hard as nearly to prove the opposite of it to the unwary. There have been few polemicists in the physical and natural sciences and mathematics; in the moral and social sciences they are legion.

berg gave an exposition of the theoretical interpretation, experimental meaning, and mathematical operation of quantum mechanics for professional physicists. The latter was the first undergraduate textbook of its kind and it still is standard.[12]

A treatise does not convey an argument for any idea or point of view. Its function is clear presentation, definition, explanation, and illustration. Therefore, its style is expository rather than discoursive. Any treatise is characterized by the subject matter competence of its author. It will reflect his simplification, organization, and explanation of his material. The word treatise implies more form and method than does the word essay. Nevertheless some classes of scientific writing commonly are designated by the phrase "systematic treatise." [13]

The report is similar to the treatise in that it is an expository form of writing. It differs from the treatise by being descriptive and historical rather than explanatory. Moreover, although intellectual achievements and scholarly deliberations may be reported, the report itself is an essentially non-intellectual form of writing. The fact that learned men make reports does not mean that their descriptive, factual statements have the quality of being learned argument and logical discourse. The essay is needed for that.[14] A report requires

---

[12] Compare George Berkeley, A *Treatise Concerning the Principles of Human Knowledge*, David Hume, *Treatise of Human Nature*, J. E. Cairnes, *The Character and Logical Method of Political Economy*, and Donald J. Dewey, *Monopoly in Economics and Law*. Cf. George Ryerson Fowler, A *Treatise on Appendicitis*, and J. M. Keynes, A *Treatise on Probability*. An example of a lengthy historical treatise is provided by Singer, Holmyard, Hall, and Williams' five-volume study, A *History of Technology*. Stroud's *Digest of the Diseases of Birds*, written by Robert Stroud after twenty years of study and experiment, is one of the most comprehensive and definitive works available on the subject. In a lighter vein, there is Richard Carrington's *Elephants*, a lucid and entertaining account of their evolution, anatomy, love life, and long association with man.

[13] Cf. the *Century Dictionary and Cyclopedia* (12 vols., rev. & enl. ed., New York: The Century Company, 1911). This point is emphasized, for example, by J. M. Keynes' two-volume study, A *Treatise on Money*, which actually is dissertational in character despite lengthy expositions. In the case of a mature student capable of a scholarly treatise in his field of academic interest, his specimen of erudition might properly be substituted for a thesis or dissertation if kept under the treatise label. This might apply especially in the case of a doctoral candidate definitely committed to teaching.

[14] Henry David Aiken points out that the essay has been employed for much of the serious philosophical writing of our time, and that the essay is the form precisely suited to both what he himself had to say and the way he wished to say it. See Henry David Aiken, *Reason and Conduct: New Bearings in Moral Philosophy* (New York: Alfred A. Knopf, 1962), preface, vii.

certain information, intelligence, organizational sense, and technical ability. In the academic life the report is produced at the empirical, not the intellectual, level of scholarship.

The main purpose here is to differentiate between a thesis or dissertation and a report by contrasting their writing styles and intellectual significance. Thesis and dissertation can be what they purport to be only if they convey their writer's own logical argument. Reports can be what they purport to be only if they do not. The essays are discursive in style; the report expository. Reports provide bases for scholarly and scientific work. Theses and dissertations represent its consummation.

A report is a formal exposition of facts or of the record or result of something. "Whatever its purpose, a report is invariably and necessarily historical." [15] A report is designed to meet the needs or interests of those to whom it is directed. Its nature and functions are derived from the division of labor principle; and its purpose is to provide bases for thought or action. Reports are made by learned men and groups as well as by students. Student reports may represent only plagiarism, or may be only counting and summing. Scholars' reports, on the other hand, often present the fruit of significant thought and judgment.[16] Even a progress report on an inquiry by a mature investigator may be more significant than a neophyte's finished statement based on a survey or other technique of data gathering.

Several factors complicate treatment of the academic report. The claims of industrial research and the pressures of "print or perish" have combined, at the faculty level, to exaggerate the importance of the research report. Student research reporting gained currency as growing numbers of professional and technical students

---

[15] Jacques Barzun and Henry F. Graff, *The Modern Researcher* (New York: Harcourt, Brace & World, 1957), p. 5. It would be difficult to get along without reports of observed facts and phenomena and summations of data in our complex life. Reports of news agencies, public administration agencies, research bureaus, and business firms daily provide valuable information for use and interpretation.

[16] A stimulating report of important ideas, which reflects skillful authorship as well as important purposes, is Howard Mumford Jones, *One Great Society: Humanistic Writing in the United States* (New York: Harcourt, Brace & World, 1959). For the able report of a widely-known sociologist on graduate education, see Bernard Berelson, *Graduate Education in the United States* (New York: McGraw-Hill Book Co., Inc., 1960). Reports of various qualities are available on a wide variety of subjects including that selected by Professor Kinsey.

began to take advanced degrees. The influence of industrial research made student research reports fashionable in the physical and natural sciences. In many instances, the reliance on reports penetrated into the rest of the liberal arts and sciences. The professional and technical schools, meanwhile, took to them wholeheartedly. Finally, some institutions grant at least the Master's degree on the basis of extra coursework and a report in lieu of a thesis.[17]

The report has its importance in academic circles. Differentiating it from the required academic essays does not belittle it. Neither does it question the validity of the true research report as a writing requirement where appropriate and desired. For example, the research report may be satisfactory in connection with output of skilled technicians and quasi-professionals at the Master's degree level. In such cases, the correct thing would be to name the research report as the writing requirement. Then neither students nor their prospective employers would be misled. Then the faculty could be true to its intellectual commitments under academic freedom.

The digression contrasting forms of academic writing was taken beyond mere comparison to make it clear why the question of definition is not easily resolved. A quotation may aid consolidation of thought at this point. In his *Notebooks* (c. 1508), Leonardo da Vinci wrote: "That is scientific which is born and ends in the mind." Like pure learning, pure science is intellectual work.

This is readily illustrated. Falling is directly observable but gravitation is an intellectual percept. Besides his law of gravity, Newton's intellectual contributions include his laws of mechanics and the calculus. He once said that he attained his intellectual findings "by always thinking unto them." [18] The empirical discovery of a mineral deposit, a new star, or life on the ocean bottom six miles deep provides for an interesting report. But no matter how

---

[17] Where admitted as alternative means of fulfilling degree requirements, so-called Master's reports usually carry one-third the credit value of Master's theses. This is a reflection of their comparative intellectual significance. Candidates in physics, chemistry, agriculture, and technical and applied fields could as well write essays as not. The requirement would enhance their intellectual skills in analysis, synthesis, induction, deduction, and logical proof, not to mention their literacy.

[18] See Sir David Brewster, *Memoirs of the Life, Writings, and Discoveries of Sir Isaac Newton* (Edinburgh: Thomas Constable & Co., 1855). Cf. E. N. da C. Andrade, *Sir Isaac Newton* (Garden City, N. Y.: Doubleday & Co., Inc., 1958).

exciting, such discoveries are reported, not argued. Supporting evidence, such as photographs or specimens, is not argument such as substantiation of intellectual findings requires. To the empirical observation that bodies float, one may contrast Archimedes' famous finding and a difference will be realized.[19] Despite the magnificent persistence of the Curies, their ultimate empirical discovery of radioactivity was not the intellectual equal either of the discovery of nuclear fission or the invention of the X-ray.

The thesis and dissertational essays now have been described as species of the essay and placed at the intellectual level of scholarship. They have been defined conceptually, functionally, and by comparison. The way is now open to define and differentiate them further by illustration. For that, return is made to mainstream.

Thesis and Dissertation
Illustrated

Acceptable theses and dissertations represent the outcome of intellectual investigations. Their bases are established when study, thought, inquiry, reflection, and insight have yielded researchable hypotheses or ideas. When research provides assurance of validation or substantiation of an inquirer's solution or clarification, his thesis or dissertation can be written.[20] Production

---

[19] Archimedes perceived that bodies float or sink in water according to their specific gravity (in contrast to the Aristotelian view that flotation was a function of shape). He associated the specific weight of gold and the displacement of bathwater and then deduced a method for determining the volume of an irregular object. Thus he found a means of determining the true value of a king's gift crown. *Eureka!*

[20] This is illustrated, for example, by the IGY verification of Henry Stommel's theory on ocean circulation. For the account, see *Life*, XLIX, No. 20 (November 14, 1960), 78. It does not suffice for the writing requirement to argue the newness of empirical data or of summations inductively derived from them, as in an expository report. Neither is it sufficient to establish an arguable view, as in a literary essay, tract, polemic. Altogether too many so-called Master's and Doctor's theses or dissertations are examples of nothing but furtive insignificance. For example, the Kantian scholar who participated in the University of Chicago Great Books project once wrote a collegiate thesis on "Misspellings in Old Southern Cookbooks." See *Life*, XXIV, No. 4 (January 26, 1948), 93. Norman Foerster has told of a doctoral candidate in English who got by with "Northern Travelers in the Southern States Before the Civil War." Foerster was disturbed by the tendency to be journalistic rather than scholarly.

of these essays is difficult and demanding, but it is highly rewarding. They require a certain scholastic and scientific maturity, for in them reasoning is paramount. They are sources of significant satisfaction because they are evidence of control of subject matter, and of competence in inquiry and written discourse.

A thesis essay is written to establish the validity of a solution to some problem by means of formal, logical argument in proof. The essence of a thesis, therefore, is conceptual or empirical analysis, deduction, and conclusion. A statement of Newton's suggests the nature of the thesis by illustrating this idea. This statement infers a researchable hypothesis derived from inquiry, subsequent research, and an essay in substantiation. In this case, the research, supporting argument, and proof were mainly mathematical. When about age 73, Sir Isaac Newton wrote the following memorandum:

> In the same year I began to think of gravity extending to the orb of the moon, and having found out how to estimate the force with which a globe revolving within a sphere presses the surface of the sphere, from Kepler's rule of the periodical times of the planets being in a sesquialterate proportion of their distances from the centers of their orbs (sesquialterate means one and a half times, or, as we say, the square of the years are [sic] as the cubes of the orbits), I deduced that the forces which keep the planets in their orbs must be reciprocally as the squares of their distances from the centers about which they revolve: and thereby compared the force requisite to keep the moon in her orb with the force of gravity at the surface of the earth, and found them answer pretty nearly. All this was in the two plague years of 1665 and 1666, for in those days I was in the prime of my age for invention, and minded mathematics and philosophy more than at any time since.[21]

This is a splendid guide for the prospective thesis writer. For this purpose its key words are: "I began to think . . . , having found . . . , I deduced . . . , and [researching!] found. . . ." Newton was working with ideas, "thinking unto them," not grubbing for data. It was intellectual work which enabled him to reach the conclusions on which he based his law of gravitation. It is interesting to note that Sir Christopher Wren, Edmond Halley, and Hook

---

[21] E. N. da C. Andrade, "Isaac Newton," in James R. Newman, *The World of Mathematics* (New York: Simon & Schuster, Inc., 1956), I, 257. The word "orbit" is now used in place of Newton's "orb." Isaac Newton was 23 years old in 1666.

reached a similar conclusion. But none of them managed the intellectual achievement of proving or demonstrating it.

Whitehead's statement in the preface to his book, *The Principle of Relativity*, is similarly instructive in this connection:

> As the result of a consideration of the character of our knowledge in general, and of our knowledge of nature in particular, undertaken in Part I of this book and in my two previous works, on this subject, I deduce that our experience requires and exhibits a basis of uniformity, and that in the case of nature this basis exhibits itself as the uniformity of spatio-temporal relations. This conclusion entirely cuts away the casual heterogeneity of those relations which is the essential of Einstein's later theory. It is this uniformity which is essential to my outlook, and not the Euclidean geometry which I adopt as lending itself to the simplest exposition of the facts of nature.[22]

Graduate students will find it useful to think of Whitehead's deduction as an hypothesis. His research is implied, and the entire statement may be regarded as a prospectus for a thesis essay. His series of three books suggests that fundamental insights usually require a mature comprehension which enables the thinker to simplify. Model-building then can help.[23] This is how it was with Kepler when he deduced that planets move in elipses. It was so with Galileo when, subsequent to his empirical discovery that the paths of projectiles are parabolas, he made his famous contribution to the laws of mechanics. So it was with Bertrand Russell when, with his Theory of Types, he "brought into philosophy a new idea of cardinal importance." [24]

Graduate students are not expected to tackle, let alone solve,

---

[22] Alfred North Whitehead, *The Principle of Relativity with Applications to Physical Science* (Cambridge: Cambridge University Press, 1922), p. iii. The two previous books were *The Principles of Natural Knowledge* and *The Concept of Nature*, both by the same publisher.

[23] Use of abstract models in thought apparently began in earnest toward the end of the last century. On models as intellectual tools, see the work of Poincaré and other French writers of the late 19th century. On economics as model-building, see Andreas G. Papandreou, *Economics as a Science* (Chicago: J. B. Lippincott Company, 1958).

[24] The quotation is from Alan Wood's preface to his projected book, *Russell's Philosophy*. This preface was published posthumously in Bertrand Russell, *My Philosophical Development* (London: George Allen & Unwin, Ltd., 1959), p. 258.

problems of the class solved by Newton, Whitehead, and Russell. But these illustrate excellently the way they must attempt to work.

For example, Metzler has raised the question whether the classical monetary theory of international economic adjustment is based on a multilateral or on a bilateral conception of international trade. A Master's candidate conceivably might lay it down as his thesis, after appropriate preparatory study and thought, that the classical theory had a multilateral (or a bilateral) basis. The position taken could be supported in an essay by proofs derived from analysis and interpretation of classical school writings. Such proofs would be couched in formal, logical argument from a set of premises to conclusions.

This would be an appropriate kind of term essay at least, at the first year of graduate study.[25] Such a studied evaluation and interpretation of an idea in its historical setting certainly could contribute to the student's understanding of Classical thought. Through clarification at least, it conceivably could contribute to general understanding of the Classical trade theory by providing a clearer light for its appraisal.

Other fields provide examples, including many at their applied levels. In the late 1950's two boys, one in a New Jersey high school and the other a freshman at the Massachusetts Institute of Technology, hypothesized that a radio signal could be bounced off an orbiting projectile by means of a certain method. They succeeded in doing this and so acquired experimental evidence to validate the solution they conceived for this problem. Now there is Telstar. Similarly, chemical compounds can be proofs of intellectually derived hypotheses as well as empirical discoveries resulting from trial-and-error procedures—or serendipity.[26]

---

[25] It is vague to speak of a "term paper" and misleading to say "term report" —unless, of course, a report is definitely the assignment. Even undergraduates should learn to set out and prove or substantiate ideas and views in essays. This kind of training is begun in grade schools in Europe: e.g., the *Aufsätze* of the German kindergarten. Cf. Max Weber, *Gesammelte Aufsätze zur Religionssoziologie* (Tubingen: Mohr, 1920-21), in which he elaborated his interpretation of religious beliefs and social institutions as different expressions of a common psychological attitude. This idea is less novel now than when he first adduced it.

[26] Serendipity is the name for an apparent aptitude for making fortunate discoveries accidentally. The term was coined by Horace Walpole: see his *The Three Princes of Serendip* (i.e., Ceylon) who made such discoveries. Fortunate

When he was a graduate student at the University of Wisconsin, Walter Heller, later a professor and chairman of President Kennedy's Council of Economic Advisers, inquired why withholding at the source could not be applied to income tax as well as to social security payments.[27] Beardsly Ruml subsequently worked the idea out in implementation of national policy.

The dissertation is a more versatile essay than the thesis. It is less rigorously formal and may serve a wider range of purposes, qualities which reflect its closer kinship to the literary essay. Although a dissertator employs the discoursive style to convey "results of experience and profound meditation," his essay differs from the literary essay in important respects. A dissertation is more dignified and formal than the usual literary essay. Its point of view is nonpersonal and its penetration is deeper. Its treatment is profound, not cursory; full, not brief; and weighty rather than light.

A dissertation is a more or less formal essay (i.e., trial or attempt) in the analysis, interpretation, evaluation, and explanation of a topic, subject, or body of knowledge or opinion. It may attempt refinement of knowledge or establishment of a point of view. In the latter sense, a dissertation may be critical, normative, conjectural, even speculative.[28] To dissertate is to discourse in a learned and formal manner, communicating a process of reasoning from premises

---

observations became the basis for Roentgen's contrived invention of the X-ray and Fleming's discovery of penicillin. Hertzian waves were discovered without any reference to their use; it wasn't at first known that they had any use. Later, however, they became the basis for the radio when the empirical finding was used creatively. Trained minds are required to take advantage of such seeds of intellectual achievement. The accidental discoveries themselves, however, can only be reported and do not provide direct bases for the required academic essays. This is generally true of empirical research.

[27] Dr. Heller has stated to the writer that the paper he gave at the 1941 symposium on financing the war was an outgrowth of his "work in Harold Groves' seminar and [his own] field investigation of a number of income tax systems in states and provinces in 1939-40, which eventuated in [his] Ph.D. thesis [Wisconsin] in 1941." Cf. 1958 *Proceedings of the Fifty-First Annual Conference on Taxation*, ed. Walter J. Kress (Harrisburg, Penn.: National Tax Association, 1959), p. 246; Walter W. Heller, "Collection Methods Appropriate to the Wartime Use of Income Taxes," in *Financing the War* (Philadelphia: Tax Institute, 1942), pp. 201-224; and *Hearings Before the Committee on Finance, U. S. Senate, 77th Cong., 1st sess., on the Revenue Act of 1941*, pp. 400-414.

[28] Consider, for example, Machiavelli's *The Prince*, Marx's *Das Kapital*, Lenin's *The State and Revolution*, Djilas' *The New Class*, Eric Hoffer's *The True Believer*, or Henry George's *Progress and Poverty*.

to conclusions.[29] A dissertator may employ premises taken from reason and which have no empirical basis. His premises need make sense only in some meaningful context pertinent to important knowledge while conforming to the canons of logic.[30] A dissertator may lean heavily upon assumptions.[31]

In the preface to his *Risk, Uncertainty and Profit,* which was his prizewinning doctoral dissertation, Frank H. Knight, widely known economist, wrote:

> There is little that is fundamentally new in this book. It represents an attempt to state the essential principles of the conventional economic doctrine more accurately, and to show their implications more clearly, than has previously been done. That is, its object is refinement, not reconstruction; it is a study in "pure theory." [32]

---

[29] Discourse is dependent upon reasoning faculty or power. It is the action or process of thinking consecutively and logically. It is also the orderly communication of thought. An example is provided by the contribution of Bertil Ohlin to international economics in his application of general equilibrium theory to international trade in *Interregional and International Trade.* Compare the work of Walras as popularized by Gustav Cassel (*Theoretische Sozialökonomie*), which permitted a revision of the science of economics by taking the principle of scarcity as a point of departure. More of this sort of thing awaits the minds of interested and able scholars. Cf. C. P. Snow, *The Two Cultures and the Scientific Revolution* (Cambridge: The University Press, 1959), p. 17: ". . . at the heart of thought and creation we are letting some of our best chances go by default. . . . In the history of mental activity . . . [the clashing point of two subjects, disciplines, cultures] has been where some of the break-throughs came. The chances are there now." Cf. John Tyndall, "All Experience is an Arch," The Belfast Address 1874, reprinted in *The Graduate Journal,* V, No. 2 (Winter 1963), 403 ff. Cf. in the same issue Howard Mumford Jones, "The Future of the Arts in a World of Science," pp. 232-39; and Whitney J. Oates, "The Humanities in Land-Grant Institutions," pp. 349-60.

[30] For example, the first canon, which is to have valid assumptions.

[31] All argument must proceed from assumptions (as final elements of premises). Therefore it is impossible to demand that all assumptions should be based on argument.

[32] Compare the concept of a dissertation provided by D. W. Sciama in the preface to his *The Unity of the Universe* (Garden City, N. Y.: Doubleday & Co., 1959): ". . . cosmology is a highly controversial subject which contains little or no agreed body of doctrine. Although most of the ideas developed in this book have been borrowed from the writings and conversations of others, the synthesis presented here is my own. This caution, however, does not apply to the first part of the book, which describes how our present observational picture of the universe has been built up. . . . The rest of the book is mainly concerned with explaining how the influence of distant matter arises and what its consequences are. No knowledge of physics or astronomy is assumed on the part of the reader, only a willingness to follow an argument to its logical conclusion."

The dissertator's counterpart of Sir Isaac Newton's famous memorandum is provided by Professor Abram L. Harris in the preface to his essay on the thought of Marx, Veblen, Commons, Sombart, and Pesch. A bit longer than Newton's, Harris' statement is as follows:

> This volume is the outgrowth of studies of the institutional and historical schools of economics which I began some years ago. The first result was an essay . . . in which I sought to explain certain variants of the institutional "approach" as departures from traditional or neoclassical economic theory. This essay was followed by others dealing specifically with the theories of Thorstein Veblen, Karl Marx, Werner Sombart, and Heinrich Pesch. . . .
>
> None of the early articles contained an examination of J. R. Commons, whose institutionalism shows traces of Veblen's influence. Commons' ideas are systematically organized around theoretical models, which is not the case with Veblen; and his treatment of the phenomenon of capitalism, although at times polemical, is devoid of Veblen's disconcerting satire and irony. . . .
>
> My original intention of expanding the essays on Marx and Veblen was gradually given up. . . . Although I did not agree with many of their theories, I was more or less in sympathy with their evaluation of our system of business enterprise, or capitalism, as Marx called it. But I came to believe that while Marx and Veblen had made some important contributions as critics and historians of capitalism, their conception of the basic defects of the system was mistaken and that their programs of economic reorganization, designed to increase industrial efficiency, lessen economic inequality, and create greater "effective" freedom for the masses of men, would achieve none of these things, but would probably create greater "evils" than those attributed by them to capitalism. And then as Sombart, Pesch, and Commons were brought into my investigation, I recognized certain resemblances between their theories and those of Marx and Veblen. In their theories, as in those of Marx and Veblen, capitalism is pictured as a system of power. Also, as in the case of Marx and Veblen, the theories of these writers support policies and programs of social action which aim to bring about greater "effective" freedom, security, and welfare for the masses either by abolishing capitalism or by redistributing power by means of various forms of collective action, all calling for or leading to increasing regulation of economic life by the state. Thus, I came to regard Marx, Veblen, Sombart, Commons, and Pesch as representatives of patterns of thought which depart not only from the analytical methods of traditional economic theory but also from the principles of classical liberalism concerning the meaning of freedom and the political conditions under which it can best be realized. In addition to setting forth the contributions of these writers and their limitations as theoretical econo-

mists, I have thought it might prove useful to examine their ideas and programs of social reform against the background of nineteenth century liberalism. In making this examination, my guiding spirit became John Stuart Mill, for whom my admiration has increased over the years, not because of his stature as a technical economist, for in this capacity his shortcomings are great, but because of his social philosophy which embraces most that is good in our nineteenth century libertarian inheritance.[33]

These paragraphs are evidence of the study, thought, and reflection which underlie a dissertation of real worth, and the steps in the process by which one is realized. Their author's premises and project are clear; and the reader is placed in position to evaluate the author's analyses and to test his conclusions. The key ideas for graduate students are: "outgrowth of studies . . . which I began some years ago. . . . I sought to explain. . . . This essay was followed by others. . . . My original intention. . . . I came to believe. . . . I recognized certain. . . . I came to regard. . . . I thought it might prove useful. . . ." The intellectual fruit was cultivated and it matured until it was ripe to pick.[34] Graduate students should work this way throughout their coursework and preparatory reading.

A wealth of examples of this kind of intellectual exercise is available in the literature of all the scientific and humane disciplines.[35] Their ideation provides more valuable reading than does the exposition and description found in textbooks. It may be of interest to note

---

[33] Abram L. Harris, *Economics and Social Reform* (New York: Harper & Row Publishers, Inc., 1958), pp. xiii-xv. Cf. Guido de Ruggiero, *The History of European Liberalism,* trans. R. G. Collingwood (London: Oxford University Press, 1927).

[34] In the Compass Books edition (New York: Viking Press, 1962) of his *The Story of Utopias* (New York: Liveright Publishing Corp., 1922) Lewis Mumford said, p. 7: "Two main positive ideas came from my study of utopias and have been supported by further study and reflection."

[35] Useful results may be derived from a study of the structure, premises, argument, and conclusions, to say nothing of the methodology, organization, and style of such works as: Jacques Barzun, *The House of Intellect;* John K. Galbraith, *The Affluent Society;* Oskar Morgenstern, *The Question of National Defense;* W. Arthur Lewis, *The Theory of Economic Growth;* Leo Straus, *Natural Right and History;* Karl R. Popper, *The Open Society and its Enemies;* Wolfgang Köhler, *Dynamics in Psychology;* Norbert Wiener, *The Fourier Integral and Certain of its Applications* and *Cybernetics, or, Control and Communication in the Animal and the Machine.* In view of the "rather forbidding mathematical core" of *Cybernetics,* Dr. Wiener wrote for the layman the related book *The Human Use of Human Beings,* in which the "not inconsiderable social consequences" of his point of view are emphasized.

in passing that a highly elaborate dissertation, involving elegant presentation of a formal and systematic inquiry into, or investigation of,
some subject, is called a disquisition.[36]

The thesis and dissertation concepts now should have emerged
sufficiently for their direct comparison by means of illustration. Comparison will heighten clarification as well as differentiation. Both
types of essay have wide applicability in all fields of knowledge; but
the remarkable suitability of the thesis to the sciences and the dissertation to the humanities must have become obvious. The value of a
good dissertation to a prospective teacher also is notable. A brief
summary here may serve as a prologue to the act of comparison.

A thesis manifests an attempt to prove the validity of the writer's
solution to a significant problem. His essay represents an intellectual
achievement in pure or applied science as well as one in formal,
logical argument. A thesis is neither conjectural nor speculative and
seldom normative or critical. Science is exclusively inquiry—setting
up problems, working at them, solving them. This novel and creative
activity is distinct from the usual textbook learning which is acquiring possession of knowledge.[37] The scientist need not be a scholar:
he may or may not be learned. He seeks knowledge that people can
acquire and make their own. The scope of his thesis may be narrow
because his singular purpose requires a single leitmotiv. The focus of
his essay should be sharp and its penetration deep.[38] The successful
thesis essayist provides an addition to knowledge in the form of a
verified idea.

A dissertation manifests a scholar's attempt to enhance learning.
His essay represents an intellectual achievement in criticism, clarifica-

---

[36] Famous examples of the disquisition are Calhoun's *Disquisition on Government*, Locke's *Essay Concerning Human Understanding*, and Voltaire's *Essai
sur les moeurs et l'esprit des nations*, an elaborate historical disquisition in 200
chapters.

[37] José Ortega y Gasset, *Mission of the University*, trans. and with an introduction by Howard Lee Nostrand (Princeton: Princeton University Press, 1944),
p. 75: "Whether we like it or not, science excludes the ordinary man." For that
matter, so does learned scholarship. Cf. Max Weber, "Science as a Vocation,"
in *From Max Weber: Essays in Sociology*, trans., ed., and with an introduction
by H. H. Gerth and C. Wright Mills (New York: Oxford University Press, 1953),
where he says that unless one has a passion for knowledge he has no calling for
science and should do something else.

[38] Understandably, a thesis need not be long, and may be much shorter than
a dissertation. The applicable rule is that the writer should say as much as he
needs to say, not as much as he can.

tion, or refinement of knowledge as well as one in logical verification. The versatility of the dissertation makes possible its use over a wide range of subjects. As an exercise in learned scholarship, a dissertation may be general in purpose and broad in scope. It will be long enough to deal fully with some complex of questions. Drawn from the analysis of the writer's subject, these questions will provide his leitmotivs and the framework of his essay. Each will be treated as a sort of "little thesis" to provide the dissertator his means of closing the ring step by step on his subject. The successful dissertator makes knowledge more widely useful and more fruitful by enriching the understanding of his readers.

The different characteristics of thesis and dissertation may be illustrated by contrasting the approaches of a thesis writer and a dissertator to a given idea. Take for this purpose the thought of Professor Gray (with support from Hawtrey and Pöhlmann) that: "The impulse to communism has come from the necessity of constant military readiness against an external enemy." [39] A Master's thesis writer, for example, could treat the statement as an hypothesis. Under some such title as "The Impulse to Communism," he would present in an essay the argument in proof of his proposition. On the other hand, a Master's candidate wishing to dissertate under the indicated title could assume the validity of Gray's idea and take it as his premise and point of view. Basing his discourse on it, he might raise and answer the question: What must one know about Communism to understand why it eventuates? He then could explain his premise and discuss its implications rather than attempt to prove it.

The difference between a thesis and a dissertation may be demonstrated in another way. It would be inappropriate for a thesis writer to speculate whether the people of the Soviet Union might one day achieve Western-style individualistic freedom. But a dissertator might properly discuss the question whether the Soviet people eventually might produce a liberal social order as a result of their rising and broadening educational achievements. In his discussion he could pre-

---

[39] Alexander Gray, *The Socialist Tradition from Moses to Lenin* (3d impression; London: Longmans, Green & Co., 1948), p. 15. Cf. pp. 13-15. Also, Drew Pearson in *The Tampa Tribune*, November 17, 1961, reported that during the 22nd Party Congress in Moscow, Pavel A. Sotyukov, editor-in-chief of *Pravda*, read a Molotov letter, a sentence of which said: "Without serious conflict, without war, advance toward Communism is impossible." This appears to be the present Chinese Communist position.

sent arguments drawn from available evidence on all aspects of the matter. He could present his own inferences and deductions derived from study, appraisal, interpretation, insight, and reflection. He could arrive at some definite conclusion via a process of logical reasoning from stated premises.

These examples show that thesis and dissertation require their own kinds of brainwork and research projects. To enhance clarification of the difference between these exercises, one might contrast R. L. Bruckberger's *Image of America*, a dissertation, and J. M. Keynes' *The General Theory of Employment, Interest, and Money*.[40]

Peter Drucker wrote a foreword to the first of these books. In it he said that the question to which *Image of America* responds is: "What must a European know to understand America?" He then said:

> The answer, the essence of America, Father Bruckberger says, is the primacy of the person, the live, real, three-dimensional man. This theme is developed like a fugue in three parts reflecting respectively on our political principles and institutions, on our economic beliefs, and on our economic and social achievements. And contrapuntally this is contrasted with the heresy of Europe: the subordination of man to abstraction.

Bruckberger does not postulate the primacy of the person in America as something to be proved. On the basis of his preparatory study, he simply takes it as axiomatic and for a premise.[41] Discussing it in three lights, he contrasts Europe's conception of man to ours. Employing it as a key, he opens the way to clarification of the culture and mentality of Americans so that this nation can be understood by outsiders.

---

[40] R. L. Bruckberger, *Image of America*, trans. C. G. Paulding and Virgilia Peterson (New York: Viking Press, 1959). J. M. Keynes, *The General Theory of Employment, Interest, and Money* (London: Macmillan & Co., Ltd., 1936). The distinction also may be aided by contrasting Haberler, *Prosperity and Depression*, to the writing of such earlier business cycle theorists as Jevons, whose sun-spot theory is well known. While Jevons theorized about the reason for the phenomenon, Haberler contributed to understanding of the business cycle by clarification, refinement, comparison, and synthesis of knowledge about it. See Gottfried von Haberler, *Prosperity and Depression* ("Harvard Economic Studies," Vol. CV [new rev. & enl. ed.; Cambridge: Harvard University Press, 1958]).

[41] Compare the assumptions set out by Professor Black in the preface to his *The Art of History*, reprinted in appendix J.

For his part, Keynes was concerned with a difficulty which imposed a different kind of task. Consequently, he did a different kind
of thing. His task, in the mid-1930's, was to establish aggregate economic analysis by validating the hypotheses wrapped in his General
Theory. His task was to validate his solution to a problem. This he
attempted via proofs deductively derived from abstract analysis and
tested against empirical evidence. This is the kind of thing done by
those who proved the earth round and part of the solar system. It
was done by those who declared that the atom could be split and
that nuclear energy could be harnessed to the will of man.

Keynes took a "macro" point of view, in contrast to that of neo-
classical and other economists, and asserted a theoretical explanation
of changes in the level of aggregate output and income in the market-
ordered economy. He was especially concerned with the implications
of his ideas for economic stabilization and growth. He placed himself
in position to ignore value; and his work induced a revision of an
incipient branch of economics and gave it new dimensions. Keynes'
task was not to explain aggregate economic analysis so that it could
be understood by students and practitioners. That he left to others,
who have provided treatises for the purpose and ultimately a "key." [42]
Meanwhile, his propositions inspired several doctoral dissertations.

These illustrations have been drawn from the moral sciences.
Illustrations of equal value and pertinence could have been drawn
from any other field of knowledge. The works of philosophers since
Descartes' *Discourse on Method* are replete with examples. One from
the work of Bertrand Russell has been presented. A wealth of examples occurs in the works of mathematicians, such as Boole. In 1854
he laid the foundations of the modern study of symbolic logic. Max
Planck's discovery of the quantum revolutionized the whole system

---

[42] The task of clarifying and explaining aggregate analysis has been under-
taken, for example, by Dillard, McKenna, the Ruggleses, and Dernberg and
McDougall. Cf. Dudley D. Dillard, *The Economics of John Maynard Keynes*
(Englewood Cliffs, N. J.: Prentice-Hall, Inc., 1948); Joseph P. McKenna, *Ag-
gregate Economic Analysis* (New York: Dryden Press, 1955); Richard Ruggles
and Nancy D. Ruggles, *National Income Accounts and Income Analysis* (2d ed.;
New York: McGraw-Hill Book Co., Inc., 1956); Thomas F. Dernberg and
Duncan M. McDougall, *Macro-Economics* (New York: McGraw-Hill Book Co.,
Inc., 1960). The "key" was provided by Alvin H. Hansen, *A Guide to Keynes*
(New York: McGraw-Hill Book Co., Inc., 1953). Cf. David McCord Wright,
The Keynesian System, The Millar Lectures, No. 4 (New York: Fordham Uni-
versity Press, 1962). For an example of a dissertation, see Lawrence R. Klein,
The Keynesian Revolution (New York: The Macmillan Co., 1949).

of physics. Norbert Wiener regards G. D. Birkhoff, of Harvard, as the first important American mathematician to have all of his schooling in the United States. He wrote of Birkhoff: "He had a brilliant dissertation [Chicago, 1907] on certain branches of dynamics, concerning particularly the mechanics of the planets, a field which had been outlined in France by Henri Poincaré." [43]

The writing requirements for graduate degrees now have been treated from a generic point of view by means of definition and illustration. Understanding of these concepts may be furthered by contrasting what is required in respect of them by Master's and Doctor's degree candidates.

Master's and Doctor's Essays Compared

The distinction between the writing requirements for Master's and Doctor's degrees is not a matter of kind but one of level of attainment. Master's and Doctor's candidates should do qualitatively the same kind of thing with the latter doing it better. In general, "the master's thesis is recognized as training in research rather than research accomplishment. Research accomplishment is the objective of the doctorate." [44]

The distinction between Master's and Doctor's level essays turns principally upon four sets of factors. Usually mentioned first are the materials with which the student works during his inquiry and the processes of his research. Second is the selected problem or topic together with the candidate's solution or arguable view. Third are the inquiry which led to the candidate's position and the research on the basis of which it is sustained. Finally, there is the essay with its argument and techniques of proof. The importance of the second and third factors is paramount, with that of the fourth next. The materials factor has least importance.

Materials usually are categorized as being original, primary, secondary, or tertiary on the basis of their authorship and derivation. Those called original are the candidate's own product, derived by his

---

[43] Norbert Wiener, *I Am A Mathematician* (Garden City, N. Y.: Doubleday & Co., Inc., 1956), pp. 27-28.
[44] "Should You Go To Graduate School?", pamphlet issued by the Graduate School, University of Florida, 1961.

own research as guided by the needs of his inquiry. Those classed as primary are basic first-hand reports and documents from which other materials may be derived. Public and private documents are regarded as primary sources of information. Writing based on such by persons other than the candidate provide secondary or tertiary sources. This is more than a matter of first-hand versus second-hand information. A more important consideration is whether the student discriminates among sources, and whether he can produce significant data of his own. What the student does with his materials is more important still.

Trouble often ensues where originality of student essays is assessed on the basis of materials alone. Such narrow focus on research materials has been productive of two sorts of difficulties for graduate candidates. First, it induces a misconception of the writing requirements which, combined with a pragmatic outlook, leads to mere compilation of data. Surveys are popular to provide bases for unimaginative compendiums which are submitted for credit as theses or dissertations.[45] In the second place, emphasis on the materials factor diverts attention from the significance of the other three. It provides a poor guide to a successful essay project compared to explanation of a subject or solution of a problem. Concern with sources and data can obscure the validity of criticism or evaluation of a body of knowledge or the works of an author. In the latter case, originality cannot be defined from the point of view of sources of materials. The writer's thought must govern.

Understanding of this point may be aided by reference to the appendices to this book which present lists of model theses and dissertations. It may be clarified here by means of illustration. For example, the author of a doctoral dissertation on the economic thought of Karl Marx had this to say in his preface:

> The purpose of this dissertation is to test Marx's predictions as logical derivations of his economic system. As such, it was found unnecessary to incorporate material other than Marx's own writings into the study.[46]

---

[45] There is a difference between information of value to a business firm, for example, and knowledge that is important from the point of view of learning and science. It does not suffice to assert the newness of data such as might be presented in an expository report.

[46] Fred M. Gottheil, "The Economic Predictions of Karl Marx: An Examination of Marxian Economic Theory" (Doctor's dissertation, Duke University, 1959), p. i.

This statement may be adduced in support of the postulate that it is more important for a student to generate an original idea and sustain it imaginatively than for him to work with primary materials. The case for the misleading influence of the materials factor and the greater significance of the other three is equally well supported by an outstanding Master's thesis on the writings of Thorstein Veblen. Its author heard it asserted that Veblen had no theoretical system. His reading and analysis of the whole body of Veblen's writings led the author to posit that Veblen did have such a system.[47] His position was effectively sustained in a brilliant essay.

Successful fulfillment of the writing requirements for graduate degrees requires that students move up from the world of facts and data to the realm of ideas and reason. It calls for achievement at the intellectual rather than the empirical level of scholarship.[48] The employment of basic or primary data, as by a thesis writer, may be illustrated by the relationship of Kepler to Tycho Brahe. Had Brahe's careful reports of his precise astronomical observations over thirty years not come into Kepler's hands, they may have lain unused for decades. As it was, they formed the basis for Kepler's discoveries and of the Rudolphine Tables. Gade writes:

> The different mentalities of the two men led each one along his own line. Kepler's unlimited speculative propensity supplemented Tycho's mechanical faculty. He found in Tycho's ample legacy of first-class data precisely what enabled him to try, by the touchstone of fact, the successive hypotheses that he postulated.[49]

---

[47] Richard Ludwick Sterba, "The Foundations of Veblen's Theoretical System" (Master's thesis, University of Texas, 1950). This essay is of higher quality than that attained by many doctoral candidates.

[48] Oliver Wendell Holmes once said: "There are one-story intellects, two-story intellects and three-story intellects with skylights. All fact collectors, who have no aim beyond their facts, are one-story men. Two-story men compare, reason, generalize, using the labors of the fact collectors as well as their own. Three-story men idealize, imagine, predict; their best illumination comes from above, through the skylight." It should be clear from the nature of Dr. Holmes' mind that this is not a prescription for augury. Kant argued that knowledge is not a collection of gifts received by the senses and stored in the mind as if it were a museum, but the result of mental activity. One must search, compare, criticize, unify, generalize to attain knowledge. The scientist and the scholar alike must take an interest and make an effort if they are to know. Cf. Joan Robinson, *Economic Philosophy* (Chicago: Aldine Publishing Company, 1962), pp. 3, 88 on conception of ideas in metaphysical form.

[49] John Allyne Gade, *The Life and Times of Tycho Brahe* (Princeton: Princeton University Press, for the American-Scandinavian Foundation, New York, 1947), pp. 190-91.

Kepler was a great mathematician. According to Gade, he also was "inventive, full of original ideas and exceedingly productive." Kepler's untiring patience in comparing and calculating the observations at his disposal made possible his revolutionary intellectual findings. His genius supplied what Brahe, whose "endowments were of a practical order," lacked. Gade's succinct summation is: "In his work with Tycho, one does not know which to admire the more, Kepler's patience or his penetration."

The ready availability of good primary data relevant to his inquiry is valuable to a scholar or scientist. If there is none relevant to his project he will have to engage in research to produce his own.[50] One also may find existing data out of date, incomplete, or otherwise faulty. To ensure himself of the accuracy of data an inquirer may have to re-research or re-work them, just as Kepler did. Anyone who seeks the intellectual mode of knowing may need to originate data of his own to pursue his inquiry or for research verification of his insight. In any case, one may be well advised to prepare for inquiry by establishing an empirical mode of knowing through study of basic source materials.

To use guild terminology, a candidate for a Master's degree is properly regarded as a novice working under the tutelage of his mentor to acquire basic methodological competence, self-discipline, the habit of taking responsibility for accuracy and validity, comprehension of subject matter, and control and use of ideas. His Master's essay is the final learning exercise by which he qualifies himself for full-fledged apprenticeship.[51] A candidate for a Doctor's degree has a different status and objective. He is an academic apprentice who seeks to qualify himself, especially by fulfillment of his writing requirement, for the status and role of journeyman. A doctoral essay must establish competence to do at least reliable intellectual work alone.[52]

---

[50] This was the case, for example, with Galileo who originated his own data by means of experiments with inclined planes and falling bodies. For an account of the Galilean problem, inquiry, and experimental research, see F. S. C. Northrop, *The Logic of the Sciences and the Humanities* (New York: The Macmillan Co., 1947), pp. 22-28 and *passim*.

[51] This does not apply in cases where students go straight to the higher degree. A Master's degree is not a prerequisite for a Doctor's degree although in many cases it is a useful preparatory step. Also, if attainment of the higher degree is delayed, one graduate degree at least is in hand.

[52] This does not suggest denial of access to appropriate guidance and advice

Master's and Doctor's essays may differ as to the quality of materials involved because of their different functions and purposes. A Master's essay may rest essentially on secondary sources, or at least on a combination of primary and secondary sources, so long as it meets form and quality requirements. An acceptable Doctor's essay, on the other hand, should be based on original and primary sources. This normal but not necessary distinction rests on the difference between research training and research accomplishment. Nothing need prevent a Master's degree candidate from doing a better than merely acceptable job. Distinguished essays win prizes as well as qualify their writers for advanced degrees. It is worthwhile to do an essay well, if possible excellently, in view of what one of real quality can set in motion relative to a career.

A graduate candidate's project of inquiry and research should be relevant to important knowledge.[53] It provides the basis for both his intellectual mode of knowing something and his essay in substantiation of it. Doctoral candidates may be expected to undertake inquiries that are new and original, and that are more difficult and significant than those which suffice for Master's candidates. Doctoral projects should be differentiated by the nature and quality of selected problems or topics, by conceptual originality in respect of the inquiry, power and penetration of analysis, level of abstraction and degree of simplification, inventiveness of hypotheses and their proof-tests, and design and control of the relevant research and experimentation.

A doctoral inquiry should be characterized by originality of thought, imaginative speculativeness, number and value of insights, and the vitality of experimentation and proofs. It should attain higher

---

during the processes of inquiry, research, and writing. Even at this stage, learning of requisite skills must be consummated and the necessary edge given to competence. Attainment of self-confidence requires access to confirmation.

[53] Bertrand Russell has illustrated this point by remarking that learning would suffer if a learned man were to improve his income by teaching brewing instead of organic chemistry. Important knowledge is exemplified by the principles, theories, theorems, axioms, postulates which provide the apparatuses of intellectual thought in all sciences; and by the ideas which are intellectual achievements of fundamental learning and basic science. Cf. Norbert Wiener, *Ex-Prodigy* (New York: Simon & Schuster, Inc., 1953), p. 194: ". . . in 1925 . . . the conflicting currents aroused by the earlier work by Bohr began to be resolved and . . . the ideas of de Broglie, Born, Heisenberg, and Schrödinger showed that the quantum theory was to mark as great a revolution in the philosophical presuppositions of physics as had the work of Einstein."

levels of abstraction for analysis and synthesis, greater elegance of model-building, and more sophisticated reasoning in induction and deduction. A certain naïveté may be permitted the Master's candidate, especially if his work at an intellectual level of scholarship contributes to his intellectual growth and methodological competence.

The intellectual achievement of a graduate degree candidate must be the logical outcome of a rational process of thought. As such, his solution should be a recognizable contribution to knowledge, his criticism or clarification a significant contribution to learning.[54]

A doctoral candidate's inquiry begins with imaginative thought on some subject reasonably well known to him, reflection on which leads to insight. This stage is followed by analytical work which may involve model building, recasting of ideas and materials, and their new synthesis. Then follow experimentation and testing. This process of intellectual work may be illustrated by an early achievement of Albert Einstein's. Concerning it, James R. Newman wrote:

> At the heart of the theory of relativity are questions connected with the velocity of light. The young Einstein began to brood about these while still a high school student. Suppose, he asked himself, a person could run as fast as a beam of light, how would things look to him? Imagine that he could ride astride the beam, holding a mirror in front of him. Then, like a fictional vampire, he would cause no image; for since the light and the mirror are traveling in the same direction at the same velocity, and the mirror is a little ahead, the light can never catch up to the mirror and there can be no reflection.
>
> But this applies only to *his* mirror. Imagine a stationary observer, also equipped with a mirror, who watches the rider flashing by. Obviously the observer's mirror will catch the rider's image. In other words, the optical phenomena surrounding this event are purely relative. They exist for the observer; they do not exist for the rider. This was a troublesome paradox, which flatly contradicted the accepted views of optical phenomena. . . .[55]

---

[54] These terms mean products of the writer's own brainwork tested by his own research. To define a thesis or dissertational essay as an "original contribution to knowledge" is absurd. Contributions to knowledge or understanding are achievements of intellectual work which it is the function of theses and dissertations to substantiate. Although both essays represent intellectual products or results, contributions and substantiations are functionally different things. So are knowledge and essays about it.

[55] James R. Newman, "Einstein's Great Idea," in *Adventures of the Mind* eds. Richard Thruelsen and John Kobler (1st. ser.; New York: Alfred A. Knopf,

From here Einstein made his thoughtful way—via the concept of simultaneity, his clarification of which charged him with the task of challenging and refuting two Newtonian assumptions—to his first postulate of his Special Theory of Relativity. This principle says that the velocity of light in space is a constant of nature, unaffected by the motion of the observer or of the source of the light. Striding intellectually to his second postulate, Einstein soon was in position to state boldly that the mass of a body is a measure of its energy content. He wrote this in a paper, "On the Electrodynamics of Moving Bodies," which he published in 1905 (at age 26) in *Annalen der Physik*. This paper included the now famous formula, $E = mc^2$. Einstein proposed that his theory could be successfully tested with bodies whose energy output is variable to a high degree. Twenty-five years later many physicists made the test, with such aids as cyclotrons, and their results verified his idea.

A doctoral candidate is expected to produce a more polished and erudite essay than that acceptable for a Master's candidate. The essay should be a more or less lively intellectual exercise in logical substantiation in either case. But the tightness of the doctoral candidate's logic, his techniques of proof, and the value of his conclusions should differentiate his essay clearly from one adequate for a Master's candidate. His argument should be characterized by lively and original expression, richness of treatment, and some elegance. His writing style should be lucid. It is proper to think that a doctoral candidate should be more precise both as a thinker and as an essayist than a Master's candidate. Nevertheless, there is no rule which requires a Master's essay to be minimal in quality. Much may be gained from a Master's essay of superior or distinguished quality.

A doctoral essay may be both narrower in scope and shorter in length than a Master's essay on a similar problem or topic. This is because of the doctoral candidate's higher level of abstraction and generalization, more heroic assumptions, more penetrating analysis, more precise argument and proof, and the simplicity achieved by a more powerful logic. Factors of size and scope thus may be irrelevant for comparison of Master's and Doctor's essays.

1959), pp. 220-21. The same kind of thing is done in the moral sciences and the humanities. For example: Gilbert Highet, *The Anatomy of Satire* (Princeton: Princeton University Press, 1962). For a short example in economics, see C. E. Ferguson, "Transformation Curve in Production Theory: A Pedagogical Note," *The Southern Economic Journal*, XXIX, No. 2 (October 1962), 96-102.

Size and scope are functions of the intellectual task being performed in the essay, and of the discipline or science within which the essay falls. Some proofs are simple and short, others complex and long. Also to be considered are the nature, characteristics, and demands of the underlying projects of inquiry, the writer's objectives, his point of view and approach, and his capacity as an essayist. Some writers are terse, others wordy. Few or many chapters may be needed for a writer to present and substantiate his position on a matter.

The proportions of an essay devoted to the presentation of empirical, historical, institutional, and other descriptive and quantitative materials and evidence in contrast to the proportions devoted to explanation of the qualitative, abstract and conceptual analysis and synthesis, to deduction of hypotheses and inferences, and to argument of proofs will vary. These proportions will be functions of the selected project and the way things are done in the writer's field of interest. In and of themselves, such proportions have no bearing on essay quality. Clear presentation of some problems requires extensive frames of reference and elaborate settings. Some proofs need large empirical bases, inductively derived, while others do not. Doctoral theses of first rank have required a single short chapter (especially in the natural sciences); while so-called theses of little or no merit have occupied hundreds of pages and two or more volumes.

Lest an erroneous conclusion be drawn from the preceding by the unwary, it may be well to observe at once that there is no necessary inverse relationship between thesis size and quality. Neither scope nor size of a thesis or dissertational essay has any necessary bearing on its quality or importance. The things which count are quality and vitality of thought, clarity and precision of reasoned argument, lucidity of substantiation, originality of the inquiry, formulation of the problem and design of the research project, and inventiveness in respect of a solution or position that is new. The basic question relative to the essay is whether it is a matter of important knowledge.

Summation

The question now to be answered relates to the lesson of these didactics. Perhaps the lesson is that to succeed, a graduate student must attain at least some level of intellectual scholarship. The first step in this direction, but only the first, is to establish an empirical mode of knowing something. Then relevant issues and uncertainties can be studied and reflected on until an answer or solution is reached via imagination, intuition, insight, logical analysis and synthesis as with models, and deduction. The intellectual result may be valid if it stands technical tests provided by research and experimentation. It is not necessary for a student to more than meet the required performance standard for his level in these respects, but it is worthwhile for him to aim high. Whether theses or dissertations, distinguished essays often become springboards to distinguished careers.[56]

A corollary to the lesson is that it is not enough to report technical achievements at an empirical level of scholarship, such as in counting and summing. The thesis is a unique product of intellect. The argument it presents calls much more upon the imaginative, intuitive, inventive, innovational, problem-solving, and other reasoning powers of the mind than does the research which provided factual tests for its hypothesis. Hypotheses are more important in inquiry than the touchstones of fact against which they are tried. The dissertation also is a product of intellect. This is as true of the discussion it presents as it is of the inquiry and research on which the discussion is based. Being essays, theses and dissertations represent exercises which begin and end in the mind. They differ in kind from reports, which are expository exercises in objective representation of empirical realities.[57]

---

[56] Cf. Rockefeller Brothers Fund, *The Pursuit of Excellence* ("Special Studies Project Panel Report V" [Garden City, N. Y.: Doubleday & Co., 1958]). Aristotle said long ago that "Excellence is an art won by training and habituation. We do not act rightly because we have virtue or excellence, but we rather have those because we have acted rightly. We are what we repeatedly do. Excellence, then, is not an act but a habit." Examples of superior and distinguished essays are available in all fields. They should not remain buried in libraries. They should be taken out and read at least as models. Lists of some such theses and dissertations are provided in Appendices G and H. Stars of the first magnitude provide better guides than lesser lights. Collections of theses and dissertations pertaining to all fields of learning are available in all good libraries. So are bibliographies of such works. Graduate schools and learned societies periodically publish lists of theses and dissertations completed and of research in progress.

[57] For clear illustration of the qualitative differentiation of data, and the difference between obtaining it and using it, see Walter A. Morton, "Wage-Push Inflation," in *Proceedings of the Eleventh Annual Meeting, Industrial Relations Research Association,* ed. Gerald G. Somers (Madison, Wis.: December 1959).

A second corollary of the lesson suggests the value of competent use of the essay form. Study and practice in the use of the essay are good ways of stimulating imaginative, speculative, creative use of the mind. Essay writing is an intellectual exercise which enhances competence in methodology, logical argument, and rhetoric as well as in grammar and literary tool skills. The vital necessity of such practice in the art and science of reasoned discourse has been emphasized by the 1956 Panel Discussions at Yale University:

> . . . the ability to express ideas coherently is not merely a problem of correct grammar, but rather involves the organization of ideas in a meaningful manner. Unless a student can express an idea clearly, he does not really understand it. Thus, the ability to express ideas coherently is highly related to the problem of substance, and is properly the responsibility of the graduate school. Some students have difficulty in writing because they have nothing to say. They have not developed habits of creative thinking, and do not know how to approach a subject.[58]

The importance of reminting the words thesis and dissertation, by reaffirming the concepts for which they really stand, arises from the uncertainty which has grown up about them. This is a troublesome feature of the contemporary academic scene. Almost any kind of writing may be called one or the other these days. Students may be

---

[58] *Graduate Training in Economics*, "Panel Discussions at Yale" (New Haven: Yale University, 1956), p. 12. Lee H. Bristol, Jr., as Creative Education Foundation president, pointed to the findings of Prof. John Arnold of Stanford University to the effect that exercise of one's constructive imagination can enable one to approach his potentiality for creative thought. University of Buffalo experiments with coursework in creative thinking, and systematic instruction in "applied imagination" bears this out. See "To Walk Taller in the World," (address by Dr. Lee H. Bristol, Jr., Fairleigh Dickinson University, November 18, 1960). Cf. Alexander Osburn, *Applied Imagination: Principles and Procedures of Creative Thinking* (New York: Charles Scribner's Sons, 1953). The entire issue of *Think* Magazine, Vol. XXVIII, No. 10 (November-December 1962) was devoted to "Man's Creative Mind." Cf. Vol. XXIX, No. 3 (March 1963). See also the discussion of reason in "Greece: Part III," in *Life*, LIV, No. 6 (February 8, 1963). There is a widespread feeling that many minds are not trained to think logically in any circumstances, and that the contemporary generation generally lacks the faculty for logical thought. Cf. Dorothy L. Sayers, *The Lost Tools of Learning* (London: Methuen, 1948). See also Carroll V. Newsom, *A University President Speaks Out: On Current Education* (New York: Harper and Row, Publishers, Inc., 1961), esp. pp. 103-106 on graduate education.

directed to produce any of several kinds of non-essay writing under a thesis or dissertation label.

This need not bewilder students who know what theses and dissertations are. They will be able to confront confusion with poise. Knowledgeable students neither become lost in semantic swamps nor involved in semantic issues. They make sound writing requirement proposals for consideration of their supervisory committees. They accept committee suggestions and modifications, and go to work on them. They avoid undue delays for useless academic backing and filling. In the end, they realize the satisfaction of fulfillment of degree requirements and embarkation upon careers in reasonable and appropriate lengths of time.

3

Readying
Oneself to Write

More than 2,000 years ago the Greek thinkers recognized that
to wonder is the primary condition that leads to inquiry.
WOLFGANG KÖHLER

The most beautiful thing we can experience is the mysterious.
It is the source of all true art and science.
ALBERT EINSTEIN

Readiness to write a thesis or dissertation is an attained condition. It is a state of mind which is reached by the intellectual route
from wondering to knowing. It follows naturally from scholarly activities pertinent to an educational process leading to a degree. It does not
necessarily follow, however; nor is it automatically realized. In many,
if not most, cases of graduate candidacy, the condition of readiness
to write is a result of conscious preparation.

The learning process by which a student prepares himself or
herself to fulfill writing requirements involves all coursework and seminars, all reading and writing, all investigations, and all thought and
discussion prior to the writing. This is not to suggest, as some apparently do, that the purpose of coursework is to prepare graduate students to write theses and dissertations. Such achievements are only
some of the results of an educational process which prepares students
to stand on their own feet in responsible adulthood. Since many students meet writing requirements successively for both Master's and
Doctor's degrees, this book is designed to aid students at both levels.

The analysis which follows may make the attainment of readiness to write seem longer and more complex than it really is. This

50

illusion appears because concurrent learning processes will be abstracted for treatment one at a time, and will be analyzed step by step. For clarity, the parts of the component processes will be illustrated as well as explained.

It may be well to keep in mind during the analysis and discussion, that Master's coursework usually is completed in one academic year and doctoral coursework in two. The Master's degree writing requirement often is met within the year of coursework or by the end of the following summer term. This means that the underlying inquiry has been concurrent with coursework. A few Master's candidates take a third semester to complete their theses or dissertations.

The doctoral writing requirement is designed for fulfillment the year after completion of coursework. Occasionally two years are taken. A longer period suggests an interval of teaching or some other occupation. In any case, doctoral candidates usually do not begin the investigative projects on which to base their theses or dissertations until after "prelims" have been passed. All this may seem elementary, but it provides frames of reference within which to consider student preparation of readiness to write the required academic essays.

Candidates for Master's degrees normally must select essay problems or topics within their first semester in residence. Despite this timing, selection need not be the traumatic experience it seems to be for many. Neither need selection be so subject to procrastination. Commitment to a problem or topic can mark the climax of a rational process, especially under informed and expert guidance. Selection can be the carefully contrived outcome of a process begun even as an undergraduate. This is especially so where upper class coursework is in the hands of professors who are members of the graduate faculty, and who encourage top undergraduate scholars to pursue graduate study. Any upperclassman with a prospect or intention of doing graduate work certainly gives some thought to the fields of his probable concentration.[1] He can give thought as well to his eventual thesis or dissertation, perhaps to the distinct advantage of his senior term essays and those of his initial graduate semester.

The Master's degree candidate who has given no thought to selection of his thesis problem or dissertational topic before enroll-

[1] On the three-year Master's degree program which begins in the Junior undergraduate year, see Oliver C. Carmichael, *Graduate Education: A Critique and a Program* (New York: Harper and Row, Publishers, Inc., 1961), Chap. ii.

ment in graduate school is not in danger of becoming lost. He can devote a program of outside reading and discussion to it. Such a program could easily be guided by his teachers and advisors; and it could provide him with ideas and material for course term essays and seminar papers.

Doctoral candidates have more difficult problems of selection than those which press Master's candidates. However, they have the advantages of more time and greater maturity. Many a doctoral essay is the offspring of an idea conceived in a Master's seminar. Unanticipated flashes of insight can enable students to intuit or induce significant and stimulating propositions.[2] The difficulty doctoral candidates appear to face in this respect often arises from their tendencies (*a*) to procrastinate, (*b*) to flounder indecisively, and (*c*) to wish for some unique problem or topic concerning which a classic may be written.[3] Like uncertainty, the fallacy of perfection is in more ways than one an enemy of intellectual achievement.[4] The purpose of a doctoral essay is to prove attainment of a certain level of intellectual and research competence, not to "set the world on fire." The so-called "*magnum opus*" concept of a doctoral essay is false.

The general process of attainment of readiness to write has similar characteristics for both Master's and Doctor's degree candidates. The difference of achievement levels for those attempting to qualify as academic apprentices and journeymen does not differentiate the kind of thing they must do. It merely implies that foundations and basics are emphasized at one level and virtuosity at the next. Preparation of readiness to write will be treated generically, therefore, from three points of view. These may be visualized as

---

[2] On the nature and possibilities of induction, see Loren Eiseley, "The Man Who Saw Through Time," one of the "Adventures of the Mind" series, *The Saturday Evening Post*, CCXXXV, No. 20 (May 19, 1962), 68 ff. On intuition, see Eugene Raudsepp, "Can You Trust Your Hunches?" *The Management Review*, XLIX, No. 4 (April 1960), 4 ff. On the "contradiction of parity," see Snow, *The Two Cultures and the Scientific Revolution*, p. 17.

[3] See Panel Discussions at Yale, *Graduate Training in Economics*, p. 16: "It is quite well known that the greater part of time now spent on the Ph.D. thesis is spent in floundering around trying to select a problem and decide just how to carry it out. More and earlier practice in research might avoid much of this floundering." So might clarity as to the essay requirement!

[4] Cf. Barzun and Graff, *The Modern Researcher*, p. 37: "The fallacy of perfection is the worst enemy of intellectual work. The effort to attain it may contribute to surface finish, but it does so at the cost of inner solidity."

three parallel columns, with readiness the attained capstone they support.

The first in the set of columns stands for mastery of the subject matter and isolation of the problems and uncertainties of some discipline or field of learning. This may be called substantive achievement. The second column represents mastery of the methods of inquiry, research, and logical argument. Mastery of methodology implies attainment of learning how to learn. It underlies capability to explain and prove the validity of what one may have learned. The third column is for mastery of the essay form of writing. The scholarly essay is the form of expression best suited to explaining the derivation and proving the substantiation of ideas. Its effective use requires integration of substantive and methodological achievements. Both from this point of view and that of writing skills, writing lesser essays provides direct preparation for writing the thesis or dissertation.

These three processes—mastery of subject matter, accomplishment in methodology, and acquisition of essayist skills—are concurrent undertakings in the general process of graduate education. For clarity, they will be abstracted from the general process and treated in separate sections in the order named.

Substantive Preparation to Write

Substantive preparation to write an academic essay in fulfillment of a writing requirement involves two objectives. They are comprehension of the body of knowledge and control of the intellectual apparatus of theory which lie within the purview of the chosen science or discipline. As bases for a thesis or dissertation, these achievements have two aspects. The first is general and primary; the second is particular and proximate.

The general and primary basis for an academic essay is acquired by means of the broad ordinary process of scholarly maturation. It is a function of growing comprehension of one or more fields of knowledge reached via coursework and related reading, and of a change from the habit of empirically knowing to that of intellectually knowing. All coursework is involved, but especially that of major fields. Early coursework often is highly descriptive and insti-

tutional in order to provide solid empirical foundations for intermediate and advanced work. Later coursework becomes increasingly
abstract and conceptual as students are brought up from the empirical to the intellectual mode of knowing by means of developing
theoretical proficiency. Textbooks are left behind and reading lists
are put to use. In this way, students gain contact with the best minds
and thought in the fields of their curricular interests. Opportunities
to analyze and compare the work and positions of mature thinkers
on various problems and topics provide them access to the intellectual scholarship in their major fields of study.

Preparation of the particular and proximate basis for an academic essay begins later than, and runs concurrently with, general
preparation. This second aspect of substantive readiness develops
as interest centers on the substance and the methods of some particular area of learned concern. This basis gains strength and importance as attention focuses more and more acutely on selected questions
and uncertainties relevant to the area of special interest.

Selection of an attractive problem to define, analyze, and attempt to solve follows naturally from thoughtful reading of learned
journals and books. Unresolved questions, doubts, and trail ends
pointed out by master investigators can be explored as bases for
possible term essays. So can the suggestions of mature thinkers.
Professors themselves often attribute to colleagues and confreres the
ideas from which their papers spring.[5]

Students have an especial advantage in this connection. Their
unforced unconventionality of thought often contrasts sharply with
that of older and committed thinkers. Many of the greatest contributions of noted thinkers came in their early years. Sir Isaac Newton
said that he achieved his best work when he was "young and full
of inventiveness." Albert Einstein challenged and refuted long-
standing Newtonian assumptions, and achieved the basis for his

---

[5] For example, C. E. Ferguson credits M. J. Farrell with the idea underlying
one of his papers. See Ferguson, "Theories of Growth and the 'Rate of Growth'
Hypothesis," in *Weltwirtschaftliches Archiv*, Band 89, Heft 2 (1962), note 1,
p. 267: "Indeed, this paper had its origin in a concluding speculation made by
Farrell: 'It would be interesting to see the effect on the many "theories of economic growth" of substituting in them the *Rate-of-Growth Hypothesis* for their
present (usually linear) consumption functions'." Cf. Schoeffler's attribution to
Adolph Lowe in Sidney Schoeffler, *The Failures of Economics: A Diagnostic
Study* (Cambridge: Harvard University Press, 1955), p. 222.

theory of relativity, between the ages of 16 and 25. The paper in which he stated that $E = mc^2$ was published when he was 26. This is about the average age of doctoral candidates today.

Focussing attention on some problem or topic can lead via study, imagination, thought, intuition, conjecture, reflection, and insight to a solution or clarification of it. Such achievement often is the outcome of a series of investigations, each dealing with some part of a problematic complex.

Achievement is more a matter of intellectual than of chronological age. For example, Sylvain Cappel, senior in The Bronx High School of Science, won first prize in Westinghouse's annual Science Talent Search with a study of the application of mathematical logic to computers.[6] He explained his project by pointing out that in logic things usually are true or false, but that there are cases where the Aristotelian law of the excluded middle doesn't hold. He dealt with these. Interviewed at the ripe age of 16, Cappel said that he had become interested in mathematics when "quite young."

It should be obvious that the general and particular aspects of substantive preparation to write are mutually reinforcing. Together they bring successful students to the enjoyment of an intellectual level of scholarship. This is a level of excellence which is rationally attainable as an academic goal, necessary personal and mental perquisites being given. Aristotle's axiom that one becomes what one habitually does applies here as a reason for optimism. Even in the academic life, heroes are made more often than they are born. This is the reason for having faculties and libraries.

The general aspects of substantive preparation emphasize the important stages of intellectual growth. The first stage is getting a solid and complete empirical background, the significance of which is that it provides a foundation for intellectual achievement in a field of interest. The next stage is acquiring control of the theoretical apparatus of one's science or discipline. Then comes study of the problems, uncertainties, issues, doubts, and errors of the science or discipline. This includes appraisal of relevant discussions, oral and

---

[6] See *Newsweek*, LXI, No. 11 (March 18, 1962), 94. Compare the case of Jean Frène, French farm boy who, upon being drafted into the French army at age 19, was found to have "a mind like Leonardo's." See *Time* LXXIX, No. 15 (April 13, 1962), 72. See also, "Case of the Reluctant Genius," *Reader's Digest*, LXXXI, No. 486 (October 1962), 107-11.

written, and analysis and evaluation of the arguments advanced by participants. Students at last begin to take their own intellectual wings when they undertake their own analyses, and build and use their own models. As facility with analysis grows, and as ability to recast data and ideas as means to new syntheses increases, their inductive and deductive powers improve. Then thought, imaginative speculation, learned conjecture, and reflection combine to provide the understanding which leads through insight to conclusions.

Preparation on particular problems and topics develops by similar stages. The process is begun by laying solid empirical foundations through background study. Generalization follows as a higher form of thought than descriptive detail. From there scholars move to levels of abstraction and conceptualization and of theoretical inquiry. Thus, particular inquiry yields particular ideas which can be developed, by means of confirmation, into particular knowledge. In this way, students make contributions to knowledge and understanding.[7]

Capacity to produce an adequate academic essay on the basis of an original individual inquiry and research effort is an essential characteristic of a finished and professionally competent scholar. The term "professional" is not used here in the popular sense, but rather to suggest a minimal level of communications competence.

---

[7] The preparation of general and particular readiness serves equally well to effectuate readiness for the written and oral qualifying examinations which mark completion of coursework requirements. For example, a doctoral candidate in economics became interested in the question of factor shares of output. Over a two-year period he pulled together all the best thought he could find on it and so formulated an excellent body of knowledge on it. Then he fitted into this frame of reference the essence of economic theory in general. He did the same with the subject of economic growth and development. In the end, he decided to write his dissertation on a topic in this area. For an excellent dissertational example of this kind of organizational work see Harold J. Barnett and Chandler Morse, *Scarcity and Growth: The Economics of Natural Resource Availability* (Baltimore: The Johns Hopkins University Press, for Resources for the Future, Inc., 1963). Cf. Mario Bunge, *The Myth of Simplicity* (Englewood Cliffs, N. J.: Prentice-Hall, Inc., 1963), p. 3: "Thinking begins with forming, associating and elaborating ideas; it culminates with synthesizing them into bodies of grounded and testable opinion. But *critical* thinking—the thinking peculiar to science, technology, rational philosophy, and rational decision making—begins when we start to analyze both initial ideas and final (but still corrigible) syntheses. Science and, to a lesser degree, technology are eminently testable and, by the same token, critical or analytic. And so is every philosophy which purports to be rational, that is, arguable—and a fortiori every philosophy which claims the right to be called scientific, that is, testable and congenial with science."

A thesis or dissertation represents more than a substantive examination. It is also a sort of superfinal examination in the art and science of learned inquiry and argument, and in the control of the crafts of researcher and communicator. Candidate grammar must be as acceptable as candidate tenets.

Methodological Preparation
to Write

There is a difference between knowing one's subject and knowing one's craft. As spelled out by Jacques Barzun, one reads to secure comprehension of accepted truths, disputed problems, rival schools, and methods in favor. While this learning will give students possession of what a discipline has to offer the world, it does not in itself enable them to contribute to what is known.[8] Students also need competence in the methodology of inquiry and research. This is a vital concomitant of substantive preparation. Without it an intellectual level of scholarship hardly could be attained. A scholar simply cannot walk on one academic leg.

Method is the life-blood of brainwork. Without it there would be neither analysis nor model-building; and learned scholarship and science would not exist. Science begins and ends in the mind, and it therefore is abstract and conceptual. Without methodology, a graduate student would be unable to find, define, analyze, research, or solve any problem of sufficient significance for an acceptable thesis. Except as a methodologist one could not effectuate the clarification, refinement, synthesis, explanation, or criticism which are the ends of the dissertator's discourse. Except as methodologist, how could one present a rational argument in formal logic in either case?

Besides comprehending the scope and methods of their own disciplines and sciences, graduate students would do well to attain familiarity with the general methods of inquiry. It would be to their distinct advantage to have explicit coursework in the methodologies of inquiry, problem-solving, and research, especially at the Master's degree level. However, it is unfortunately true that many graduate

---

[8] Jacques Barzun, *The House of Intellect* (New York: Harper and Row, Publishers, Inc., 1959), p. 12. By comprehension, as of accepted truths, both knowledge and understanding of them is meant.

students lack access to coursework in the general theory of inquiry
and problem-solving. Many even lack direct access to the general
methods of their fields of concentration.[9] Despite faculty intentions
and planning for incidental presentation of relevant methodologies as
part of coursework, it frequently results that they are not effectively
taught in this way.

For many students, study in methodology is not an official requirement. But for all it is an intellectual requirement. It is vital
that graduate students learn how to learn, and how to pursue learning, if they are to be successfully educated for intellectual work.
Self-teaching often is the most realistic means of attaining methodological competence. The earlier it is begun, the better.

Graduate students would be well advised to read and study the
literature of scientific investigation. Such reading would significantly
enhance preparation to fulfill writing requirements because it would
aid intellectual development and scholarly maturation. A basic list
of titles might include: F. S. C. Northrop's *The Logic of the Sciences
and the Humanities*, W. I. B. Beveridge's *The Art of Scientific Investigation*, Karl R. Popper's *The Logic of Scientific Discovery*, W.
B. Cannon's *The Way of an Investigator*, R. A. Fisher's *The Design
of Experiments*, Arthur Koestler's *Insight and Outlook*, N. R. Hansen's *Patterns of Discovery*, Ernest Nagel's *The Structure of Science:
Problems in the Logic of Scientific Explanation*, R. B. Braithwaite's
Scientific Explanation, M. R. Cohen's *A Preface to Logic*, Rudolph
Carnap's *The Continuum of Inductive Methods*, and John Dewey's
Logic, The Theory of Inquiry. These can lead to others.

The basic book for graduate students in this list probably is
Dewey's. However, some may have to lay a foundation for it. Students whose coursework in "methods" will have covered only techniques of expertise in doing things may well find themselves in this
category. Study of Dewey would be enriched by reading such books
as that of Koestler's, and by study of Stephen Körner's *Conceptual
Thinking: A Logical Inquiry*. Two paperbacks of especial helpfulness
in this connection are Lizzie Susan Stebbing's *Thinking to Some*

---

[9] Cf. Sayers, *The Lost Tools of Learning* (London: Methuen, 1948), esp.
pp. 7 ff. This little booklet is available for one shilling. The application of its
ideas is not limited to England. Compare the growing rejection of "progressive
education" in public schools.

Purpose (Penguin), and Alfred Jules Ayer's *Language, Truth and Logic* (Dover Publications).

The importance of general methodological study is emphasized by Barzun and Graff. They say:

> . . . methods of work, that is, devices of investigation and expression, follow from the characteristic features of typical problems. These devices . . . are the general ones of scholarship, not the particular ones of statistical or mathematical work, nor the field or laboratory techniques of testing or interviewing.[10]

General methodological competence is underlain by coursework such as that in grammar and mathematics, which are logical methods and systems.

Besides general works, those pertinent to a student's own field or fields of interest should be studied. These provide means of particular methodological preparation. This idea may be illustrated by means of examples drawn from a few fields. Books bearing on particular field methodologies include John Hylton Madge's *The Tools of Social Science*, Edward A. Freeman's *The Methods of Historical Study*, and Marc Bloch's *The Historian's Craft*. Another is *History: Methods and Interpretation* by William Leo Lucy, S. J. *Master's Essays in History* by Allan Nevins includes a select bibliography on historical method. Graduate candidates may value R. A. Close's *English as a Foreign Language: Grammar and Syntax for Teachers and Advanced Students*. This list may be extended to other fields with Wolfgang Köhler's *Dynamics in Psychology*, Leon Festinger's and Daniel Katz's *Research Methods in the Behavioral Sciences*, Ludwig Wittgenstein's *Tractatus Logico-Philosophicus*, and Jacques Hadamard's interesting but controversial *The Psychology of Invention in the Mathematical Field*. George Polya presents two works for the mathematician: *How to Solve It: A New Concept of Mathematical Method*, and *Mathematics and Plausible Reasoning* (2 vols.). Heinz W. Brand has written *The Fecundity of Mathematical Methods in Economic Theory*. Treatises on the scope and method of economics were listed in Chapter One.

Similar guides are available in the physical and natural sciences,

---

[10] Barzum and Graff, *The Modern Researcher*, p. xii.

the social and behavioral sciences, and in the humanities.[11] Comparison of the methodological requirements of economics and other sciences has been made by Prof. R. F. Harrod. He states that:

> . . . the fact that the achievements of economics are exiguous and the tools used simple makes it necessary to concentrate all the more closely on what there is. Their complex technique of proof provides the conclusions of the more highly elaborated sciences with a defense against the inroads of charlatans. In economics fools are only too ready to rush in.[12]

For his part, in his Introduction to the Cambridge Economic Handbooks, J. M. Keynes wrote:

> The theory of economics does not furnish a body of settled conclusions immediately applicable to policy. It is a method rather than a doctrine, an apparatus of the mind, a technique of thinking, which helps its possessor draw correct conclusions.[13]

Particular methodological preparation to fulfill writing requirements calls for understanding of the research concept. The term "research" has fallen into ambiguous usage such that clarity and agreement on the matter have been lost. Confused and contradictory or inconsistent statements about "research" are the rule. A thesis or dissertation, for example, is not a "piece of research" but a piece of writing based on inquiry. This sort of thing follows pragmatic interests and influences and the recent proliferation of research reports, which may indeed be "pieces of research."

To help students secure a straighter view of the research concept, it may be useful to deal with some examples of the ambiguity with which they have recently had to deal. What really is research?

---

[11] These include articles, such as Dwight J. Ingle, "Testing Claims to Knowledge in Biology and Medicine," *Perspectives in Biology and Medicine,* V, No. 1 (Autumn 1961), 65-85 [also in *The Graduate Journal,* V, No. 1 (Spring 1962), 112-132]. See also the essay of Frank H. Knight, "Methodology in Economics," Parts I & II, *The Southern Economic Journal,* XXVII, Nos. 3 & 4 (January & April, 1961).

[12] Roy Forbes Harrod, *International Economics* (Chicago: University of Chicago Press, 1958), p. 2. Cf. Fritz Machlup, "Are the Social Sciences Really Inferior?" *The Southern Economic Journal,* XXVII, No. 3 (January 1961), 173 ff.; and his "The Inferiority Complex of the Social Sciences," in *On Freedom and Free Enterprise: Essays in Honor of Ludwig von Mises, presented on the occasion of the 50th anniversary of his doctorate,* ed. Mary H. Sennholz (Princeton: D. Van Nostrand, 1956).

[13] Vol. 1 (1922), p. v. Quoted by C. W. Guillbaud in Harrod, *International Economics,* p. ix.

Opinion is divided as to the definition and scope of research. Does it include inquiry, which leads to intellectual findings, or only the clerical and technical work which eventuates in empirical certainty? Would it be helpful to distinguish between the intellectual work of inquiry and the technical work of research? Should these scholarship activities be regarded as parts of an overall process of investigation?[14] A problem exists here because these activities can be separate and distinct, and never brought together. For one example, bibliography is an important product of empirical scholarship which *per se* is not necessarily representative of intellectual achievement. For another, scholarship offers this generation more knowledge on the Kentucky rifle than was possessed by those who made and used it. Interesting as this may be, it is not important knowledge.

Faculty views on research frequently tend to be subjectively attained. Under the pressure of the so-called "print or perish" rule, it has been asserted that research is publication—"whatever is gotten into print." Declaimers for this approach assert that "research" includes even articles written "off the top of one's head." Within large institutions of late, "research" has been cynically defined as "looking for the guy who moved the files," and clarified by means of a contrast: "Plagiarism is stealing from one author; research from two or more." [15]

The upshot of all this is that as graduate academic essays and

---

[14] Dewey would hold that inquiry and research are components of a continuous process. See John Dewey, *Logic, The Theory of Inquiry* (New York: Holt, Rinehart and Winston, Inc., 1938). The requirement for graduate students is to relate these functions appropriately in investigations and not to get lost in mere empirical searching for merely useful information. The historical unfolding of the physical, natural, and social sciences since Bacon suggests that knowledge is a function of methodology. Professor Frank H. Knight apparently differentiates between inquiry, the goal of which is an answer or a solution— an intellectual finding—and research, the goal of which is relevant data for empirical proofs or substantiation. He states that methodology cannot be separated from research which is methodical—or methodological.

[15] Cf. John T. Connor, President, Merck & Co., Inc., "Research: The New Dynamo for Economic Growth," pamphlet, p. 4: on what Dr. Sumner Slichter called "the industry of discovery" an anonymous composer of doggerel has written:

> "In modern industry, research
> Has come to be a kind of Church
> Where rubber-aproned acolytes
> Perform their Scientific Rites
> And firms spend funds they do not hafter
> In hopes of benefits Hereafter."

the Ph.D. have become protean to an absurd degree,[16] the research concept has been similarly misused. Some apply the term inclusively, some exclusively, and others just vaguely.

Dr. J. H. Means takes an inclusive position. He says cogently with respect to the concept and scope of research:

> In its essence research may be said to be man's conscious effort to find new facts by exploration, to relate them to one another, and to derive from them new principles and generalizations. It is the consequence of man's insatiable curiosity and of his innate desire to improve his own lot.[17]

In contrast to Dr. Means, Dr. John C. Almack takes an exclusive position and presents a limited view of research. Upon defining the concept as a search for facts from which principles can be formulated, he posits that: "Research employs the inductive method; only incidentally does it have anything to do with deduction." [18] This would limit research to empirical undertakings. Deduction would enter only where choice among alternative research procedures would be involved, and where alternative or successive lines of attack would have to be decided. Dr. Almack quotes C. A. Jacobson to the effect that "Scientific research is the slow, laborious process of laying bare, one by one the facts and truths of nature, which have a definite bearing upon the *fundamental principles* involved in a problem." [19]

---

[16] Protean: Exceedingly variable, readily assuming different shapes and forms. Proteus was a prophetic sea-god in the service of Poseidon. When seized by someone wishing to know the future, he would assume different shapes as a means of trying to escape having to prophesy. Hence, protean applies to anyone who easily changes his appearance or principles—or anything which does. The concept is negative. The academic essays have been "proteanized" by insinuation of other forms of writing under their labels as means of escaping the rigors of the requisite performance standard.

[17] Quoted by Sanford S. Atwood, "Graduate Education and Research," *The Graduate Journal*, Supplement to Vol. II (1959), 161.

[18] John C. Almack, *Research and Thesis Writing* (Boston: Houghton Mifflin Company, 1930), pp. 11-12. See pp. 12-16 for a distinction between pure and applied research. On deductive method as the basis of economic theory see Schoeffler, *The Failures of Economics*, pp. 222 ff. On deduction of physical principles see the work of Newton, Einstein, etc. See also Clay Blair, Jr., "Two-Hundred-Year-Old Mystery Solved," *The Saturday Evening Post*, CCXXXIII, No. 9 (August 27, 1960), 20 ff. A striking difference may be noted between the empirical discoveries, examples of serendipity, reported at the end of the article, and their implications. Cf. Ernest Dichter, "Seven Tenets of Creative Research," *The Journal of Marketing*, XXV, No. 4 (April 1961), 1-4.

[19] Almack, *Research and Thesis Writing*, p. 12.

This conception would exclude inquiry and limit research to empirical undertakings to establish empirical modes of knowing. There being no general agreement on the matter, this view may be as valid as that of Dr. Means.

It is acceptable to suggest that the researcher, like Tycho Brahe, limit himself to gathering data for a Kepler to use. This is the way much research is done in industry and government. However, any given inquirer may play the part of Brahe for himself. This is what graduate students have to do. But a question arises concerning Dr. Almack's treatment because his limited view of research is not maintained. A conflicting idea is presented in the context with the statement that "Investigations of every kind which have been based on original sources of knowledge may be styled 'research'." [20] Citing H. O. Severence and Dr. E. Emmet Reid, Dr. Almack defines research as "the trained scientific investigation of the *principles and facts* of any subject, based on original and first-hand study of authorities, or on experiment." [21] The contrast with his basic view is developed with the declaration that "Two points of emphasis are noticeable: the results are *facts* and *principles*; and they must not have been discovered before." [22] These ideas imply an inclusive position and the view that inquiry is covered by the definition of research. They

---

[20] *Ibid.*, p. 11. To be part of intellectual work, investigation must be a means to an end and not an end in itself. Knowledge and data are not the same, nor are all ideas knowledge. Only proved ideas are knowledge. Ideas open doors to knowledge because they are sources of insights and hypotheses. The latter are tentative knowledge. Together with dreams, imaginings, intuitions, insights, theories, they provide material for intellectual work. By means of scientific methods, such creative endeavors can be made to yield contributions to knowledge and to its refinement, improved understanding, and better use. Scientists are concerned with ascertaining whether ideas can be turned into knowledge. Therefore, they are somewhat more restricted in dealing with ideas than are non-scientist intellectuals. While science involves objective verification, art, such as that of management, for example, involves subjective confirmation.

[21] *Ibid.*, p. 11. On this basis, how could one meet Harrod's proposition that: ". . . it is commonly agreed that in philosophy the prime method of research is neither the study of the printed word nor the conduct of experiments, but reflection"? Would it be denied that philosophers do research? Has global use of this term been a step to inexactitude? See Roy Forbes Harrod, *Foundations of Inductive Logic* (London: Macmillan & Co., Ltd., 1956), p. v. Cf. Frank E. Lazowick, *The Science of Philosophy* (New York: Philosophical Library, 1959).

[22] *Ibid.*, p. 11.

reveal the difficulties involved in attempts to achieve comprehensiveness by means of descriptive definition.

The limited literature which purports to guide graduate students as to their thesis and dissertational essay projects includes a number of inconsistencies on this topic. Conflicting ideas often make apparently inadvertent appearances in explanations of given concepts. For example, Cole and Bigelow state that:

> . . . a scholar is impartial, and the clear objectiveness of his viewpoint prevents him from minimizing or distorting any pertinent facts. His aim is never to *prove* anything—the sign of the propagandist—but to *discover* something, *to find out* something. In his search for truth, he ignores or suppresses no fact, regardless of how violently it may militate against a favorite hypothesis.[23]

The first and last statements in this excerpt are indeed acceptable. But what about the interior sentence? Relevant research is undertaken to supply the touchstones of fact by means of which an inquirer's conjectures may be proved or disproved. The authors' intentions undoubtedly are right. They may wish to obviate a priori reasoning. Nevertheless, the meaning is not clear. Definition that is not appropriate and accurate can produce uncertainty for graduate students; and such uncertainty works against invention.

Research may be defined either from an inclusive or from an exclusive point of view. It may be defined descriptively or functionally. Whatever the point of view or method, definition must be consistent if it is to be helpful. It is important that graduate stu-

---

[23] Arthur H. Cole and Karl W. Bigelow, *A Manual of Thesis Writing for Graduates and Undergraduates* (New York: John Wiley & Sons, 1960), p. vii. This generally valuable booklet is characterized by several contradictions. The authors in 1935 asserted that a thesis originates in a problem or not at all. Now they say, p. vii: "A thesis may be defined as the report of a scholar upon some piece of research he has completed [Not a report, an essay!]. It is the culmination of a devious process extending from the initial insight into the opportunity for investigation to the insertion of the final footnote. Many elements are involved. . . . Most important of all in determining the character of the result, however, are the fundamental aims of the writer which should be an undeviating search for truth, and originality in substance." Although this statement keeps the investigative and writing projects separate, it calls for a research report rather than an essay. Yet, the truth or validity of intellectual findings must be argued and proved logically, even by novices. Moreover, the real process extends from the initial insight not to the final footnote but to the final proof of the solution achieved.

dents perceive the difference between the inquiry and research concepts, and that they understand their functional relationship. What frequently passes for "research" usually is aimless study because it is unguided by the needs of some definite inquiry—for example, as to the explanation of some phenomenon. Except for a need to test hypotheses and other sorts of tenets for validity, student investigators can have little notion as to what data to secure or any experimental basis for employment of factual material in proof tests. Graduate candidates must play the roles of both Kepler and Brahe. With students just as with Tycho mere production of data, mere projects of counting and summing, contribute little to intellectual competence or achievement. It is the intellectual function of inquiry which provides their researchable hypotheses and so their steps to success.

Clear understanding of the research and inquiry concepts is possible despite the amount of confusion which clouds the subject. It may be all right to have a broad view of research and use the word to include both inquiry and relevant data collection and experimental work. But such inclusive usage might better wait the day when the intellectual work of inquiry shall have been so well learned that the "academic shorthand" will not be misleading. Academic novices also may find it to their advantage to emphasize functional rather than descriptive definition of the inquiry and research concepts. This will help them to prepare effective bases of methodological competence through coursework and reading. There is much that is clear and valuable in the literature. For example, Dr. Guy Stanton Ford once said on this matter:

> Whatever the field, the method and spirit, if it is to be graduate in a true sense, will be the method of inquiry and research, the accumulation of data, the testing by experiment and observation that we call scientific, and the fearless drawing of new conclusions no matter how sharply they traverse accepted maxims and practices.[24]

---

[24] *Journal of Proceedings and Addresses of the Association of American Universities* (1930), p. 104. Quoted by Henry E. Bent, "Professionalization of the Ph.D. Degree," *The Journal of Higher Education*, XXX, No. 3 (March 1959), 141. Dr. Ford was Professor of History and Dean of the Graduate School, University of Minnesota, 1913-1938. He was president of Phi Beta Kappa, 1949-1952.

Dr. Ford's conception of a continuous process of inquiry from wondering through theorizing, research, and proof-testing to conclusion requires no statement about kind or quality of materials. Like that of Dr. Means, it is mindful of the intellectual work of Kepler, Newton, Einstein, Russell, Keynes, and others in that it properly relates the technical work of testing inferences and hypotheses to the conceptual and conjectural work of intellectually attaining them.[25]

Essayist Skill Preparation

One of the premises for this guide to the graduate writing requirements is that investigation and essay writing are separate intellectual exercises. The essay must follow the successful inquiry and cannot be well or expeditiously written until the underlying project is at least largely complete. On the supposition that the methodological aspect of readiness preparation has been clarified, the relationship of investigations to writing now must be drawn.

It is not enough to provide oneself with good ideas and materials. Ideas have to be "hitched as well as hatched" if they are to be put to work. At least some modest level of mastery of the essay form is required for this. Writing competence is the third of the major components of readiness to fulfill the writing requirements for graduate degrees.

Theses and dissertations have been described as intellectual achievements in discourse which are derived from intellectual achievements in inquiry. The purpose of requiring them from degree candidates is to ensure that degree recipients can achieve and uphold in-intellectual findings of their own. The applicable axiom for this is

---

[25] Cf. Herbert J. Muller, *Science and Criticism: The Humanistic Tradition in Contemporary Thought* (New Haven: Yale University Press, 1943); and Alan Pasch, *Experience and the Analytic; A Reconsideration of Empiricism* (Chicago: University of Chicago Press, 1958). It may be at least as important to develop critical competence as to develop scientific ability, especially in the case of scholars and teachers. Criticism is a source of both understanding and expansion of knowledge. For a book of essays on the idea that we can learn from our mistakes, see Karl R. Popper, *Conjectures and Refutations: The Growth of Scientific Knowledge* (New York: Basic Books, Publishers, 1962). Cf. Ivor Armstrong Richards, *Principles of Literary Criticism* (New York: Harcourt, Brace & World, Inc., 1963).

that one really doesn't know what one may have achieved until one can explain and defend it in writing. Mere reporting of accomplishments in inquiry, in problem-solving, criticism, clarification, refinement, is not enough. To be acceptable, theses and dissertations must provide evidence of comprehension as well as of acquisition of knowledge.

The criterion that a graduate student is ready to write a thesis or dissertational essay when he has formulated something of value to say is a meaningful one. But success can elude those who do not know how to say what they have discovered, how to explain the derivation and to argue the validity of an intellectual achievement. Ability to relate intellectual findings to other knowledge is also important. Capacity for skillful presentation of a logical argument is indispensable as one of the three pillars described as supports of the readiness capstone.

The heading for this chapter raises the question: readiness to write what? It is not enough to name the stipulated essays, and their generic definition leaves the matter open. So do such illustrations as have been used to clarify the academic essay concepts and functions. The didactics of Chapter Two are necessary but not sufficient for the topic of Chapter Three. The best way to resolve the question of *what* one must prepare to write may be to proceed through a generalized essay by taking generalized writing steps. If the required kind of writing can be clearly visualized it can be well done.

Didactics requires that the epitome of the thesis and dissertation be illustrated by means of a generalized model. The description here fleshes out the abstract model on page 19. The Ferguson articles noted on pages 54 and 69 provide real-life models, as do the prospectuses in Appendices I and J. The essence of the thesis and dissertational essays has been given in the light of their distinguishing natures and characters. It now can be stated in terms of their common underlying or basic form. This can be done by presenting their general structure and organization.[26] One epitomizing model will do for both because both are essays and, as has been shown, the dissertational essay provides the model for the thesis essay. The model

---

[26] Analytical treatment of any literary form calls attention to its principal aspects. The substance, tone, and style of the thesis and dissertation were treated in Chapter Two. Their structure and content are described in detail here. Cf. Hughes and Duhamel, *Rhetoric*, pp. 11-25.

will be spelled out because so little material is directly available on this subject.

The title of a thesis or dissertation should convey a fair idea of what it is about. The essay itself should begin with an introduction which puts the reader in position to appraise and enjoy the intellectual fare to come. The introduction may take the form of an expository overview which sets the stage for the exercise. As explanation, it reveals the thesis or dissertation as the culmination of a process of achievement extending from the preliminary preparation, through the insight which provided the opportunity for investigation, to the final logically-deduced conclusion.

Explanation of why and how the exercise was undertaken helps to clarify what the essayist is trying to do and to place the attempt in its proper setting. This should include the frame of reference and benchmarks for the undertaking, the writer's investigative methods, and the structure of his inquiry. The objectives and rationale of the exercise should be stated clearly and unequivocally. Then should follow exposition of the basis for the exercise in the relevant literature, other materials and data, and the writer's own thought. The questions and uncertainties which attracted his attention and stimulated his interest should be pointed up. This provides a basis for explaining the investigative take-off and the progress of the inquiry from there.

The climax of the introduction is reached when the essayist states what he proposes to achieve in his essay. Thereupon he presents the premises for his forthcoming argument. He must say where he begins, with what he begins, and why he does so.

The premises for an essay, like those of the underlying investigation, include the conditions and propositions which were antecedent and basic to its argument. Their exposition should begin with a showing of what is taken as given or granted. Examples include Einstein's proposition that the speed of light is a constant of nature, and Bruckberger's that the fundamental difference between Europe and America lies in the latter's appreciation of the real individual in contrast to the former's abstraction of man. What is given may include existing conditions or situations, relevant knowledge such as theorems, theories such as "so-and-so's hypothesis," and any relevant axioms. Here one may find a statement of relevant parameters which may include constraints and boundaries relevant to the system within which the exercise is set.

Thereafter come the writer's selected variables and his own postulates and assumptions. The latter usually are stated in some such form as "suppose that." They may relate to conditions, purposes, goals. They give the argument its nature, shape, and direction. While they need not be argued, assumptions must meet the canons of logic: to be worth anything they must be valid. The more heroic the assumptions, the higher the level of abstraction may be. *Ceteris paribus* (other things remaining the same) is a famous assumption of this sort. Mathematicians routinely begin by stating their assumptions—as well as other premises.

These steps prepare the way for the writer's statement of his hypothesis if he has solved a problem, or for his declaration of position or intention if he intends to substantiate a criticism or a clarification.

The essayist moves from the introduction to the main body of his essay as soon as he has taken his stand and declared what he will attempt to do. The body of the essay has two main parts whose lengths are a function of the subject and of the essayist's objectives and skills in discourse. In the first part, he will explain the derivation of his hypothesis or position. In the second he will attempt to substantiate his thinking by validating it with proofs derived from his research. Each part involves presentation of a reasoned, logical argument from stated premises to logically drawn conclusions. One or two chapters may be required, or several. On the other hand, the entire essay may be presented in a single, even short, chapter.[27] Much depends upon the writer's task, his intellectual maturity, and his grammatical skills.

The body of the essay is comprised, thus, of the writer's formal

---

[27] As scholarly essays, the brief intellectual exercises listed below illustrate, as does Einstein's famous article of 1905, the kind of thing here being described, even though they are neither theses nor dissertations. Their analogue in music (taking them as models) may be the sonata form. All of the following are essays in economics by C. E. Ferguson of Duke University: "An Essay on Cardinal Utility," in *The Southern Economic Journal*, XXV, No. 1 (July 1958), 11 ff.; "Inflation, Fluctuations, and Growth in a Dynamic Input-Output Model," in *The Southern Economic Journal*, XXVIII, No. 3 (January 1962), 251 ff.; "On Theories of Acceleration and Growth," in *The Quarterly Journal of Economics*, LXXIV (February 1960), 79 ff.; and "Theories of Growth and the 'Rate of Growth' Hypothesis," in *Weltwirtschaftliches Archiv*, Band 89, Heft 2 (1962), p. 266 ff. Cf. C. E. Ferguson and Ralph W. Pfouts, "Aggregate Production Functions and Relative Factor Shares," in *International Economic Review*, III, No. 3 (September 1962), 328 ff.

and more or less learned argument. This he develops by logical stages. The main components of the argument are presented sequentially, each being followed by such detailed development and elaboration as is necessary and sufficient for it. In many cases a paragraph or a sentence or even a formula will do. The logical sequence of topics should present an orderly process of reasoning from premises to conclusion. The argument should be syntactical and be characterized by coherence and congruity.

The third main section of the academic essay follows the drawing of the conclusion which provides the basis for validation of the writer's position or tenet. It may begin with a reformulation of the hypothesis or position placed in argument at the outset. The inferences of the defended proposition should then be stated and clarified; and the implications of each should be drawn and evaluated. These steps provide a basis for assessment of the value of the defended position and a judgment concerning it. Thereupon decisions can be made as to the use or application of the results of the investigation. The significance of these steps is that in their light the circle can be closed. The essayist can refer to the matter with which he began and show that his problem has been solved, his uncertainty eliminated, his refinement consummated, or his criticism upheld.

The definition of the thesis and dissertation in Chapter Two has been supplemented by this description of their structure and organization. This description states no hard and fast rule concerning these concepts. It places no limits of content upon them. Their length will vary with writers' tasks. It should be remembered that while the academic essays have certain set-form properties they also are characterized by flexibility.

This highly generalized model has been presented because such analytical and explanatory works as may be found on the essay pertain to the literary essay. The distinction between the literary essay and the scholarly academic essay is important.[28] The literary essay is more or less casual and conversational, and discursive in the sense that it may ramble. Theses and dissertations are characterized by

---

[28] Because theses and dissertations are essays, it is useful to read what the principal encyclopedias have to say on the essay, and such books as R. D. O'Leary, *The Essay* (New York: Thomas Y. Crowell Co., 1928). Cf. Professor O'Leary's *Essay Writing: A Handbook for the Use of Teachers,* by the same publisher. It will be necessary to note the differences between the literary essay and the scholarly academic essay.

their presentation of logical and more or less formal reasoning. They are discoursive in the sense that their essence is systematic argument.

The academic essays are literary forms in which competence can be acquired by two principal means. First, one can read and think about the literary essay. Reading and appreciative analysis of good examples can establish its concept and fix its model in the student's mind. The process can be helped along by careful reading and analysis of good articles from learned journals and scholarly books.[29]

A certain amount of interpolation is necessary here because there seems to be little that one might call a literature of thesis and dissertational essays. The process of learning can be climaxed by reading model theses and dissertations. A recommended list may be found in Appendix I to this book.

The second means by which the skills of an academic essayist can be acquired is through practice. The concept and the model of the essay can be applied as soon as they are understood. Rather than "term papers" or "term reports," which names suggest no intellectual challenge, one can write "term essays." The latter would provide opportunities to practice explaining the derivation and arguing the validity of positions taken on matters of interest. Practice in essay writing enhances all skills of intellectual scholarship.[30] Skillful reasoning in analysis and synthesis, in induction and deduction, and in argument of explanation and proof enchances the capacity to learn. Enrichment of capacity to learn works to the general advantage of scholarship and scientific achievement as well as that of writing competence.

Even a modest accomplishment in essay writing can provide valuable preparation for fulfilling writing requirements. The writing of scholarly term essays of even approximately learned quality involves

---

[29] Learned journals are not the only source of good examples of this kind of thing. For a logical argument based on and derived from reasoning, see Dr. Robert J. Huebner, "Cancer as an Infectious Disease," the November, 1960, Harvey Lecture, New York Academy of Medicine. This address was reported by Albert Rosenfeld, "Clues to a Deadly Riddle," in *Life*, LII, No. 25 (June 22, 1962), 76 ff. Dr. Huebner achieved a logical refutation of objections to the single-cause theory of cancer and to viruses as a cause of human cancer.

[30] Cf. O'Leary, *The Essay*; esp. Chap. ii, "The Essayist Type of Mind." See also note 26, p. 67. Cf. Robert R. Rathbone and James B. Stone, A *Writer's Guide for Engineers and Scientists* (Englewood Cliffs, N. J.: Prentice-Hall, Inc., 1692), esp. Chap. ix, "Techniques and Devices to aid the Writer." Cf. Ivor Armstrong Richards, *The Philosophy of Rhetoric* (New York: Oxford University Press, 1936).

integration of all substantive and methodological preparation. By discoursing in writing on their analyses of problems and substantiation of tenets, by presenting arguments from premises to conclusions for, against, or in clarification or criticism of ideas, graduate students would be doing precisely the kind of thing called for in their final writing requirements.

The direct and most obvious gains from practice in essay writing are attainment of writing skills and improvement of writing style. These gains will be reflected in appropriate and consistent style sheet and mechanics, aptness and precision of statement, enhancement of vocabulary, and fluidity of expression. But the gains from essay skills do not end here. The nature of the scholarly essay is such that it takes the essayist into the realm of ideas at an intellectual level of learning. It is in this sense that scholarly essays are miniature works of thesis and dissertational essay nature. Moreover, one or a series of term essays can provide both the empirical bases and intellectual preparation for a thesis or dissertation of real value. Beyond conceptualization of significant essay projects, the essayist candidate gains advantages of timing and position. He learns to know when the fruit of an investigation is ripe to pick for his academic essay; and his complete preparation enables him to write his essay quickly. It is said, for example, that Oppenheimer wrote his thesis in physics at Göttingen in two weeks.

The capacity to formulate academic essays on the basis of results of preparatory investigations is a derivative of acquired general competence in conceptualization. Such facility is fundamental to simplification of complexities and to expert teaching. It also is the foundation for continuous production of learned essays during an academic career. Meanwhile, it is a basis for confidence on the part of graduate students that they need not try to say in their essays all that they know. It is important to know when enough has been said and "when to put the period." Ability to recognize the completion of an argument is an important indication of maturity and degree qualification.

An Academic Essay
Prospectus

The pillars of readiness to write have been shown to be substantive and methodological preparation and attainment of essayist skills. The capstone of readiness crowns them. It will be manifest by a proposal for a thesis or dissertation called a prospectus. The prospectus is a description of the main features of a candidate's proposed literary undertaking. It will include a statement of an investigative project and a summary outline of the essay to eventuate from it.

Between a short introduction and a short conclusion, an academic essay prospectus should contain descriptive expositions of the candidate's inquiry and intended essay. His explanation of the inquiry must make clear its nature, reasons, objectives, and plan, and the design of the relevant research. The function of the inquiry is to set up the essay to which it leads. Therefore the model of the essay should show its relationship to the described inquiry. The model of the essay will take the form of a summary outline, the content of which will be a series of general propositions. Even though only suggestive of the ultimate essay, it will provide the supervisory committee aid for interpretation of the underlying investigation. It also will provide the committee a framework within which to guide the student's work and interpret his progress.

A graduate student may at first find it difficult to say precisely what he would like to do and how he would do it. He may be so close to his project that simplification requires considerable effort and thought. It may help him to discuss the idea and structure of his incipient prospectus with his major advisor, other faculty, and fellow students before its finalization is attempted. In many cases the degree candidates must present and defend their prospectuses in seminar. However it is done, presentation, explanation, and defense enable one to pin his thinking down. It may help to visualize the prospectus as a model comprised of two interrelated models: one of the inquiry and one of the essay.

When a candidate feels that he is ready to write a prospectus, he should take a draft of it to his major advisor for criticism. In final form it becomes the basis for his presentation of his proposed essay project to his supervisory committee. A good prospectus will help the committee to visualize what it may expect from the candidate.

The faculty supervisory committee which meets to consider a candidate's essay proposals will think of them first from the point of view of appropriateness and adequacy. The committee will then consider whether the candidate can complete the project with materials and equipment available to him in some reasonable length of time.

If the project is too ambitious the committee will make suggestions for its reduction. If the project appears to be inappropriate or unworkable the committee will suggest that it be abandoned for another. Once the committee accepts a candidate's proposals his problem or topic is registered with the graduate school. The candidate then must proceed on the basis of the agreement. He may not change his project without approval, and that may not be easy to secure.

The prospective essayist will be required by his supervisory committee to consider the value of his intended achievement. He will need to consider early whether the outcome of his project may provide an adequate contribution to knowledge or to learning. He should carefully consider whether, and to what possible extent, the project might enhance his own competence and development. At the time of his examination on and defense of his essay he will need to know the significance of it, especially with reference to its probable meaning in some specific context, its implications, and possible usefulness.

A candidate's career and other objectives reasonably may be taken into account when choice between thesis and dissertation is made, just as they are when decisions are made as to his coursework program. Either thesis or dissertation may be selected at both Master's and Doctor's degree levels.[31] It could make sense for a would-be scientist to elect to solve a problem and write a thesis, and for a would-be scholar and teacher to elect a refinement or criticism as a basis for a dissertation.[32]

A difficulty often intervenes at this point. A serious shortcoming of many graduate students, especially at the Master's degree level, is that they do not undertake adequate and pertinent preparation to fulfill their writing requirements. Many either limit or foreclose their prospects of deducing meaningful problems or topics, or of adducing acceptable hypotheses or explanations. Too many students do nothing but plead for assignment of projects by faculty supervisors, apparently having been somehow conditioned by the "system" to do this.

Many essay advisors assign studies either as means of getting their own research done or as means of keeping "on top" of student

---

[31] Cf. T. S. Painter, "First You Must Catch Your Hare," *The Graduate Journal*, I, No. 1 (Spring 1958), 41 ff. On pp. 48-50, Painter deals with the different motivations, objectives, and abilities of graduate students seeking the Master's degree; and with the different Master's degrees being awarded.

[32] Cf. Everett Walters, "What Degree for College Teachers?" *The Journal of Higher Education*, XXXI, No. 2 (February 1960), 69 ff. See esp. pp. 72-73.

projects without having to undertake related special studies of their own.[33] Some advisors design large projects of empirical research as bases for grants of funds and, in effect, employ graduate students to do project units. Harmful practice is involved where graduate students are permitted to dress up their reports and submit them in lieu of, but under the labels of, theses or dissertations. Empirical studies made to provide useful knowledge as bases for business and public routine or policy decisions are not necessarily appropriate for academic essays. These comments should not detract from the splendid situations in which students derive notable benefit from participation in faculty projects relevant to important knowledge. A good example of the latter is provided by the work of Yuk-Wing Lee under Norbert Wiener at the Massachusetts Institute of Technology in the early 1930's.[34] Similar examples are current in all good graduate schools in fields ranging from statistics to metaphysics.

A candidate for a graduate degree becomes ready to write a prospectus of his academic essay when he has reached a state of confidence about a meaningful intellectual achievement of his own. He then will have moved from perception and comprehension of critical uncertainties in some field to resolution of a difficulty on which his thought has centered. At least he will have attained the threshold of an achievement, from which vantage point his intuition and insight enable him to explain his projected inquiry, the design of his relevant research, and the model of his probable essay.[35] The candi-

---

[33] The latter reason seems to be the more prevalent one. This practice apparently results from heavy, especially miscellaneous, teaching loads, committee responsibilities, and research tasks. Some faculty members are too busy under "print or perish" rules or as consultants to give students much time or help.

[34] On the subject of faculty interest, appreciation, and stimulation, see Professor Wiener's accounts of his work with Carl Muckenhaupt, Shikao Ikehara, and Yuk-Wing Lee. His work with the latter was especially rewarding. Professor Wiener conceived the problems and formulated them for Lee to solve within a given frame of reference. See Wiener, *I Am A Mathematician*, pp. 132-35. Compare also the relationship between Morris Cohen and Ernest Nagel.

[35] Cf. Panel Discussions at Yale, *Graduate Training in Economics*, pp. 15-16: "It is very important that those embarking upon research recognize the importance in the research process of the original conception of the problem and the design of the research to fit the problem." Cf. James, "The Dissertation Requirement," *School and Society*, LXXXVIII, 147-48. His five steps in the formulation of a dissertational inquiry and research project include: "the identification of a problem or purpose; the formulation of a clear statement of the problem; the justification of the problem as one worthy of research time

date's conception of his fulfillment of the writing requirement for his degree is a natural outgrowth of his general and particular preparation for it.

The final step in the process of degree attainment is based on the candidate's competence to choose a project which warrants a thesis or dissertation at his level. By "warrant" is meant justify. It is important to choose a problem or topic worthy as well as capable of treatment for such purpose. It should provide a basis for an adequate and appropriate academic essay at an intellectual level of scholarship; and it should be neither too large nor too long for the candidate to handle more or less alone, with the materials and equipment available to him, within a reasonable length of time. An important criterion is the capability of separate and adequate treatment by the student concerned. Unless one can exercise such choice he cannot place himself in position to write the necessary essay. Neither can he demonstrate intellectual maturity appropriate to the degree sought. Competent Master's and Doctor's degree candidates also take account of the technical and data requirements of a proposed project, availability of materials and means, quality of library and laboratory facilities, and the interests and competence of their academic advisors. Time requirements and expense also must be considered. Besides representing an adequate level of intellectual scholarship, the project must be one a student can handle and complete within an appropriate length of time.

It may be helpful to recall here how a series of term essays can set up a thesis or dissertation if they are not merely miscellaneous. For example, a set of term essays written to meet course or seminar requirements can serve to clarify the interrelationships among the components of some problem complex. The current literature of any field can yield a list of critical questions, issues, problems, which may be defined, analyzed, compared, and arranged in order. They can be examined in the light of relevant systems and ideas, and evaluated on the basis of thought and discussion. Should a project warranting

---

and as one that has not been done previously by some other scholar; a plan of procedure or research design; and proposed deadlines. If the project requires financial aid, then a sixth step is the presentation of a budget. All of this the candidate should do for himself. Of course, the advisor may advise, he may encourage—he may exhort—but he must not hold the candidate's little hot hand as the advance statement is being written."

thesis or dissertation and within the competence of the candidate not exist within one area, a search of the literature pertinent to another may enable the candidate to infer or deduce one there. Any research librarian can guide candidates to the lists of completed theses and dissertations as well as to the lists of those in progress.

Good possibilities for theses and dissertations are legion. The academic world is replete with examples at an intellectual level of scholarship. Jacques-Yves Cousteau has posed a question for the pathologist. Why, he asked, does animal life below certain depths in the sea show no evidence of cancer? One or more expensive expeditions may be required to secure the necessary information. When the empirical basis for an intellectual achievement is complete, some new approach may provide a vital insight. The answer to the question could have impressive implications for an understanding of cancer in humans.

A distinguished chemistry professor has provided a suggestion for the biologist. Upon learning that Florida citrus trees varied in their resistance to freezing temperatures according to the ways in which they had been fertilized, he observed: "Bet they don't know why!" Basic research in biochemistry may enable someone to find out why.

The use of models in intellectual work might be taken as a topic for an interdisciplinary dissertation. A series of term essays over a year or two on the use of models, by fields or groups of fields, could prepare the empirical basis for an intellectual achievement in methodology. Or one could treat the changing notion of property in economics and in law. This might be done by a series of essays tracing the shift from a concept of real property to that of earning power as property, say, from the tenth to the twentieth century.

This sort of thing has been done with notable success in all fields of learning. A real life example is provided by E. H. Chamberlain's doctoral essay in economics. The idea which became the basis for his prize-winning thesis at Harvard was conceived by him during a transportation seminar under Prof. I. Leo Sharfman, at the University of Michigan. It is interesting that Professor Sharfman rejected young Chamberlain's suggestion that he write a term paper on it. Perhaps the initial formulation of the idea of monopolistic competition was naïve and crude. Sharfman may have felt that his student was not then ready to work at a high enough level. The important consideration, however, is that Chamberlain was stimulated by Sharfman's remarks and his own thinking to stick with the idea and work it out.

In the preface to the book which grew out of his Harvard thesis, Chamberlain wrote:

> The title of this book is apt to be misleading, since I have given to the phrase "monopolistic competition" a meaning slightly different from that given it by other writers (Professor Pigou, in particular, has used the term to describe what is here regarded as only a portion of the problem, *viz.* oligopoly).
>
> Professor Young once suggested "The Theory of Imperfect Competition," and this, although it had to be discarded as inaccurate, comes close to describing the *scope* of the subject. The book deals, not with a special and narrow problem, but with the whole of value theory. Its thesis is that both monopolistic and competitive forces combine in the determination of most prices, and therefore that a hybrid theory affords a more illuminating approach to the study of the price system than does a theory of perfect competition, supplemented by a theory of monopoly. The analytical technique which emerges is distinctive, both from that of the familiar theories of competition and monopoly, and from any simple compromise between them. A comparison of the conclusions with those of pure competition indicates that economic theory is often remote and unreal, not because the method is wrong, but because the underlying assumptions are not as closely in accord with the facts as they might be.
>
> This study first took form in the two years preceding April 1, 1927, at which date it was submitted as a doctor's thesis in Harvard University. Since that time it has been completely rewritten. Chapter III has appeared, in substantially the same form as now, in the *Quarterly Journal of Economics* for November, 1929.
>
> In the revision the scope of the problem has been more rigidly defined, and the argument throughout has been re-oriented in order to achieve greater unity and logical consistence. Much that was irrelevant to the main conclusions of the theory has been eliminated, gaps have been filled in, and the methods of approach to different phases of the problem have been brought into agreement with each other. Sometimes the conclusions have been slightly altered, but on the whole, the argument as it now appears is merely a more tenable formulation (I hope) of the thesis advanced and filed in Harvard University Library in 1927.[36]

---

[36] Edward Hastings Chamberlain, *The Theory of Monopolistic Competition*, ("Harvard Economic Studies," Vol. XXXVIII [7th ed., Cambridge: Harvard

The idea of the prospectus for a thesis or dissertational essay might be made clearer by comparison of Chamberlain's statement with those of Whitehead and Sciama, Knight and Harris which were presented in Chapter Two. It also could be aided by comparison of model statements of this sort contained in the appendices below on thesis and dissertational essay prospectuses. All of these reflect maturity of thoughtful preparation. Careful consideration will show them to be helpful guides to project formulation.

A first-rate prospectus has several values for the graduate candidate. An unambiguous statement of the main features of his proposed undertaking requires that he be clear in his own mind about what he intends to do. Distinct perception of an essay in intellectual scholarship is a long step toward its successful completion. A good prospectus provides strong aid in overcoming obstacles to commitment to action.

Another value of a good prospectus lies in the fact that it provides a basis for meaningful discussion of the student's proposal with his advisor and supervisory committee. A precise, intelligible statement implies that he knows fairly well what he is doing and that he is at least about ready to go ahead. A clear and definite presentation prevents misinterpretation and obviates intra-committee disagreement over what the candidate intends. If the candidate's proposals withstand committee scrutiny and can be defended against committee challenge he has reasonable assurance that he is attempting the right kind of thing. Besides wanting to know whether the candidate knows what he wants, the committee seeks assurance that the candidate's project is a workable one that he can handle alone with the school facilities available to him. Then steps in direct fulfillment of the writing requirement can begin.

A third major value of an approved prospectus is that it provides the candidate specific guidance as to his inquiry. The student who keeps the plan and schedule of his investigation in mind will tend

---

University Press, 1956]). The first edition was published in 1933. This extract reveals (1) that a thesis originates in a problem which it states, whose analysis it explains, and the validity of whose solution it proves; (2) that a well chosen problem is one which gives the basis for a study of ideas and their interrelationships rather than of facts, and which invites and deserves further study; and (3) that a doctoral essay is not required to have the finished quality expected of the work of a mature professional who, on the basis of post-doctoral work, has attained his *Meisterschaft*.

to get on with it. He will be able to keep on the track of it and not become lost in time- and energy-consuming side-issues and irrelevancies. Clear retention of the design of his research will facilitate his exploitation of methodological opportunities and other leads and ideas. The experimentation involved can enrich conceptions, yield valuable insights, suggest new approaches, provide new analytical models, and aid comprehension. It may be useful to prepare charts of the entire project and of subordinate component projects to be pinned up above one's desk for continuous reference. This would guide the integration of thought and reflection on the endeavor; and it would aid perception of the inquiry and research as steps in a process from question to conclusion.

These matters suggest important functions of appraisal after a candidate has provided himself at least a reasonably firm basis for a commitment decision. Then the defined and delineated study begins; and the voyage of investigation is pursued to its destination. Some intellectual voyages are long, others short, depending upon the problem or topic and the ability and resolution of the candidate. When a candidate reaches a point, on the basis of his underlying investigation, where he can produce a detailed outline of his intended essay he has attained readiness to write it. His prospectus now provides a fourth value, since he will be guided by both the description of his inquiry and the model of his intended essay.

Careful outlining and re-outlining in accordance with the original model of the essay should be done at two-to-four-day intervals. Successive attempts at detailed outlining should be made in the light of the general model but without reference to preceding detailed outlines. This focuses the full powers of mind on each outline attempt and brings all thought and learning to bear on the incipient essay. Comparison of outlines, upon completion of each succeeding one, can provide continuing bases for attainment of a final detailed outline. The process of outlining and re-outlining need continue only until the candidate has provided himself sufficient rechecks of his thinking to be sure his outline is as good as he can make it.

Time and care taken to produce a good outline are well spent. The outline is the structure upon which the essay will be fleshed out.[37] It conserves time and energy; and it serves as a guide to

---

[37] James, "The Dissertation Requirement," *School and Society*, LXXXVIII, 148: "Writing must involve outlining, so that the ideas are arranged in some

completeness. Particularly, it guides expression of the writer's argument by logical sequential steps from his premises to his conclusions. In most fields the first draft of the essay may best be written without notes or only a few. After studied reconsideration, upon passage of a week or two, a more elaborate draft can be fleshed out with the aid of notes. This draft or a third can be worked over and footnoted as it is researched. Finally, a draft essay can be prepared for submission to the student's advisor for his criticism. It should be grammatically correct, coherent, and syntactical to enable the advisor to concentrate on the candidate's argument.

After consultation with his advisor, the candidate can return to his desk for work on the final draft which, when checked, may be sent to the typist. It should conform precisely to all style sheet and other requirements of the given graduate school. As finally typed, copies of the essay are distributed to the candidate's supervisory committee and become the basis for their final examination of the candidate.

The suggestion of several essay drafts need not be alarming. They may seem to be time-consuming but they really will be time-conserving. Moreover, they enhance essay quality to the immediate and future benefit of the essayist. Besides conserving time, they also conserve energy and space. In so doing they reflect maturity. A well-written essay on a meaningful intellectual achievement can be short. The quality of a thesis or dissertation is not a matter of some large number of pages and tables. The basic question concerning the essay is whether it presents a clear and complete argument on behalf of an intellectual achievement. How long was Einstein's famous 1905 essay in *Annalen der Physik?* [38]

A well-formulated prospectus for a thesis or dissertation aids a candidate in both his investigative and writing undertakings and in his relationship with his supervisory committee. It aids the supervisory committee in its appraisal of both the candidate and his

---

kind of logical or compelling order. I am a devotee of . . . the topic sentence. I would urge that paragraph one on page one of an acceptable dissertation should include a statement of the problem or purpose; and that on the same page there should appear a concise statement of the results. . . . In scholarly writing the story should be told on page one, and the remainder of the dissertation should elaborate and support the opening statements in a carefully conceived sequence of paragraphs and chapters.

[38] *Annalen der Physik,* Band 17 (1905), pp. 132-48. In typescript it might require 50 pages.

proposals. A clear, precise, carefully drawn prospectus reflects sound and complete preparation and intellectual maturity. From all points of view, a good prospectus suggests a high potentiality for success. Graduate students will find it valuable to think in this direction from the start.

Summation

Readiness to write a thesis or dissertation has been clarified as a condition attainable by means of a three-fold preparatory process. The first and most significant component of the process is substantive achievement. The second, methodological achievement, includes competence in grammar, logic, and mathematics. The third is competence in essay writing which involves writing style and style-sheet and production mechanics. The latter are what usually are described in graduate catalogues and in graduate student handbooks.

Preparation of readiness at the level of style-sheet and production mechanics is a simple matter. These technicalities can be learned from guides provided by graduate schools and by practice in connection with term essays. When thesis and dissertation drafting begins, the forms of headings, subheadings, footnotes, pagination, etc. can be brought together on individual style sheets and posted above typewriters for reference.

Preparation of readiness at the methodological level requires time for attainment of skills in analysis and synthesis, research and proof, definition and delineation, and formulation and use of assumptions. Term essay writing provides opportunities for practice in these matters and in discourse. Such skills can be achieved concurrently with preparation of readiness at the substantive level. This is why study of method and essay writing should parallel coursework and other subject matter studies.

Readiness to write a Master's essay is not the same as readiness to write a Doctor's essay, since they represent different levels of competence and academic achievement. Whatever his academic level, however, the ideal graduate student is intellectually curious and continuously inquiring. The processes of his getting into position to write are the increasingly exciting ones of progressive maturation. The climax comes when the student knows what he wants to do and what he can do. Then his problem will be less one of competence than of desire to do more than is required. It is important to know where and when to stop. Clear guidance and regular progress checks can help. Most students need to be pushed as well as guided toward full realization of their potentialities. They need to be aware that the matters of administrative routine which are involved differ from the substantive factors which they are designed to support but not to replace.

This chapter has presented a generalized explanation of the process by which one can ready himself to write a good thesis or dissertation. Its expositions have been spelled out with care because of the importance of the undertaking with which they are concerned. Nevertheless, this generalized model of the preparatory process should not be interpreted too literally or applied too strictly, since all graduate schools have and state their own requirements which degree candidates are obliged to learn and follow. However, this presentation has been generalized from the practice of the best schools. The excellent faculties of the top colleges and universities teach their students to proceed along these lines.

The faculties are there to teach, but it is the students who must learn. One reason for the writing requirements' being hard obstacles to degree attainment is that many students prepare poorly and inadequately to meet them. Graduate students need more than the scholar's equivalent of the surveyor's chain and transit, the sextant and barometer, to lay out their fields of thought. They need reference points and benchmarks before they can describe the boundaries of their fields, let alone lay in contour lines and the main features of terrain and topography. Antecedent to these steps there must have been some overriding concept, some general frame of reference within which tasks are perceived and performed. Graduate students must bring to essay projects understanding of some body of knowledge, both per se and in reference to others, together with reasonable control of basic research methods and skills. They must acquire the "mind of the essayist" and become able to write.

The lesson of this chapter is straightforward. Capacity to fulfill the writing requirements for graduate degrees involves the building up and arrival at a certain minimal level of competence in intellectual scholarship. The methods and projects of Paul Erlich and Thomas Edison, who respectively found 605 and 1743 things that wouldn't work, are inappropriate for graduate students. The proper business of graduate students is reasoning, not trial-and-error or serendipity. In his famous essay, "The American Scholar," Emerson described the scholar as "the delegated intellect," and said that in "the right state he is *Man Thinking.*" [39]

Readiness to write a thesis or dissertation is the fruit of a combined process of intellectual maturation and substantive achievement. It is a quality compounded of a fundamental intellectual achievement and of ancillary technical and artistic competence. The corollary to this lesson is that readiness to write the required essay cannot be provided by an empirical mode of knowing something, or by merely useful information. Science and scholarship are inseparable from a sense of method. Readiness to write a thesis or dissertation depends upon some achieving of important knowledge via the reasoning powers of the mind. The necessary achievement comes by brainwork. To be guided by less is to be guided by a false doctrine which would belie academic freedom. A lesser guide would be unintellectual at best, and anti-intellectual at worst. Academic freedom at its best is intellectual freedom, not clerical or technical freedom even though this may be involved. The basis for academic freedom is intellectual responsibility in both learning and teaching. A student hoping for a career of achievement in the intellectual life of his society must begin by learning to do intellectual work.

A further corollary of the lesson is that intellectual work is within the reach of any adequately intelligent graduate student who has the mentality for it and the necessary interest in it. Mentality is discussed on pages 142-144. This sort of thing is not reserved to rare and occasional geniuses. It is open to many if they will be rightly oriented, sufficiently motivated, and adequately disciplined. Knowledge is comprised of ideas that have been derived and confirmed by intellectual work. Whoever can do such work of deriving and confirming can fulfill writing requirements for graduate degrees.

The range of opportunities to do the exciting work of ideation and intellection increases with attainment of successively higher levels of intellectual scholarship. The discipline which exalts the

---

[39] Besides being thoroughly familiar with "The American Scholar," graduate students will find it helpful indeed to study Emerson's essays entitled "Intellect" and "Self Reliance." They will find it helpful as well to read Karl Jaspers, *The Idea of the University*, ed. Karl W. Deutsch, trans. H. A. T. Reiche and H. F. Vanderschmidt (Boston: Beacon Press, 1959).

mind and binds it to the ideal is a source of increasingly rich rewards and satisfactions. The significance of learning to do effective
intellectual work lies in the fact that the essence of intellectual work
is learning how to learn. Its value lies in the fact that it is the
source of all important knowledge now possessed, and it will be the
source of all its extensions.

4

Performance Standards

After all, only he who handles his ideas lightly is master of his ideas—and only he who is master of his ideas is not enslaved by them. Seriousness is only a sign of effort, and effort is a sign of imperfect mastery.

LIN YUTANG

Somewhere along the line our signals seem to have gotten mixed and we have begun to ascribe to an academic degree a significance which it can never really have.

W. ALBERT NOYES

Graduate students need to know the answers to three basic questions if they are to fulfill their writing requirements effectively. The first two have been treated. They are the questions of "What?" and "How?" The third question is "How well?" Readying oneself to write includes acquiring and understanding a reasonable answer to this third question. The purpose of this chapter is to aid this process.

Whether large or small, and whether calling for brainwork or not, assignments are composed of at least two elements. These are "what" and "how well." As soon as "what" has been made clear, "how well" must be specified. This latter usually is done by setting tolerance limits or by describing, perhaps defining, minimal acceptable quality. This quality may be exceeded but it must be attained. Values to be gained from exceeding it must be assessed in the light of the costs of doing so.

Performance standards exist wherever and whenever student work is graded. They are implicit in both coursework and writing requirements. To some extent, coursework standards vary with institutions. To some extent they vary with departments and professors.

86

They are more definite in some fields and less so in others. Nevertheless, they are there. The rather extensive unwillingness to set standards as clearly for graduate writing requirements as for graduate coursework requirements remains a curious fact of academic life.

Certain writers, some whose works have been cited, have turned earth in the field of "what" by defining and differentiating theses and dissertations. There has been considerable cultivation of the writing style and style-mechanics fields. However, the field of performance standards, that of "how well," has been left largely untilled. A spade has been put in here and there, as will be shown; but this field seems not really to have been worked. Neither has the related field of the criteria to be employed to determine whether the required standards have been attained or exceeded. Therefore, certain preliminaries shall be entertained before going to work in these fields.

Performance standards for Master's and Doctor's essays are as readily determinable as are the definitions of the two sorts of essays by which writing requirements are fulfilled. Evaluative criteria for use in testing performances with reference to the standards are equally determinable. Determining such criteria does not pose a difficult philosophical question. It merely calls for terminological decisions. Graduate students can provide themselves the vital answers through reading and thought. Those who do will enjoy distinct advantages in fulfilling their writing requirements.

The standard of excellence which graduate students must attain is that implicitly set and operative within the best graduate schools. Like the golfer's par, it is no higher for top schools than for lesser. The idea current in certain circles that lower standards should prevail in lesser schools is false. The "magnum opus" idea is equally mistaken.

The standard of acceptable performance for thesis and dissertational essayists must be seen in the light of the threshold analogy. Whoever gets over gets in. Prizes may be awarded those who clear the threshold high. But while prizewinning essays often provide excellent models, they do not set the performance standards for Master's and Doctor's essays. These standards are concepts of excellence of a different derivation. Before dealing directly with standards and criteria, it may be helpful to take a look at the purposes of the graduate schooling to which these are relevant.

The Rationale of
Graduate Programs

Collegiate schooling in the United States has been frankly oriented toward the widest possible attendance. Entrance examination scores and other factors are coming into growing use, however, to modify "widest possible." Between the undergraduate and graduate levels of schooling the concept of the optimum student body changes markedly. At the graduate level it becomes limited to the minority of any generation which is capable of being educated for intellectual work.

The Provost of Cornell University, Sanford S. Atwood, has said on this point:

> Special instruction for the gifted is an inherent principle in gradu-ate education, and the system should be flexible enough to allow the best possible training in creative scholarship for each individual.[1]

Charles E. Odegaard, President of the University of Washington, declared:

> . . . the long-established state university has peculiar resources and peculiar opportunities for students of superior intellectual ability, and should by all means be enabled to serve them well.[2]

A distinction between undergraduate and graduate education has been ably made, meanwhile, by Professor Henry G. Booker of the Department of Electrical Engineering, Cornell University. He explained:

> The principal function of undergraduate education should be to develop the mind of a student by having him think through things that other people have frequently thought through before. It should be the object of undergraduate education to pursue this process to the point where it is no longer worth the student's while to think through well-known thoughts merely to develop his mind. Gradua-tion should signify that a student's mind is about as developed as it can be merely by studying what is well known. By contrast it

---

[1] Quoted by Reece McGee, "The State University: A Prolegomenon," *The Graduate Journal*, II, No. 2 (Fall 1959), 238.
[2] *Ibid.*, p. 238.

should be the object of graduate education to develop the student's mind by having him think through things that have not been completely thought through so far as the student is aware. Research should thus be the principal tool of graduate education.[3]

Policies regarding graduate school programs and selection of their students make it clear that admission requires both a high intelligence and demonstrated competence in the acquisition and comprehension of knowledge. Students sought for graduate programs include those eager for what someone has called "the discipline that exalts the mind and the freedom that binds it to the ideal." In sum, enrollment requires some indication of competence to do intellectual work, originally and creatively.[4]

Dean Bent of the University of Missouri Graduate School has studied the opinions of a number of graduate school deans expressed since 1904. On the basis of his study, Dean Bent says that: ". . . there is a striking consistency in the statements which we find regarding the fundamental character of the program for the Ph.D. degree." [5] The definitions of thesis and dissertational essays, research, and intellectual education, which have become neglected and deserve reaffirmation, find support in these quarters.

In a well-known report on policies in graduate education, which is often referred to as "The Report of the Four Deans," it was said:

We reaffirm what we take to have been the original idea and intent of the Ph.D.; namely, to train men to do advanced work of an original nature, without maiming them spiritually or assuming that they are Methuselahs. Such training should obviously include a wide grasp of what is already known . . . and it should equally include strict introduction to methods and tools.

The degree . . . implies a high *technical* ability—and, we hope, taste and skill in the art of written and oral communication. The result should be *original* work, especially in the sense of having the

---

[3] *Ibid.*, p. 225. Cf. *The Components of Graduate Education* (Atlanta: Southern Regional Education Board, 1954).

[4] Better graduate schools require that a student have a "B" average or better, at least during the third and fourth undergraduate years, and that he graduate at least in the top 20 per cent of his class.

[5] Henry E. Bent, "Professionalization of the Ph.D. Degree," *The Journal of Higher Education*, XXXI, No. 3 (March 1960), 142 ff. Dean Bent's explanation of the present impasse of the Ph.D. and his conclusions and proposals are presented on pp. 144-45.

work reported with individuality. We cannot require a man to be creative.[6]

Much hinges on the words *original* and *creative* in this statement. Besides observing that the work should be presented and argued with individuality (in an essay rather than a report!), it may be useful to question the idea that a candidate cannot be required to be creative. Intellectual work and intellectual results are called for. The real idea, as suggested by use of the word original, is that expression of creative capacity is sought. The goal is originality, novelty, and individuality by means of imaginative and intuitive employment of reason in intellectual work. A candidate may properly be required to use his reasoning and methodological abilities to be a critic, clarifier, originator, or a problem-solver. This is what graduate education may be assumed to be for. It is only improper to require more creativeness of a Master's or Doctor's degree candidate than is appropriate for his level of achievement. If candidate creativity exceeds requirements, that can be cause for rejoicing but not a basis for new performance standards.

The creativeness requirement needs to be in keeping with the objective of graduate study to develop students to where they can invent, innovate, and originate with some degree of reliability and dependability. Professors Cole and Bigelow, of Harvard and Columbia, address this point as follows:

> Originality in research may be said to consist in the discovery or analysis of new data by old or new methods, or in the manipulation of

---

[6] "Report of Committee on Policies in Graduate Education," *Journal of Proceedings and Addresses . . . Ninth Annual Conference of the Association of Graduate Schools* (1957), p. 38. This report is reprinted below as Appendix A. Its authors were J. Barzun, J. P. Elder, A. R. Gordon, M. E. Hobbs, Chairman. See p. 189. Compare the Cornell University policy stated by Provost Atwood, viz. "It is the purpose of the [Cornell] Graduate School to offer facilities for advanced study and research so that students may obtain a comprehensive view of a field of knowledge and receive the training required for independent investigation in that field. In providing this opportunity, the School makes it possible for the students to associate freely with mature scholars who will give them such aid and direction as they may need. Accomplishment is judged primarily by the evidence of growing capacity for critical thought and mastery of subject matter in a selected field of study and not by the fulfillment of routine requirements." This statement suggests goals and the nature of standards and criteria in general terms, but it is not precise as to the quality requirements or measurements needed as guides by supervisory committees and students.

old facts by some new technique, or from some fresh point of view. Such discovery or manipulation need not be peculiarly difficult, nor require especial maturity in the investigator. Inventiveness is not an instinct which appears in man only with the attainment of some particular age, and originality of thought in matters of research is similarly unrestricted.[7]

The best graduate schools perceive graduate schooling as a process of education leading to the doctorate. What, then, is the best available thought as to what should be done, by stages, as this process moves toward consummation? What should be required as indication of fruition, and how should that indication be judged?

The answers to these questions may be provided in the light of the facts that: 1) the creative process is mental, and it is imaginative and intuitive; 2) the creative process is individual and not social; 3) the world of the intellect is abstract and qualitative, and not the real world of the senses which it contemplates and explains through analysis and deduction; and 4) insight, which is an attribute of creativity, is a function of intellect.[8] Graduate study has been

---

[7] Cole and Bigelow, *A Manual of Thesis Writing for Graduates and Undergraduates,* p. viii. Perhaps in carefully restricted situations it *may* or *can* suffice for a Master's degree candidate to produce new data and draw conclusions from it; but a Doctor's degree candidate should go beyond this to draw inferences from his conclusions which may serve as basis for a significant criticism or to confirm a new idea. It may be useful to suggest here that in many places the phrase "analysis of the data" lies in the realm of academic cant. This "analysis" often represents mere posing, or at best only summing and speculating. All except a few who are "analyzing the data" seem to stop short even of interpretation. This can open a way for counting projects at an empirical level of scholarship for the unwary and ill-advised. Such phraseology can misinform.

[8] These ideas are supported by the thought of Richard T. LaPierre, Professor of Sociology, Stanford University. Cf. Glenn Negley, *The Organization of Knowledge* (Englewood Cliffs, N. J.: Prentice-Hall, Inc., 1942), p. 63: Thinking is done by individuals. To be significant it must have deliberation and intent—i.e., interest, reason, purpose. Otherwise it is idle and not analytical but only imagination or fantasy. Cf. Homer G. Barnett, *Innovation; The Basis of Cultural Change* (New York: McGraw-Hill Book Company, 1953), in which the author attempts "to formulate a general theory of the nature of innovations and to analyze the conditions for, and the immediate social consequences of, the appearance of novel ideas." There is no innovative "faculty" but only learned innovative use of faculties; innovation is not a unique property of Master's and Doctor's degree candidates, for whom graduate schools provide especially propitious conditions. C. Northcote Parkinson has pointed out that the relation between the number of persons engaged in a job and the productivity of each is inverse. Consult his *Parkinson's Law and Other Studies in Administration* (Boston: Houghton Mifflin Company, 1957).

designed to enhance intellectual competence, and to build bases for independent intellectual achievement. What the doctors do after attaining their degrees is largely up to them. Some go to seed, many remain indifferent, while a few make masterful scholars and scientists of themselves.

The careers of such men as Allan Nevins, H. S. Commager, Max Lerner, Arthur F. Burns, Morris Kline, Ernest Nagel, Edward Teller, Robert Oppenheimer, David Riesman, Lionel Trilling, and Crane Brinton illustrate the latter. Their careers also make it clear that the doctoral thesis (or dissertation) is a test, and that the successful essay indicates that a foundation is at last complete on the basis of footings laid down at the Master's degree level (the ground having been prepared in undergraduate years). To employ guild terminology, we have the levels of the novice, the apprentice, and the journeyman. It is up to the holder of the doctorate whether he remains a journeyman (*Geselle*) or becomes a master of his craft (*Meister*).

Referring to the present protean Ph.D., which he describes as "both a professional and a nonprofessional degree," Grayson Kirk writes:

> Here, the great barrier so far as student time is concerned is the dissertation. It is defined everywhere as an original contribution to knowledge, and many young men put in years of dreary drudgery upon a subject that is of little or no significance to anyone. Few dissertations do contribute anything of value to the sum total of human knowledge; the young man is not ready to make a major contribution, and he may not be ready until he is a mature scholar some years hence. Would it not be better if we were to regard the dissertation merely as a trial-run in scholarship, giving satisfactory evidence that the student can do competent research on an assigned topic, and that he can write his conclusions in clear, effective English? If we agreed upon this, we could shorten the doctorate time, and we would lose nothing of importance.[9]

In support of this position, Norbert Wiener stated his opinion forthrightly in the first volume of his autobiography, where he said:

---

[9] Grayson Kirk, "Education for the Future," *The Graduate Journal*, II, No. 2 (Fall 1959), 260. Cf. note 38 p. 35.

It is often supposed that a man's doctoral thesis should be one of the best things he ever does, and should give the full measure of the man. I do not believe this. A doctor's thesis is nothing but a specific piece of work by which a journeyman qualifies himself to become a master of his craft; and if he does not exceed this level a dozen times in the course of his career, he is a very poor master indeed. . . . It is only when a man has his dissertation behind him and is not pestered with the prospect of future formal requirements to fulfill that he can do his best work as a free man, with his task itself as the goal and not the spurious goal of a certain academic and social position. The thesis should be good, but if the scholar's work does not soon exceed the level of the thesis, the candidate is well on his way to becoming one of those desiccated homunculi you find in faculty meetings of our third-rank colleges.

If my own dissertation had been the only piece of scientific work I have ever produced, it would have been a most unsatisfactory ticket of entry to a career of learning. However, as the facts have developed, it did give me the training in the organization of scientific material which led me in the next two years to a series of papers that I should much prefer to represent my induction into a scholarly career.

I have known more than one student who has waited to present a thesis for his doctorate, even after he has produced a number of acceptable papers, until he can write that one paper that will allow him to break into print in the learned world with a maximum of impetus and *elan*. It is of course a fine thing if a youngster can establish himself as an important figure with his first work. Nevertheless, I feel that many a student has placed too much emphasis on this point, and has wasted years waiting for the great idea to come to him, which he might have devoted to experience in publishing and in receiving the public criticism of his printed work. It is altogether too much to expect to become a great man on the first try; and if the course of one's late work contains such material as need not be a matter of shame, it makes very little difference whether the first paper is excellent or barely conforms to the necessary standards for the doctorate.[10]

Messrs. Kirk and Wiener are supported in their views by the Trustees of the Carnegie Foundation for the Advancement of Teaching. On the overemphasis of research at the expense of college teaching, and the impossibility of resolving "the conflict by turning out

---

[10] Wiener, *Ex-Prodigy*, pp. 174-75. Cf. his second autobiographical volume, *I Am A Mathematician*, pp. 21-22.

a certain number of creative researchers and in addition producing a certain number of college teachers," they held that the graduate school "must seek to inculcate scholarly research interest and standards in every man it turns out."

Thereupon they stated:

> Any discussion of the role of research in graduate education leads to the question of the dissertation. A sound conception of the dissertation recognizes that it should be a trial run in scholarship and not a monumental achievement. Some graduate departments have magnified the thesis beyond reason, both in size and in emphasis upon it as an original contribution. There is no demonstrable relationship between the size of the dissertation and its quality. Some believe that the emphasis on an original contribution to knowledge is the most important factor in forcing students into more and more abstruse and narrow topics.
>
> The important thing to keep in mind is that it is not so much what the individual can "prove" or "contribute" that counts in a dissertation; it is what the individual shows of how his mind works, of his literacy, of his quality of thought. Students must not be encouraged in the pretentious habit of trying to put everything they know into the thesis. . . .
>
> Published contributions are only one desirable consequence of research training. Other consequences are scholarly judgment, critical acuity, knowledge in depth, and the capacity to teach in an inspired fashion.[11]

The novice, or candidate for a Master's degree, is required to achieve certain things.

First, he should complete the acquisition and consolidate his comprehension of a chosen body of knowledge, both per se and in its relationship to other bodies of knowledge.

Second, he should attain mastery of the methods and techniques by which knowledge is tested and additions to it are made. As control of the methods of scientific investigation is acquired through explicit coursework in inquiry and problem-solving, the candidate should begin to exercise his initiative and intellectual ability by working as independently as he can on small problems, as to meet seminar requirements.

---

[11] Fifty-third Annual Report, esp. pp. 19-20 of the section entitled "Proposals for Reform of Graduate Education."

Third, he must learn by experience with the essay form how to write an acceptable thesis or dissertation.

Ultimately, under instruction and with guidance, he is expected to learn by experience how to formulate and carry out a project of critical and constructive inquiry, and to argue the validity of his project and findings in an essay. While the Master's essay of his choice may not represent research in the sense of originating facts and materials on the basis of which to explore new territory, his doing the underlying job provides valuable training in, and a reasonable test of, use of research skills. It also provides training and a test of his ability to employ the reasoning powers of his mind.

The important point, here, is that the student should acquire ability to express *his* ideas coherently and to move easily between the empirical elements of his problem and the abstractions posed by analysis or synthesis. He must learn to organize ideas and to develop perspective and capacity for insight.[12] He must learn to deduce hypotheses and to draw conclusions. He must learn to test the hypotheses and conclusions he formulates by applying them to the touchstone of fact. He must learn that conceptual brainwork precedes empirical work.

Throughout his program, the Master's degree candidate should be permitted as much freedom of choice and thought as is consistent with his abilities, personality, and competence to use it meaningfully, on the one side, and with his acquisition of scholarly self-discipline on the other. In all, his preparation is for successful embarkation on the arduous but thrilling voyage to his doctorate.

Dean Elder of Harvard's Graduate School of Arts and Sciences asserts the contrasting view that "Master's programs ought to be entities in themselves, devised *de novo*, each having its own pattern, and each its own beginning and end." [13] His position that "these

---

[12] Leonard B. Beach, "Freedom and Discipline in Graduate Programs," in *The Journal of Higher Education*, XXX, No. 3 (March 1959), proposes on p. 172 that: "Since it [Master's thesis] must continue to be a venture in depth rather than in breadth, a highly personal and somewhat impressionistic essay, and in this respect different in kind as well as in scope from the doctoral dissertation, I would assume that we may here again encourage the spirit of free (and still, possibly, naïve) inquiry which we hope to fan into the flame of independent research at a later stage."

[13] J. P. Elder, "Reviving the Master's Degree for the Prospective College Teacher," *The Journal of Higher Education*, XXX, No. 3 (March 1959), 133 ff.

programs should not be attached like a poor cousin to the Ph.D. programs" has the support of Dean Everett Walters of the Ohio State University and of Dr. Oliver C. Carmichael, consultant to the Fund for the Advancement of Education.[14]

Truly devised *de novo* to meet the requirements of individual students, a Master's degree program can take its candidate to a degree which may serve him either as an academic destination or way-station. Perhaps what we really need is a two-year Master's degree program which would provide some approximation of comprehension of the subject matter of a chosen field together with at least minimal competence in scholarship to do directed research, and to teach subject matter effectively at the college level.[15] The quotation from Lin Yutang with which this chapter began throws suggestive light on this matter.

The basic concerns of a course of graduate study are the same no matter whether it is pursued only through the novitiate or to completion of the apprenticeship. These concerns include comprehensive mastery of some body of knowledge sufficient for its controlled use, and a degree of mastery of the crafts of inquiry and research. For some students, competence in the art and craft of pedagogy will be important. The Report on Panel Discussions at Yale provides an interesting comment on progressive attainment of research competence:

---

[14] Everett Walters, "What Degree for College Teachers?" *The Journal of Higher Education*, XXXI, No. 2 (February 1960), 69 ff., and Oliver C. Carmichael, "A Three-Year Master's Degree," *The Journal of Higher Education*, XXXI, No. 3 (March 1960), 127 ff. See also Paul Woodring's comment on Dean Walters' proposals and Dean Walters' rebuttal, *The Journal of Higher Education*, XXXI, No. 5 (May 1960), 282 ff.

[15] The present one-year Master's program provides a complete basis for none of these; it affords no time for methodology, for learning how to learn, and none for digestion of knowledge. Even the "staff of life" serves life only upon reduction to amino acids and such. A suitable program for the first year might include: 12 semester hours of advanced coursework, 6 of theory of inquiry and problem-solving, 6 of research seminars in the subject and related fields, and 6 for the language requirement or a free elective. The second year's work could include: 6 semester hours of advanced coursework, 12 of research seminars, 6 of guided reading under the major advisor, and 6 for the thesis or dissertational essay. Such a 60-hour program could provide not only for scholarly research and teaching competence; it could provide a basis for a doctoral program both better and shorter; doctoral coursework requirements could be reduced by a year; and doctoral candidates would have greater methodological competence as well as stronger substantive foundations. The longer Master's and shorter Doctor's program is prevalent elsewhere. It could as well be here. Apex realization requires well-laid foundations.

One of the major objectives of research training should be practice in the handling of empirical materials of all sorts . . . [The graduate student] should gain experience in the critical evaluation of definitions and concepts, and in the manipulation and recasting of material.

The form of research training should probably differ at different stages of the graduate training process. . . .

The Ph.D. thesis [or dissertation] should serve a major function in research training, and should provide a test of whether the student has achieved research competence. But the primary research training should be begun much earlier in the student's career; it should not fall upon the thesis [or dissertation] alone. The thesis [or dissertation] may well emerge as an outgrowth of some earlier project.[16]

It is clear and widely accepted that the candidate for a Master's degree must attain comprehension and control of some basic body of knowledge, assured self-discipline as a basis for precision, and mastery of the basic research methods and tools of his field of interest. What, then, reasonably may be required and expected of the doctoral candidate?

A candidate for a doctorate must of course consolidate his knowledge and understanding of the substance of his chosen discipline or science—its ideas and materials, its methods and techniques, and its rules and standards. While attaining mastery of large segments of knowledge he must assimilate them into comprehensive patterns. In contrast to the more or less casual empiricism of the Master's level, he must learn the scientific testing of hypotheses and conclusions.

The successful doctoral candidate who emerges from graduate schooling and apprenticeship into the capacity of journeyman should be characterized by fully competent knowledge and understanding of his field. He should as well be professionally competent in the crafts of inquiry and research at least as these relate to his field. He should be able independently to structure and carry to fruition a project of research in a systematic and meaningful way; and to clarify his research and his results in a meaningful essay. He should be able to evaluate his achievements.

By means of a thesis, the doctoral candidate proves his compe-

---

[16] *Graduate Training in Economics*, p. 17.

tence to research and solve a problem not previously solved; and shows his capacity for originality by imaginative, speculative, and inventive employment of his mind and facilities in locating, approaching, and analyzing his problem. By means of a dissertation, the doctoral candidate proves his comprehensive understanding and control of the substance of some subject and reveals his capacity for originality and novelty by means of perceptive insights and imaginative innovation in recasting and synthesizing ideas and materials. In either case, he proves his competence in argument and discourse; and he proves his competence to write a coherent, intelligible, significant, scholarly essay on the basis of his own thought and work.[17]

In qualifying at last for his *Gesellenzeit*, as with apprentices everywhere, the doctoral candidate must provide final proof of his establishment of the necessary levels of competence. Every candidate for journeyman status must satisfy the *Kunstverständinge*, the "knowers of the job" or craft, that he has qualified himself to play the role by ability to perform its functions dependably. The new doctor is not called upon at this point to qualify for his *Meisterschaft*. It is left to him whether, on the basis of his achievements as a journeyman, he ever will.

Performance Standards
for Academic Essays

Performance standards for Master's and Doctor's theses and dissertations must be perceived as minimum quality requirements. There is no necessary limit to the amount by which the thresholds of acceptability may be exceeded. This minimum, however, properly is the same for all aspirants at each degree level.

Thesis or dissertation, the graduate academic essay must measure up against two categories of performance standards. One of these relates to the essay as a medium or vehicle of communication. The

---

[17] Even casual thought suggests that fewer possibilities may be open to doctoral candidates for writing theses than dissertations. Candidates should be allowed to choose between these two kinds of essays and their different underlying projects. The terms *Master's essay* and *Doctor's essay* may provide better usage than the prevalent *Master's thesis* and *Doctor's dissertation*.

other pertains to the quality of whatever is being communicated. Of the two sets, the latter is the more important. However, because the vehicle becomes apparent before its burden, treatment of these categories will be in the order in which they were named.

The regulations which graduate schools publish concerning format, paper, illustrations, title page, headings and sub-headings, pagination, and the like represent local standards of one sort. Graduate students must learn them in order to meet them. Copies of such regulations are obtainable at all graduate school offices. They usually include some such instruction as:

> It is the candidate's responsibility to study theses selected by his supervisor or recommended by the Graduate School to find the acceptable form for presenting his material, to proofread the material carefully, and to present his thesis in good form free from errors.[18]

Acceptance of thesis and dissertational essays by graduate schools requires, first of all, conformity with regulations as to mechanics and style sheet. The attractiveness of good form makes a manuscript easy and pleasant to read and appraise. Besides facilitating faculty evaluation, it reflects graduate school performance standards and control, and it simplifies inter-student comparison. The values of good form for students are that it reflects careful preparation, orderliness, recognition of appropriateness, and maturity, dependability, reliability and precision. Good "packaging" reflects appropriate work habits, poised awareness and sureness, and it helps put ideas across by inducing focus of attention on them. But good style sheet and mechanics are only the first of the standards in this category to be perceived, learned, and met. The phrases "in good form" and "free from errors" signify much else.

Good form relates also to such matters of grammar as syntax, the rules of which must be complied with. Besides right sentence structure, this involves apt phraseology and correct word usage. The language should be expressively employed and the vocabulary well chosen. Freedom from errors relates to grammatical correctness and

---

[18] "Graduate Student and Faculty Handbook," pamphlet issued by the Graduate School, the University of Florida, p. 34. Such statements continue by recommending some style manual as showing acceptable form. For a list of these, see Appendix K.

right spelling, to adherence to the style sheet, to agreement of chapter headings and subheadings with table of contents, to correctness of all quotations and all citations, and to all other elements of content.

Good form relates, in the third place, to effective application of the essay model. This requires that the thesis or dissertation be correctly structured as an essay, and that its contents be well organized. It should be borne in mind that to discourse is to present a process of reasoning from premises to conclusions in the form of a well-reasoned, logical argument. To be in good form, the argument should be consistent and coherent, and its premises should conform to the canons of logic. It is vital that the organization of ideas and material within the essay be such as to yield inner consistency and overall integrity. Good form requires that the essay be clearly coherent.

Finally, good form relates to the quality of rhetorical style. The writer of a thesis or dissertation must be able to convey his mental actions and intellectual achievement to the reader. This requires enough facility of expression to be clear, if not interesting, and to make ideas march. It will help to remember that usually in scholarly writing the whole story should be told in summary form at the outset. If the project is clearly stated in the introduction it will be a guide to coherence in the body of the essay for the writer; and it will be a guide for the reader's orientation and appraisal.

Performance standards are applied not only to the candidate's mastery of the essay form and style but also to the quality of what he is communicating. He is not, as a clerk, to make a report. As a novice or apprentice scholar or scientist he employs the essay to display a reasoned argument in proof or validation of an intellectual achievement. This may be an intellectual discovery, as a law or principle, or it may be an invention, innovation, clarification, criticism, refutation, refinement, or synthesis. In his essay he explains what he did and argues for acceptance of his result as valid. He must avoid incorrect conclusions, inferences, or solutions such as might arise from erroneous logic, loose argument, or inconsistencies. By the fluidity of his style, the aptness of his expression and choice of words, the organization and ease of handling of his ideas, he provides evidence of mastery of both the essay form and the subject treated, to a degree appropriate to the Master's or Doctor's degree level.

Excellent theses represent significant achievements in inquiry and problem solving. Good dissertations are derived especially from relatively full knowledge of discipline and subject, experience, wisdom, insights, and profound reflection and meditation. Especially at the Master's degree level there is little of this. For example, what inexperienced candidate would be capable of the insights which made possible *Hadrian's Memoirs*, so sensitively written by Marguerite Yourcenar? Or those which made possible J. B. Bury's *The Idea of Progress*? Or Arthur Koestler's *Insight and Outlook*? Or W. J. Cash's *The Mind of the South*? Or Howard Mumford Jones's *The Theory of American Literature, The Pursuit of Happiness,* and *American Humanism*?

These questions are not raised to suggest that unattainable standards be set. Nor are they raised to suggest that lesser projects are inappropriate, even at the doctoral level. Rather, they suggest that some graduate students are permitted, even encouraged or required, to attempt too much. Few graduate students have either time or the opportunity to attain wisdom and capacity for fine judgment. Artistry and achievements of virtuoso quality call for maturity and care. Such attributes characterize few academic journeymen and seldom an apprentice. This is the perennial problem of youth: scientific problems are difficult, and dissertational qualities are acquired with experience. The concept of necessary excellence for students has been clarified by Dr. H. H. Andersen:

> There is admittedly too much to know for any individual to achieve distinction in all areas, some of which will lie beyond his concern and capacities. But except for such natural and inevitable limitations, he should be disciplined where possible to the fullest extent of his potentialities. It is not enough that he stand high in the grade-curve for his group, for he must finally be measured, not by what others can or cannot do, but by the standards required by the subject. It is not enough for a student to be better than others in mathematics unless he can solve the problem. That is the test life administers. . . . Superiority that does not make a difference in the outcome is a distinction without significance.
>
> Actually, the standards of excellence are not hard to identify. They are the standards by which the ends we strive for are achieved.[19]

For what ends do we strive by means of graduate schooling? Concurrence on this matter will help significantly to clarify the stand-

---

[19] H. H. Andersen, "Democracy's Fateful Flaw," *Phi Kappa Phi Journal,* XXXX, No. 4 (Winter 1961), 14-15.

ard of minimum acceptable excellence for graduate research and
academic essays. Is it a function of graduate schooling to yield Par-
nassian achievement or only solid journeyman competence? Frederic
W. Ness, editor of *A Guide to Graduate Study*, states:

> There is difference of opinion among many American educators
> as to whether the Ph.D. ought to be awarded in recognition merely
> of a substantial advance along the road to educational fulfillment;
> or whether, as in certain European academic systems, it should
> symbolize arrival at a Parnassian peak of solid accomplishment.
> Since the latter ordinarily calls for many years of preparation and
> effort and since the demand in our country for Ph.D.'s vastly
> exceeds the supply, the former concept is the one which dominates
> most of the doctoral programs in American colleges and universities.
> The Ph.D., then, signalizes a high level of preparation rather than
> a lifetime of significant contribution; but, hopefully, it looks for-
> ward, rather than backward, to a career of enlarging usefulness.[20]

Acceptance of and concurrence in the idea that graduate schooling is designed to provide training and education for careers would
make it easier to see that the Ph.D. degree is taken generally to signify journeyman competence rather than the *Meisterschaft*. This
would make it clear that individualistic insistence on the "great work"
concept of a thesis or dissertation is invalid, poor pedagogy, and an
arbitrary and improper exercise of "academic freedom." This also
would simplify the task of establishing research and essay standards
both relevant and valid.

A notable shortcoming of the studies of graduate education in
America is their lack of attention to the Master's degree. It is true
that students may go straight to the doctorate, but in the cases of the
majority of those who attain the doctorate, the Master's degree is a
milestone on the way. If the intermediate degree is not taken, the

---

[20] *A Guide to Graduate Study: Programs Leading to the Ph.D. Degree*, ed.
Frederic W. Ness, p. 5. Cf. Howard Mumford Jones, "A Friendly Guide
into the Graduate School," *Bulletin of Birmingham Southern College*, XXXIX,
No. 4 (1947), 14: "The doctorate is conventionally the mark of the trained
scholar, scientist and research worker. . . . For a permanent career in the
college or university world, despite constant complaints by deans and presidents
that this is so, a Ph.D. in the subject of one's choice is a prerequisite. It is also
that mark of mature professional training required for a life-long career in
industrial laboratories, government bureaus, some kinds of medical research,
international organizations or other professional posts within the gift of government, industry, philanthropic organization, or professional association."

coursework must be done, while the investigative training is missed.

Berelson points out that the Master's degree "is deteriorated or confused, or both. It is half way to becoming a wholly owned property of the Education Department, and it may go all the way." [21] Meanwhile, Dr. Oliver C. Carmichael declares: "The current standards of the Master's degree are so varied, that it is an untrustworthy qualification for college and university teaching." [22] Too often, also, it is an untrustworthy qualification for any doctoral program.

The Doctor's degree also is in many cases open to doubt by reason of the shortcomings of underlying programs. Berelson finds it "unclear in objectives and especially in requirements, and it takes too long." [23] The 1956 Panel Discussions at Yale University on Graduate Education in Economics found that the Ph.D. thesis is "all too often . . . a traumatic experience which leaves the student scarred but untrained." [24]

Besides the prestige delusion which induces a focusing of attention on the doctorate to the neglect of the Master's degree, there are curious delusions about the standards for the apprentice doctor. One of these is expressed in a study of graduate education for women. The authors unhesitantly assert:

> The candidate working on his thesis is no longer a student: he is a scholar, elbowing his way into the professional market-place and hawking the products of his research in competition with the wares of more experienced scholars. To the confident and resilient candidate the process may provide the stimulus to a lifetime of scholarship. To the uncertain and the inflexible, the years spent in preparing a thesis may stifle the creative intellectual drive or limit its ultimate productivity.[25]

---

[21] Bernard Berelson, "The Studies of Graduate Education," *The Graduate Journal*, I, No. 2 (Fall 1958), 161.

[22] Carmichael, "A Three-Year Master's Degree," *The Journal of Higher Education*, XXXI, 128. Cf. his *Graduate Education: A Critique and a Program*, chap. xi.

[23] Berelson, "The Studies of Graduate Education," p. 161. This is the eighth of his ten major criticisms of graduate education. He goes on: "As for the dissertation as an original and independent contribution to knowledge, it is a facade on one side of the campus, whereas on the other it has somehow managed to achieve a striking correlation between length and triviality." It must be clear that there are some who do not know or do not care what they are doing.

[24] *Graduate Training in Economics*, p. 12.

[25] *Graduate Education for Women, the Radcliffe Ph.D.*; a report by a faculty-trustee committee (Cambridge: Harvard University Press, 1956), p. 23. The first sentence of this quotation is nonsense. The Ph.D candidate is an

Provost Atwood may have seemed to some to have placed himself on the side of the romantic notion contained in the first sentence of this quotation when, declaiming against the "Report of the Four Deans," he asserted: ". . . the Ph.D. must be riddled with uncertainties if the objective is to explore the unknown and to produce original research and scholarly effort." [26] He did not, however, since he limited himself to the necessary uncertainties relevant to substance and method. He did not consider the unnecessary and irrelevant uncertainties that often are produced by invalid notions, human failings, and poor human relations. A page later Provost Atwood said:

> In essence, graduate education is an apprentice relationship. The student learns how to do research—how to think analytically and originally—by doing it. . . . *Under the guidance of his mentor*, he establishes both the skills and the quality of his scholarship.[27]

Every proper academic apprentice relationship should be a secure one, related to known requirements and performance standards, and to certain criteria for evaluation of performance and output. Students will find themselves in a different position from that they now occupy when threshold concepts of necessary excellence are established and made clear respecting their required thesis and dissertational essays. Then they will have the assurance of at least reasonable and approximate clarity from the faculty side; and they then may find themselves subject to more or less equal treatment as under a rule of laws. In such event they will be able to get on more readily than they now do with the intellectual business of graduate degree qualification. Until then, however, graduate students shall have to provide themselves

---

apprentice scholar attempting to qualify for the status and recognition of a journeyman scholar, as marked by the award of his degree. *Thereafter* it is up to him to become a master scholar or not. Novice and apprentice academicians should not be irrelevantly and unnecessarily baffled. Poor teaching and bad handling of students and requirements occur in the environment of an uncertain curriculum, and are abetted by wrong notions about fundamentals. The authors state in their final sentence the inevitable results of their misconception.

[26] Sanford S. Atwood, "Graduate Education and Research," *The Graduate Journal*, II, Supplement (Spring 1959), 158. Graduate students can live with the uncertainties relevant to inquiry and project results. In their report, the "Four Deans" were addressing the frustratingly troublesome, needless, and irrelevant uncertainties with which students cannot cope.

[27] *Ibid.*, pp. 159-60. It was Mentor to whom Odysseus entrusted his house and the education of Telemachus when he set out for Troy.

clarity as to their writing requirements on the basis of their own study of the matter. They can stand on their own feet to do this. Their guide in the endeavor will be the postulate that graduate work is essentially brainwork.[28] Besides intellectual gifts and appropriate mentality and discipline, substantive and methodological achievements are necessary for the requisite work in the realm of ideas at an intellectual level of scholarship.

Graduate students may find it useful in this to take the position of the faculty and ask themselves some questions. Why should graduate students be trained in substance and methodology and then tested via theses and dissertations to determine whether the training has been effective? What should be expected of Master's degree level performances in respect of such essays? Of Doctor's degree level performances? By what lights should performances be judged to determine whether candidates have met required performance standards? How shall the relative excellence of acceptable work be determined?

Answers to these questions and other similar ones will bring graduate students, in sum, down to two others. With what criteria should the quality of their academic essays be evaluated and judged? How should such criteria be employed? The answers to these questions can provide excellent guides for meeting the required performance standards for the writing requirements. Graduate students are as capable of providing themselves clarity about evaluative criteria as about performance standards. The following section provides a look into the matter.

Criteria for Evaluating
Writing Performances

Important as it is for the graduate essayist, the category of standards of mechanics, style, and form of

---

[28] Someone who well knew wrote: "Creative intellect is the finest flower of race. It is by such . . . —and they are rare—, that the direction of our cultural evolution is determined. It is such as they who set our finest standards and who by their example inspire and hearten others in their striving for what always lies ahead, —renewed and ever greater accomplishments." Quoted by R. E. Langer in his Birkhoff obituary, published in *George David Birkhoff, Collected Mathematical Papers* (3 Vols.; New York: American Mathematical Society, 1950), I, xiii. Here is another indication of the scholastic standard for graduate degree candidates.

the essay is not as meaningful as the category of standards which applies to the substance of the essay. Style-sheet mechanics too often are overemphasized and blown up out of all proportion. It is senseless for students to become lost in a forest of mechanical details.

It has been shown that an essay is a manifestation of an intellectual exercise of greater or less significance. In addition to the requirement that the writing be of publishable quality, most graduate schools require that the underlying intellectual work and achievement represent a project of inquiry and research worthy of publication.

Having selected a project suitable as the basis for a Master's or Doctor's essay, the prospective writer faces his first substantive requirement. He must have sufficient clarity and assurance about his project to be able to make clear to others what it is. The process of clarification begun in the prospectus, which was one of the bases for approval of his essay project, now must be consummated in the introduction to his thesis or dissertation. The value or importance of the selected problem to be solved, matter to be clarified, or knowledge to be refined is not here in question. That was considered when committee approval was secured for the candidate's project as a basis for his essay. The criterion here is clarity of definition and description sufficient to enable the reader to know what he is getting into. Only if he knows what lies ahead can the reader place himself in position to appraise the argument of explanation and proof or substantiation to follow.

The second requirement in the substantive category is that the writer's argument be clearly expressed. He must be clear with respect to his definition and description of his problem or project, and clear as to its relationship to others, perhaps as a part of some complex of relationships within a larger frame of reference. The analysis of his problem or subject must be clear and unquestionable as well as adequately incisive, penetrating, and completely dissecting. His syntheses must be coherent and logical.

Employment of models for separate and discrete treatment of problem or subject elements must be meaningful. Besides being relevant, models must enhance the analysis by means of simplification. In short, use of models for deduction of implications, inferences and solutions, and for drawing of conclusions must make sense. The importance of analytical clarity and synthetic ability is suggested by a statement of John A. Morrison's: "Knowledge comes by taking things apart: analysis. But wisdom comes by putting things together." [29] The level of abstraction of the conceptual analysis must be appropriate to the candidate's level of schooling. So must the quality of his logic in inquiry, and the imaginative speculativeness of the deductive processes of his hypothesization, or of his drawing of inferences and conclusions.

Having explained his analysis and argued its validity, the essayist next must argue the validity of his solution or conclusions. The effectiveness with which he establishes a basis for the empirical testing of his hypotheses or conclusions, and the simplicity and directness of his procurement of relevant data for this, now come under scrutiny. Does he do this work well or not? Are his research procedures smoothly effective and efficiently productive? Or are they bumbling and unsure? Does he move easily between the conceptual and empirical elements of his exercise, or does he confuse them? Is his research relevant to his task; and does he employ the product of his research as a touchstone of fact against which to test his hypotheses or his conclusions?

What this comes down to is that the argument of proof, substantiation, or validation must be well reasoned, coherent, and logically consistent. That is, it must do what it purports to do.

In the end, the thesis writer or dissertator must establish beyond doubt that he has conceived a meaningful intellectual exercise and carried it through gestation to fruition. The requirement is that brainwork be adequately manifest. Serendipity is not enough. The writer's solution, explanation, clarification, or refinement must have been the contrived product of deliberate brainwork. It must be a sought-for and not an accidental derivative.

If accidental discoveries are made during work on the essay project, these can become the bases for post-degree papers and further work. This idea suggests a basic test of justification for supervisory committee approval of the candidate's selected problem or topic in the first place. A problem or topic of genuine thesis or dissertational essay warrant will be one on which the successful essayist can do further work to the advantage of his doctoral or post-doctoral schol-

---

[29] Quoted in *Operation Understanding*, a publication of the State Farm Insurance Companies, January 1961, p. 5.

arship.[30] In such light as this, perception of a valid contribution to knowledge or to learning will not be difficult for the *Kunstverstän-dinge*. These latter then will be in a position to decide whether the candidate's essay provides evidence of his competence to reason from some significant beginning to a meaningful end, and to communicate this process of reasoning via his discourse.

The ultimate criterion is a capacity to convince others of the reality and validity of an intellectual finding. In contrast to empirical discoveries which may be shown and reported, intellectual discoveries must be proved by means of logical argument couched in discourse. Whether empirical and objective, or conceptual and intellectual, ". . . discovery concerns a phenomenon, a law, a being which already existed, but had not been perceived." [31]

Invention differs from discovery in that the thing or process invented did not previously exist. The same may be said for innovation. Like discoveries, however, "inventions" and "innovations" may be accidental. The Malay fire stick and the Amazonian blow gun were accidental inventions. The European fire piston and the pneumatic hammer were achievements in applied science on the basis of prior knowledge of physics. An empirical discovery or invention may be reported, shown, or even demonstrated.[32] Substantiation of an intellectual discovery or invention, however, is an intellectual and literary exercise in explanation and proof.

True excellence in a thesis or dissertational essay requires intellectual originality on some account relevant to important knowledge. The requisite originality will be shown by the production of a new idea and its confirmation, which validates it as knowledge. Such idea may be a solution to a problem, a clarification of something previ-

---

[30] Compare, for example, the doctoral and post-doctoral work of such men as Wiener, Birkhoff, Riesman, Crane Brinton, and Paul Samuelson. Names of younger men join this group annually.

[31] Jacques S. Hadamard, *An Essay on the Psychology of Invention in the Mathematical Field* (Princeton: Princeton University Press, 1949), p. xi.

[32] Accidental discovery and invention seem fairly frequent in the so-called data sciences. If some such empirical achievement is regarded as sufficiently important a report of it, if well enough written, conceivably might be acceptable in lieu of a thesis or dissertation. However, it would have to be recognized that the report would have no intellectual content and could not have equal credit value with a thesis or dissertation. To name such report a thesis or dissertation would be intellectually false and academically fraudulent. Such report should be called what it is—a report.

ously unknown, a refinement, or a significant criticism. The essay must reflect originality in style and in argument of explanation and substantiation, just as much as the investigation on which it rests.

Because they are conceptually and qualitatively different sorts of essays, theses and dissertations require different sorts of underlying investigative projects. They also require different sets of criteria for their evaluation.[33] Confusion of substantively different means of fulfilling writing requirements has often led to the perplexity and bewilderment, frustration and failure of candidates. Lack of knowledge of evaluative criteria appropriate to each case is an additional source of uncertainty. Such lack of knowledge can provide no understanding of the light in which faculty judgment of student work is undertaken. With such knowledge, however, candidates have light in which to see the ways in which to achieve success.

Summation

The elements of basic conceptual and functional instruction on the writing requirements for graduate degrees now have been presented. Mastery of their implications can put graduate students well on the way to success as significant academic essayists. This is like going up on a mountain to have a wide look. By getting above their projects, candidates for advanced degrees can recognize the value of their occasional and often sudden intuitions and flashes of insight. They then can make use of them in the right places.[34]

---

[33] Because both thesis and dissertation apply the essay form and similar methodology, certain criteria apply to both, especially grammatical correctness, coherence, rhetorical facility, appropriateness of usage, style sheet, and mechanics. Criteria by which the dissertation further is evaluated include: significance and validity of premises, clarity and quality of reasoned argument, validity and importance of conclusions, and quality of the contribution to learning (especially the candidate's learning!). Criteria by which the thesis is judged, in addition to the common criteria, include: structure of the inquiry, use of scientific—especially deductive—methodology, power and penetration of analysis, employment of insights (if any), quality of formal argument in proof of a meaningful hypothesis, and whether an adequate contribution to knowledge is made. These lists provide merely a suggestive start. The matter of right criteria demands careful thought. Cf. Almack, *Research and Thesis Writing*, Chap. xi.

[34] Arthur Koestler has compared the intuitions of some scientists to sleepwalking. See the preface to his *The Sleepwalkers* (New York: The Macmillan Company, 1959). Discussing intellectual discovery and its attainment by deduction, Koestler said, p. 14: " . . . the psychological process of discovery . . .

This facilitates reflection and simplification. It tunes the mind to the frequency of one's essay project much as a mother's ear is tuned to the frequency of her child's cries and needs.

Once launched upon the writing, candidates will find it valuable to keep continuously in mind the models of their intended essays. Once into them, their minds will work at subconscious levels to startle them with sudden clarifications and formulations.[35] Here and there in coursework and reading, in conversations and discussions, ideas will be encountered which will be useful in various parts and stages of the tasks. Candidates who are in position to perceive the value of such ideas and constructs can capture them and file them appropriately for use.

The performance standards for thesis and dissertational essayists may be taken as norms to which the threshold analogy applies. For obvious reasons, however, standards of minimum acceptable performance for Doctor's degree candidates are higher than those for Master's degree candidates. But at either level appropriate performance standards will be the same for both thesis and dissertation. This holds despite the fact that different criteria are employed in grading thesis and dissertational essay performances.

Performance standards for academic essays are only in part quantitative. In the main, they are qualitative. Such standards are derived from meaningful conceptions of necessary levels or grades of excellence for fulfillment of graduate educational purposes.

Performance standards in general use can be neither arbitrary

---

[is] the most concise manifestation of man's creative faculty." Cf. Northrop, *The Logic of the Sciences and the Humanities*, p. 10. It may be well to reemphasize that much of research and origination of data is related to the matter of proving hypotheses or of validating conclusions rather than to that of conceiving them. Methods are indicated by Morris Cohen, Ernest Nagel, John Dewey, and others. In the event of several hypotheses, for example, deduce from each what would follow if it were true and put the deduced consequences to empirical tests, at least to simulated ones. Thus the hypothesis that is correct or best, or whether any is correct, may be found. On this point see Northrop, *The Logic of the Sciences and the Humanities*, p. 25.

[35] Cf. Wiener, *Ex-Prodigy*, p. 46. Discussing the processes of intellect, Wiener tells how his mind goes to work on problems at a subconscious level, and how ideas form patterns in his sleep. For the way James Watt got the idea of a condenser for his steam engine upon walking in and out the gates at opposite ends of an Edinburgh park, see W. H. Dickenson, *James Watt* (Cambridge University Press, n.d.), cited in N. W. Dougherty, "Discovering and Nurturing Originality," *Phi Kappa Phi Journal*, XXXX, No. 3 (Fall 1960), 3-9.

nor capricious because they are not likely to be subject to individual discretion, notion, preference, or whim. While definite, they are not despotic. While requiring conformity, they do not demand uniformity. It is worth reiterating that, as lower limits, as threshold parameters or constraints, while they must be complied with they may be exceeded. Except for standards, how could exceptionality or brilliance of achievement be established?

Performance standards are at least implicit in all grading. So are the evaluative criteria by means of which work is tested for conformity with standards. Although grading of human effort or achievement probably cannot be as objective as, for example, the grading of wheat, it nevertheless can be more effective than it is. The grading of thesis and dissertational essay performances is improving in the light of their educational rationale. It can be more objective than it is and, so, more reasonable and significant than has been the case. The requisite quality of a thesis or dissertational essay is as capable of conceptual and postulational definition as is the nature of each of these essays.

Here, again, is a problem that is one not of definition, but of recognition and acceptance. Graduate students can recognize and make use of the performance and criteria concepts relevant for their essays as well as anyone else. They will serve themselves well if they do. Employed as guides in their efforts to fulfill writing requirements, these concepts can enable them to produce better results than otherwise. Such use of criteria is evidence of maturity.

PART TWO

The
Writing
Environment

5

Overture to the Writing Environment

The vital principle of a liberal university is its concern for Man and his fulfillment.

J. DOUGLAS BROWN

Solitude is needful to the imagination as society is wholesome for the character.

JAMES RUSSELL LOWELL

The first part of this book was concerned with helping graduate students set sail upon their personal voyages of writing requirement fulfillment. It also provided them some navigational aids. This part of the book is concerned with their academic sea, the environment in which they must work. This environment often is ideally described as a "community of scholars." For convenience here it shall be called graduate academe—or just academe.

Most beginning graduate students seem to have romantically biased notions about their brave new world of graduate academe. Their conception of the graduate school is an abstraction from reality built on the ideal model of a community of novices, apprentices, and masters engaged in learning, imparting, and extending man's knowledge of himself and his universe. Novice graduate students do not at first perceive academe as the very real world of very real human beings in which they must learn to live. To live and work in it effectively they must adjust to it. To adjust to it they must understand it. To understand it they must know it.

Graduate schooling can provide stimulating steps toward

meaningful intellectual independence for those who understand it, and who undertake fulfillment of their academic requirements with self-disciplined energy and determination. At the other extreme, hesitant students who are not fully cognizant of academic requirements may find that the typical graduate school's vagaries and inconsistencies occasionally provide all the frustrating tantalizations of an "academic snake pit."

This term has been used to express a sort of wry humor by doctoral candidates whose fulfillment of writing requirements has been delayed. Frustrated graduate students have used the term in expression of their disillusionment. Unsophisticated ones have used it in connection with bitter complaints about being "cut adrift" to do their theses and dissertations. Right or wrong, these groups are in difficulties from which they can be extricated. They can extricate themselves. They can begin by learning the nature and significance of their writing requirements, and by realizing that they are supposed and expected to stand more or less on their own feet in fulfilling them. These matters were treated in Part I. For poised effectiveness, graduate students need also to learn the nature and characteristics of the academic environments in which they have to work.

Graduate students must think for themselves but they must perform in an academic society. Some graduate schools approximate the ideal model in most of their aspects. Others approach it in some ways and to limited extents. Many reflect the model only dimly or in distorted image. Imperfections exist which have been obstructing scholastic achievement and, in many cases, extending unduly the time needed to complete writing projects. Their heavy impact, especially on attempts to meet writing requirements, has contributed to high rates of attrition of candidates for advanced degrees. For this reason, and because the values of all that is well and good speak for themselves, a central concern of Part II is with what has been called the pathology of graduate education. Student sailors may have better chances of reaching their academic landfalls if they understand their academic seas.

The positive values of the ideal conception of graduate education are widely known and understood. They have inspired generations of graduate students. Little need be said of them here nor of the top schools which approximate the model and yield its values. They deserve their prestige and their praise. Nevertheless, even they at times exhibit some of the irrationalities of graduate academic environments which are not widely known except by initiates. Obscurantism has been at work to hide them. Some students gain early awareness of them and deal with them more or less deftly. Other students learn about them late, and often through bitter and disadvantageous experiences. Most of these irrationalities appear in situations involving human relations. They arise because of human failings and weaknesses with which it is necessary to be patient. Other difficulties are inevitable results of academic growth and change.

The significance of graduate schooling is so great that its attractiveness obscures its shortcomings. Its strengths and values are notable, but its weaknesses detract from them. The mushroom growth of graduate education in recent years has permitted graduate degrees and degree requirements to become a miscellany of traditional, experimental, dictatorial, and expedient factors. These vary among universities and among colleges and departments within universities. They set the stage for a play of needless difficulties which hamper and dissuade students, especially when they attempt their theses and dissertations.

The purpose of this discussion is constructive and optimistic. It can be helpful for graduate students to be informed of the worst features of graduate schools as well as of the good ones. The good aid them and the bad trouble them. The faculty may know their milieu and how to perform effectively in it, but novice graduate students do not. Their purpose is to obtain an education on the basis of which to qualify for graduate degrees. Their close focus on purpose and on the good features of academe can cause unawareness of potential difficulties. Defeat comes easily to those taken unaware. Walking in a forest in the dark, one may stumble over things not seen. Informational forewarning can serve as a light in the hand.

The confusion to be described encompasses various difficulties which *may* be encountered in academe. Students must be mindful of the fact that they may encounter only a few or—happily—none. They must realize also that honest mistakes may occur in spite of good intentions of both students and faculty. Perhaps a student's own emotional outlook may falsely color his view of his faculty or of school regulations. Irregular eating and resting habits and accumulations of weariness reinforce such attitudes. Students who give way to resentment impose unnecessary hardships on themselves. Honest complaint is one thing; festering animosity is another.

Students should be warned not to delude themselves with excuses about the conditions of academe. Regulations are needed to systematize large organizational operations. Other things being equal, it may be that unhappiness and boredom are signs that one is forcing himself into a wrong field. Before attempting to meet writing requirements, it might be well to take time for re-evaluation and re-assessment to remove any doubt. Then, or earlier if possible, is when the decision should be made whether one is in the field of his best ability and interest. Acquired knowledge and abilities are transferable, and changing to another field may, in the end, be more economical of time and effort than staying where one is. False pride should not be permitted to force premature or unwarranted attempts to meet writing requirements. Neither should undue humility and fears of frustration or failure deter students from meeting the high challenge for success in chosen fields.

Many of the environmental uncertainties which trouble academic novices and apprentices could be made to disappear. The writing requirements could be clarified, the relevant performance standards could be made explicit, and the criteria used in appraisal of student work could be indicated. The reasons why the academic masters have not done these things may be traced to *their* academic environment. So may the causes of other aspects of student uncertainty. Graduate students can contribute significantly to reduction of their environmental uncertainties by learning enough about their academic environment to understand such relationships as these.

A good way to learn enough about anything for its understanding is to read about it. An ample literature on American scholarship is readily accessible.[1] It includes studies of academic freedom, the condition and essence of higher learning enjoyed by graduate students and graduate faculties.[2] It also includes historical and critical studies of both general and particular aspects of graduate

---

[1] For example, from Ralph Waldo Emerson's essay, "The American Scholar," to *American Scholarship in the Twentieth Century*, ed. Merle E. Curti (Cambridge: Harvard University Press, 1953).

[2] Russell Kirk, *Academic Freedom: An Essay in Definition* (Chicago: Henry Regnery Company, 1955); and Richard Hofstadter and Walter P. Metzger, *The Development of Academic Freedom in the United States* (New York: Columbia University Press, 1955).

schooling in the United States.[3] Other countries possess similar literatures which may be read for interest as well as for guidance.

Reading can provide access to understanding the graduate academic environment just as it can to understanding substantive matters and methodology. To gain a conception of the ideal, one could begin with such books as *Mission of the University*, by José Ortega y Gasset, and *The Idea of the University*, by Karl Jaspers. These could be followed by Thorstein Veblen's *The Higher Learning in America*, John D. Millett's *The Academic Community*, Paul Goodman's *The Community of Scholars*, and Alfred Whitney Griswold's *Essays on Education* and *In the University Tradition*. Other books will be helpful, such as James A. Davis' *Stipends and Spouses*. It will be especially useful, in the end, to read completely and carefully the catalogue and other publications of one's chosen graduate school. It is a curious fact that this sort of meaningful preparation for graduate schooling seldom is undertaken. Such lack of enterprise can result in misconceptions and may come from the lack of interest which underlies self-defeat.

Nearly all students who enroll in graduate schools complete course requirements for their degrees; indeed, most of them pass their comprehensive qualifying examinations. Thereupon, released from direct faculty control and cast free to fulfill the writing requirements on their own, they confront uncertainties almost at once. The first of these may be the substantive and methodological ones inherent in selection of projects and pursuit of inquiry. Then the *needless* uncertainties with which academe is "riddled" begin to produce their debilitating effects by militating against achievement.

---

[3] A significant general study is Oliver C. Carmichael, *Graduate Education: A Critique and a Program* (New York: Harper and Row, Publishers, Inc., 1961), which won the 1962 American Council on Education Book Award for the most "outstanding published work contributing importantly to the knowledge and advancement of higher education in the United States." See also Bernard Berelson, *Graduate Education in the United States* (New York: McGraw-Hill Book Co., Inc. 1960); Earl James McGrath, *The Graduate School and the Decline of Liberal Education* (New York: Published for the Institute of Higher Education by the Bureau of Publication, Teachers College, Columbia University, 1959); and Isaiah Bowman, *The Graduate School in American Democracy* (Washington, D. C.: U. S. Government Printing Office, 1939). *The Graduate Journal* (Austin, Texas: Graduate School of the University of Texas) is an excellent quarterly source of information. Cf. James H. Blessing, *Graduate Education: An Annotated Bibliography* (Washington, D. C.: U. S. Department of Health, Education, and Welfare, Office of Education, 1961).

The writing requirements thus become obstacles upon which many students collapse, rather than opportunities to prove intellectual prowess.[4]

Extrinsic and supervenient uncertainties are needlessly present in graduate schools of all quality ranks in all countries. Unprepared and ill-equipped students often unwittingly contribute to such uncertainties which harass them irrelevantly and unduly. Principally, however, they are unintentional products of perverse pedagogy by graduate faculties. A distinguishing characteristic of these uncertainties is that they center on the writing requirements, which often are vague and obscure and treated with extraordinary ineptitude. Students may become victims of faculty disagreements and arbitrariness whenever faculty concurrence on the nature and significance of these requirements is lacking. Students cannot effectively fulfill vague and shifting requirements, nor can they intervene and settle faculty disagreements. Like Tantalus, many become doomed to strive for what is always out of reach.

It is a recognized and proper function of graduate councils to define the graduate degree requirements they set. This includes definition of the writing requirements, for which it also is their function to set and clearly state performance standards.[5] Specification of per-

---

[4] Panel Discussions at Yale, *Graduate Training in Economics*, p. 13: " . . . a large proportion of students who have completed everything but the thesis never finish it." Cf. p. 20: The Ph.D. thesis (or dissertation) is viewed as "both a test of and means of acquiring core knowledge, clarity of expression, and research competence." See also pp. 23-24, and Howard R. Bowen, "Graduate Education in Economics," Supplement to *The American Economic Review*, XLIII, No. 4 (September 1953), 36-37, & 92-93. Bowen estimated, p. 92, that "out of 100 students admitted to graduate standing in economics: 60 will be awarded the master's degree or will complete the first year of graduate work successfully [;] 20 will take preliminary examinations [;] 17 will pass those examinations [;] 10 will receive the Ph.D." The attrition rate declines as one moves toward the natural and physical sciences and it drops in the applied fields. The *World Almanac and Book of Facts for 1963* (New York: New York World-Telegram and Sun, 1963), p. 540, reports that in 1959-1960, earned Master's degrees were awarded in 74,499 cases and earned Doctor's degrees to 9,829 recipients in the United States.

[5] For example, see the "Bulletin of the Graduate School," *The University Record of the University of Florida*, LV, Series 1, No. 3 (March 1, 1960), 7: "The Graduate School consists of the Dean, the Assistant Dean, the Graduate Council, and the Graduate Faculty. It is responsible for the establishment and enforcement of minimum general standards of graduate work in the University and for the coordination of the graduate programs of the various colleges. . . ." This pertains to standards for thesis and dissertational essays as well as to those for coursework and admissions. Other universities publish similar statements.

formance standards requires designation of criteria to be used in judging and grading writing performances. Neglect of these functions is one important source of needless uncertainties for graduate students. Faculty disagreements which follow neglect of these functions is another. Graduate students who are overly dependent upon their advisors, and upon their supervisory committees, may be seriously handicapped in such circumstances.

Graduate students need adequate help and appropriate guidance to avoid succumbing to the ravages of their environmental uncertainties. Their perplexity and bewilderment about what they *really* must do, and *really* how well, to qualify for advanced degrees can be overcome. They need not depend entirely on the faculty to set the matter right. In any case, the necessary faculty studies and actions will take time. Meanwhile, graduate students have ample opportunities and facilities, as well as a pressing need, to overcome the disadvantages that indifference and lack of initiative impose on them. Just as they can turn their minds to learning the nature and attributes of their writing requirements, they can turn their minds to learning the qualities and characteristics of their writing environments. Once their understanding is clear on all relevant counts, their performance can be fully motivated to meet academic challenges with vitality and perseverance. Excellence and success can be attained.

Graduate schooling is the most expensive and rewarding of all schooling. It attracts and provides intellectual outlets for many of the best minds. Graduate students and faculties work together to enhance the most precious form of capital that can be possessed, trainable intellect. Their joint concern is the establishment of foundations for learned careers in the sciences, humanities, letters, and arts. The demand for men and women with advanced degrees far exceeds the number of those who have them or are acquiring them.

The graduate faculties are the splendid strength of academe and the source of most of its valuable qualities and characteristics. Because they are human, they also can be the source of most of the difficulties which needlessly induce exhausting anxieties and frustrations in the minds of graduate students. This is less anyone's fault than it is the result of circumstances which just got out of hand. The problem of needless environmental uncertainties cannot be dismissed by denying it or ignoring it. This is a matter for faculty thought and action. It is a matter for immediate student understanding.

This is a book of a different kind than most written expressly for graduate students. It is not a manual on thesis and dissertation writing but a guide to the substance of these essays and the milieu in which they are worked out. As such it is designed to enable graduate students to overcome the disadvantages under which they now labor in their efforts to meet writing requirements for their degrees.

The purpose of Part II of this book is to alert graduate students to certain characteristics of graduate academe that they will not be otherwise prepared to perceive and understand. Its function then will be to light the way of students through what frankly may be called difficult passages. Like Bunyan's Pilgrim, they must avoid or conquer them. Each successful traverse should increase fitness for the next. A student's maturation will be, at least in part, a function of success in responding to environmental dangers and pitfalls. Academe is a human society, a life environment in microcosm, into which students pass from their academic chrysalis. Students who equip themselves with a vision of what they may expect there should be able to contend more or less effectively with its exigencies. If they can cope with academe, they should be able to cope with life.

6

Inside Academe

What man does not alter for the better, time alters for the worse.

FRANCIS BACON

We show, as a nation, laudable energy and persistence in walking according to the best light we have, but are not quite careful enough, perhaps, to see that our light be not darkness.

MATTHEW ARNOLD

Big changes occur when graduate students complete coursework and turn to fulfillment of writing requirements for their degrees under their own management. The discipline of scheduled meetings and assignments ends, and clock and calendar become less urgent when faculty direction and control subside. It is a long step for the student from the mere making of determinations in response to assignments to the making of decisions on the basis of his own solutions to his problems. Many who have demonstrated substantive and methodological competence lose out now because they are unable to cope with the circumstances and conditions of work on their thesis or dissertational essay projects.

Candidates who have selected their investigative and writing projects earlier will have an advantage at this point over those who waited until after "prelims." Nevertheless, most will have a sense of being cut adrift without vital navigational aids. However, graduate students need not be passive on this account. Unreadiness for independence can be overcome. Knowledge of tides and shoals, currents and winds can help them survive even in rough academic waters. Students can orient themselves in academe by learning to understand its relevant frames of reference and then by adjusting to them. Although most collegiate catalogues are of little help in this, alert candidates have other sources available which reveal the character-istics and qualities of their working environments.

The graduate academic environment is called a "community of scholars." It is a human society whose prime component is the teaching faculty. A graduate faculty is made up of human beings who perform under a variety of pressures and who have problems of their own. The groves of academe present pitfalls and difficulties for them as well as for the students.

The literature about graduate education says little about its negative aspects, so this book must. Completeness requires it to. A note of caution is sounded here because this chapter deals with some of the pathological aspects of academe. It should be read as explanation and not as criticism. Readers will err if they infer mere critical intention or call for reform. The purpose of the straight-forward exposition is to supply students with pertinent information on the environmental difficulties as well as the definitional ones which may be encountered. Those who achieve social as well as in-tellectual maturity attain a degree of poise that will improve their chances for academic success.

The Situation

Graduate students cope with two kinds of un-certainty in academe. One is inevitable and vital. It is necessary. Being intrinsic to learning, which indeed it enhances by intensifying its processes, this kind of uncertainty is inherent in and appropriate to academe. The other kind is extraneous and needless. It is inappro-priate to academe. It impedes and frustrates attempts at degree qualification because it intrudes upon and obstructs learning.

Unnecessary uncertainties of the second sort are symptomatic of pathological conditions of graduate academe. The cure will have to come from the faculties, but graduate students are at least re-sponsible for first aid. They certainly can protect themselves from succumbing to the effects of needless environmental uncertainties. Explanation and differentiation of the two kinds of uncertainties they face in academe can aid their adjustment to them.

In the first place, graduate students must face uncertainties which are inherent in and appropriate to the processes of their edu-cation. These are the natural, relevant hazards of their occupation;

and the source of the healthful and exhilarating anxieties which induce full use of talents in the vital tests of competence. They temper student mettle. Ways to meet them were explained in Part I.

The luster and satisfaction of the victor's crown are proportionate to the difficulties of the course. Students who feel that they have the requisite intellectual faculties, maturity, and drive to obtain degrees, and who aspire enough to the roles of Masters and Doctors, adjust willingly to these uncertainties. Under such pressures they can prove their capacities to become scholars and scientists, and to attain intellectual independence and recognition. These appropriate uncertainties include those relevant to the students themselves. Have they the necessary qualities of mind? The determination and capacity to persevere? The courage to be valiant? The time? The funds? Necessary health? Requisite physical strength and energy? Meaningful post-degree goals? These are the attributes that count rather than thickness of skin or opportunistic ingenuity.

Assuming proper selection of students for graduate schooling, the uncertainties which contribute to learning are functions of attempts to fulfill conceptually clear and meaningful requirements, and to meet known and positive performance standards. Such desirable uncertainties give meaning to attainment of distant, difficult, and rewarding ends via significant performances. They could be eliminated only by establishing innocuous requirements and setting ridiculous standards. That would be a course of deceit.

On the other hand, many graduate students are being required to face uncertainties which are inappropriate to academe. This is wrong because such uncertainties violate canons of pedagogy and reason. Needless and disagreeable, they confuse, perplex, bewilder, and obstruct. Uncertainties which are foreign to the ideal learning process and environment provide trials of endurance rather than tests of patience, poise, discipline, and intellectual ability. They are sources of exhausting and abrasive anxieties. They establish veritable snake-pits in academe by converting humane achievement courses to inhumane obstacle courses.

Needless academic uncertainties have made graduate work "inefficient and traumatically disagreeable" to many students, as a notable study soon to be quoted has shown. Their cost in energy, ambition, time, and money is high. In combination with lax admissions practices and faulty guidance of graduate students, they support high rates of attrition of candidates for advanced degrees. The tragic fact is that there is neither necessity nor rationale for their more than minimal existence. Academic snake-pits are unnecessary, inexcusable, and a disgrace. Yet they exist, and students must beware of them. Hope remains that in time they may be eliminated. Until then, graduate students must equip themselves to avoid becoming trapped in them.

Again assuming proper selection of students, the inappropriate uncertainties are those which are produced by the perverse ways in which graduate schools often operate and their faculties frequently perform. Such uncertainties are less the functions of schools and faculties taken totally than of particular situations and performances which are inconsistent with logic and good practice. They appear most often where students must try to fulfill indefinite requirements; and where faculty direction and appraisal of their work is casual, capricious, arrogant, quarrelsome, vague, or arbitrary.

The pathology of graduate schooling is a function of things graduate faculties and students do and fail to do within the academic apparatus. The faculties can reduce their contributions to needless student difficulties. Many try and many undoubtedly succeed. That is beside the point. Concern here is with the fact that some do not, but especially with what graduate students can achieve for themselves on this account. A publication of the Association of Graduate Schools which was mentioned in Chapter Four provides a good starting point for appraisal of the contemporary academic environment. It draws attention to some of the long-standing problems of graduate education, and provides a focus for a look inside academe.

This thoughtful report was published in the fall of 1957 and was widely publicized.[1] It dwelt in particular upon the length of time required to attain the Ph.D. degree, the uncertainty of its attainment, its cost in money and energy, and the attrition of candidates for it. The report gave reasons for the difficulties with which graduate study is fraught. It raised the question of how the time required to complete work for the doctorate, the uncertainties involved, and the candidate drop-out rate might be reduced. Not the first of its kind,

---

[1] The report is reprinted below as Appendix A. It appeared in *The New York Times*, November 13, 1957, p. 28. Cf. editorial in *The New York Times*, November 14, 1957, p. 32; and a report of a luncheon talk by Jacques Barzun, *The New York Times*, May 15, 1957, p. 36.

even during the 1950's, it nevertheless represented a kind of climacteric.[2] In view of its authorship, graduate students would do well to study it.

The report was discussed by the AGS conference but not adopted by the Association. Although not representative of official AGS policy, the report had an impact which was indicated by its widespread discussion following publication. That discussion, however, had a strange quality, at least to the extent of this writer's knowledge of it. Despite the implications of the report which induced it, the discussion turned mainly on quantitative rather than on qualitative factors. Concern was essentially with how much time and money the Ph.D. required and how much it ought to require; and with candidate attrition as a function of time, funds, and frustration. Much was made of the fact that many candidates are married and have families to support. All of this led to the solution: more and larger subsidies for graduate students.

The discussion waned and ceased with failure to determine adequate sources of funds. Little thought was given to the idea that some things are beyond the reach of money—to the idea that supplying funds is not invariably an efficient, effective, or even appropriate method for attaining ends. Hence, a really important point received little consideration. Graduate students are less in need of further financial help than of relief from the irrational academic vagaries and uncertainties which plague them.[3]

Reviewing the discussion, one can only be amazed at the scant attention given to such matters as more careful selection and better guidance of graduate students; clearer definition of and reasons for the thesis and dissertational essay requirements; more precise indication of essay performance standards and of criteria for evaluation of student performances; more vital Master's degree programs including better schooling of students, especially in methodology; and

---

[2] Cf. Berelson, "The Studies of Graduate Education," *The Graduate Journal*, I, 155 ff. The "Four Deans' Report" was preceded by the "Report of the Committee of Fifteen," which will be considered below.

[3] Graduate students traditionally have been willing to endure temporary financial stringency in view of the rewards for success and of their lack of time for much else than their books. Cf. Don Quixote's discussion of the condition of students in Miguel de Cervantes, *The History of the Valorous and Witty Knight-Errant Don Quixote of the Mancha*, trans. Thomas Shelton (London: Macmillan and Co., Ltd., 1900), II, Part I, Book IV, Chap. X, 32-33.

better faculty selection and pedagogy. The discussion appeared to proceed on the assumption that in these respects all was well.

The reality is that in these respects all was not well. It still is not. Academic environments have grown haphazardly and too often are characterized by confusion, inconsistency, disorganization, and uncertainty. They too often are productive of student doubt and perplexity. The reasons are clear but the necessity is not.

Graduate students share responsibility for this reality with graduate school faculties and administrations. Their poor intellectual and social preparation and their persistence in sycophancy are impressive faults. Nevertheless, their bewilderment and perplexity are in large part caused by faculty idiosyncracies, inconsistencies, arbitrariness, and arrogance within an amorphous academic structure and organization. It is unreasonable to insist that graduate students qualify for advanced degrees by meeting vague requirements which often receive capricious handling. Such factors and others underlie needless uncertainties which raise student costs in time and money, and which maintain high candidate attrition rates.

The "Four Deans" addressed themselves to this condition in their widely-read report:

> We must ruefully conclude that the Ph.D. is tortuously slow and riddled with needless uncertainties; that it is frequently inefficient and traumatically disagreeable to the bewildered and frustrated candidate. The basic flaw is: we have never cleanly *defined* this protean degree.[4]

Perhaps the concluding sentence of the statement was misleading. It is indeed true that the Ph.D. has become protean and, therefore, neither easily nor meaningfully definable. The degree is awarded not only in the natural and physical sciences, the social sciences, and the humanities, but of late in professional, quasi-professional, and other applied fields as well. The Ph.D. has been made available where philosophy is neither taught nor well known. It has been made incongruous.

This is a fact of academic life with which graduate students

---

[4] See Appendix A, p. 189. The Master's degree should not be overlooked; this statement applies also to it. On the condition of the degree environment, see also "The State of Graduate Education," four articles in *The Graduate Journal*, IV, No. 2 (Fall 1961).

must cope. However, there need be neither taking of sides nor invidious comparison in observing, in the interest of student clarity, that there is a notable difference between a "learned" man and a "professional" man. The point is that the valid and meaningful differences between these concepts have been blurred and neglected.

Proteanizaton of the Ph.D. has been accompanied by proteanization of the once clean-cut thesis and dissertational essay concepts. These are cases where casualness and laxity have opened the door to bad usage. Such usage militates against clarity and reasonableness and makes it difficult for graduate students to have true perceptions of what they must do. Usage that is bad or obscure gives rise to needless and irrelevant uncertainties.[5] Inappropriate usages and abuses represent another fact of academic life with which students must cope.

Such confusion is much less frequent in schools of top quality than in those of lesser quality. Especially in schools of middle and lower standing, the required essays, the performance standards relevant to them, and the use of evaluative criteria in judgment of them, are not everywhere clear to students. These matters cannot be made clear by faculties who do not concur in their clarification. Mixed and conflicting instructions as to the writing requirements simply defeat students. Success often depends upon student self-help to clarity. Clarity in these respects is found elsewhere in the university —to say nothing of the professions, business, and industry. Many of the most capable prospective graduate students simply turn elsewhere when they see what this aspect of graduate schooling involves.[6]

---

[5] The writer has heard a member of a graduate faculty assert in argument that "A thesis is anything a candidate submits and can get away with." This "fact of life" is a manifestation of protean concepts, requirements, standards, and criteria. It is a rule which is applied with alarming frequency. But who could work effectively on the basis of it? Other cynics have expressed similar opinions. Cf. Carmichael, *Graduate Education*, p. 48: "The character and purpose of the dissertation itself are not agreed upon." See also pp. 24, 47, 55-56, 111, 147-48, 153-54, 180, 196, 197.

[6] Stuart Sherman's sardonic exaggeration of a half-century ago is relevant: "The very best men do not enter upon graduate study at all; the next drop out after a year's experiment; the mediocre men at the end of two years; the most unfit survive and become doctors of philosophy, who go forth and reproduce their kind." Quoted by Norman Foerster, *The American Scholar: A Study in Litterae Inhumaniores* (Chapel Hill: University of North Carolina Press, 1929), p. 65. Cf. pp. 65-67.

This renewal of the discussion of the problem posed by the "Four Deans" seeks to divert attention from quantitative to qualitative factors which underlie academic difficulties. The remainder of this chapter is comprised of a discussion of the characteristics and qualities of the principal components of academe. These are the graduate schools, their faculties, and their student bodies. They will be treated in the order named in considering their contributions to needless student uncertainties. The endeavor is merely to describe generally what often is the case. The purpose, once again, is relevant information.

Graduate Schools

University graduate schools differ significantly from undergraduate and professional colleges. They are not unified, well integrated or closely-knit entities. Instead, they are complex agglomerations of heterogeneous interests seeking diverse ends. Their central and general interests are differently perceived, interpreted, and supported by their competitive departmental components. Internal stresses and strains push and pull them in all directions at once.[7] Howard Mumford Jones observes:

> Despite the wild illogicalities of their makeup, existing graduate schools of arts and sciences perform too useful a function and are too deeply imbedded in university structure for an immediate alteration. If they change, they will change with glacial slowness.[8]

All of the departments of the various colleges of a university which offer graduate work participate in its "graduate program." The components of a graduate school, however, are a dean, a graduate council, and a part-time faculty. These provide within the institu-

[7] On the chaotic inconsistency and confusion of graduate schools, see Carmichael, *Graduate Education*, Chap. iii but esp. pp. 4-5, 46-56, 58, 60-61, 111, 140, 160, 179, 195. Cf. Newsom, *A University President Speaks Out: On Current Education*, pp. 103-106. See also Jones, *One Great Society*, esp. Chap. xi: "How Scholars Are Trained."

[8] Howard Mumford Jones, *Education and World Tragedy, The Reishton Lectures* (Cambridge: Harvard University Press, 1946), p. 147. Cf. Richard J. Storr, *The Beginnings of Graduate Education in America* (Chicago: The University of Chicago Press, 1953).

tional structure a sort of loose fluxional arrangement for processing graduate students and handling "research." The present role and significance of graduate education often find this arrangement at least somewhat inadequate. Dean Jones speaks on this point, too, saying:

> In the long run, the graduate school is the most influential single element in American education and conceivably in American culture, but the paradox is that it really does not exist. . . .[9]

For example, the graduate dean has little real authority; collegiate departments can easily thwart decisions he and the graduate council make. For another, the graduate faculty is mainly only a part-time faculty; its members owe primary allegiance to their undergraduate and professional school departments. For a third, a graduate school lacks the usual collegiate budget. Faculty appointments to departmental positions often are made without approval of the graduate dean even though appointees are to teach graduate work. All of this underlies a lack of consistency in institutional practices which permits variation of standards as well as variation in realization of standards among departments.

Criticism of a colleague's handling of graduate students, meanwhile, has become *ultra vires*. Anarchy and individualistic arbitrariness make it possible for individual professors to divert and hold up graduate students without informing either the graduate faculty or the graduate dean. Students have poor access if any to academic redress. Finally, since it has only part-time faculty members, the graduate school lacks authority to institute reforms. For change and reform it is dependent upon actions taken within the several undergraduate colleges on which foundation it rests.

The miscellaneous composition and structure of most graduate schools mitigate against their having singular characteristics and unified purposes. Many have grown too rapidly and have become "jerry-built." Professional training and work in applied fields have attained "graduate status" alongside scholastic learning and pure

---

[9] Howard Mumford Jones, *American Humanism: Its Meaning for World Survival* ("World Perspectives," ed. Ruth Nanda Anshen, XIV [New York: Harper and Row, Publishers, Inc., 1957]), 63.

science. Implementation of the "provision of service principle" works against unity.[10]

Proponents of professions and quasi-professions want for their groups the prestige of the Ph.D. Many seem unwilling to accept the proposition that professional training is not graduate education. Their argument is that scholastic learning and pure science are not the only interests proper to the graduate schools.

The state of affairs which has been attained reflects a lack of decision as to the purposes and objectives, and the scope and functions of graduate education. There is no agreed definition of graduate education. The truth is that its nature and qualities are as unsettled as whimsy. Graduate schools are as protean as the Ph.D. or the writing requirements, and they seem destined to remain so until these matters somehow are decided. Academic snake-pits will occasionally appear until they are.

General propositions about graduate schools must be modified by appreciation of quality differentiation among institutions of upper, middle, and lower academe. Assuming a scale of ten quality levels, the institutions of upper academe will be ranked in the top two. Those of middle academe will have quality rankings from third to sixth. Schools in lower academe will be ranked in the seventh quality level or below it.[11] Universities continue to be distinguished by their libraries, faculties, and student bodies. Their quality rankings are in part functions of what happens within student bodies as a result of interaction with libraries and faculties.

The institutions of upper academe are characterized by excellent

---

[10] Such implementation may be interpreted as giving people what they want, a development especially within the newer and middling schools since World War I. Law, medicine, theology, and other professions such as engineering long since have established their own technical schools and degrees. However, vocations and incipient professions such as education, business management, and public administration insist on access to the Ph.D. via the graduate school.

[11] For a list of graduate schools in the upper six quality ranks, all of which grant earned doctorates, see Berelson, *Graduate Education*, pp. 280-81. Cf. p. 35: In 1958, 175 institutions granted earned doctorates and 569 granted earned Master's degrees. Of the former, 92 occupy the top six quality ranks and 83 the lower four. The *Educational Directory, 1952-53 through 1960-61* (Washington: U. S. Department of Health, Education, and Welfare, Office of Education) Part 3, gives 99 public and 120 private institutions for a total of 219 which grant the doctorate. See also Clarence E. Lovejoy, *Lovejoy's College Guide*, Part Two: Rating Colleges (New York: Simon and Schuster, Inc., 1961-62), p. 51 ff. For the size and growth of graduate enrollments, see Carmichael, *Graduate Education*, pp. 136-38 and 188.

libraries and superior faculties able to provide environments conducive to high achievements by the ablest student bodies. Their ratios of top faculty and top departments to lesser are very high. Even the least of their faculty and departments tend to be "upper division" when compared with those of all graduate schools.[12]

A significant change is seen when attention is turned to the institutions grouped in the third to sixth quality ranks. While those of third rank are near top quality especially as to libraries and faculty, the others are not. Library quality usually declines as the ranks of middle academe are descended; and homogeneous high quality of faculty and students gives way to mixed and lower quality. The proportions of middle academe faculties drawn from top-ranked schools declines with middle academe graduate school quality levels. So do the proportions of faculties drawn from top-ranked graduates of whatever schools. This is adequately explained by the variation in the capacities of schools to compete for first-rate professors.[13]

Graduate schools ranked in the top two quality groups have about completed their growth in size. Those ranked at the third level soon may. Rather than increase further in size, top schools are becoming increasingly selective. They seek the best of student talent and are concerned with maintenance of quality leadership. Their situation contrasts sharply with the dynamic prospects of middle academe schools.

Graduate schools now grouped in the fourth to sixth quality ranks have prospects of impressive growth of enrollments during the 1960's and 1970's.[14] The schools of middle academe will be expanding their facilities and increasing their faculties. They will be having significant opportunities to improve their academic qualities and to strengthen their academic environments. The advantages they can

---

[12] These comments apply as much to the colleges of top and middle quality which grant earned Master's degrees as to the universities of top and middle quality which grant earned Doctor's degrees as well.

[13] For example, the University of California is said to have had three times as many Nobel Prize winners in the sciences on its faculty in 1962 as all of the universities of the eleven southeastern states together. None of the latter were then included in upper academe. Cf. Gordon W. Blackwell, "UF and FSU: Partners in Florida's Future" (Phi Beta Kappa Address, Gainesville, Fla., May 18, 1962).

[14] Cf. Berelson, *Graduate Education*, pp. 101-102: There will be expansion of graduate work in the next few years everywhere but especially "in the public institutions, in those below top rank, and in the newer entrants."

derive from a variety of academic bloodlines, under dynamic conditions, are as apparent as the dangers of academic in-breeding in upper academe.

In-bred faculties have raised questions of policy within institutions of the highest quality ranks.[15] But the wide range of faculty academic lineage within the institutions of middle academe presents a different difficulty. Diversity and heterogeneity of faculty increase as the quality levels of middle academe are descended; and schooling that is truly graduate in character becomes increasingly spotty. Faculty quality variation underlies the diversity of views and approaches to graduate education in middle academe. This diversity requires a special quality of leadership in shaping academic requirements, performance standards, purposes, and objectives. Vital leadership of graduate councils and deans has not everywhere been forthcoming. Middle academe is becoming increasingly replete with opportunities—and demands—for significant academic leadership.

The institutions of highest quality provided approximately half of all United States doctorates up to 1963. Their proportion of Masters was nearly as great until the 1920's after which it fell sharply as the newer schools took over. Recently, with upper academe enrollment and output holding steady, the top schools' proportion of doctorates has been declining at an increasing rate as middle academe output has grown. This supports the expectation that the schools of middle academe will improve in academic quality and significance.[16] Able and well motivated students are a key factor in the enhancement of academic quality.

The schools of upper academe attract top-quality students whose undergraduate schooling has prepared them more or less effectively for advanced work. Like the faculties of these schools, their student bodies are characterized by homogeneous high quality. It has been different with middle academe. Here student quality has varied, as has faculty quality. The ratio of high-quality students to others de-

---

[15] Berelson, *Graduate Education*, p. 116: The inbreeding of the top 12 institutions is high because they supply themselves with talent. The oldest institutions, they "have been the major producers; . . . . they have had to inbreed, as a statistical consequence of their dominant position as producers." Berelson states p. 126 that he has "personally concluded that some of the departments in some of the lesser schools do at least as good a job of training as their counterparts in the prestigious institutions."

[16] Berelson, *Graduate Education*, pp. 106-107 and 116-18.

clines as school quality ranks are descended. But this is changing for the better. The proportion of top-quality students in middle academe is growing. Rapid improvement of student bodies will make graduate academe increasingly competitive to the advantage of higher learning.

The academic environment of middle academe is emphasized here for two reasons. The first is that graduate students have experienced the widest range and highest frequency of needless uncertainties in schools of this quality grouping. The second reason is that their burgeoning growth causes emphasis on procedural questions at the expense of quality considerations. There is a focus of attention on bricks instead of brains. The improvement of middle academe is a source of hope for the future; but trouble lies ahead if schools of this group become characterized by mere academic sprawl.[17]

Especially within middle academe, few graduate schools have clear and agreed philosophies of graduate education in the light of which cross-purposes might be shelved and unity achieved. Few have clear and positive policies in the light of which faculty performances can be made consistent with definite and meaningful norms.

Contradictory voices express claim and counterclaim as to what graduate schooling is and is not. Graduate councils often are no more agreed than are most interdisciplinary supervisory committees. Where graduate councils are weak, inept and compromising, their graduate deans—who properly are their executive secretaries—either must wring their hands in frustrated futility or assert themselves arbitrarily. When unguided by meaningful counsel, policy, or philosophy, the members of graduate faculties take their own counsel and act anarchistically and arbitrarily. Depending upon the quality of departmental faculties, divergencies of view may leave few bases either for interpersonal or interdisciplinary communication.

The true nature and purpose of graduate schooling and of graduate work are not widely understood or agreed within middle academe.

---

[17] See Berelson, *Graduate Education*, p. 104 and *passim* for the poor faculty, financial, and growth prospects of lower academe schools. The Southern Regional Education Board estimates that there will be over 100,000 graduate students in Southern institutions by 1970, in contrast to over 40,000 in 1954 and only 9,000 in 1938. Student body growth in other regions may be more rapid. Total United States graduate enrollment in 1963 exceeded 300,000. Canadian graduate enrollment exceeded 6,000. North American graduate enrollment, not counting Mexican, may exceed 500,000 by 1970-1975. Graduate enrollments also are increasing in the young universities of the world's new nations.

This may be said fairly because of the impressive lack of concurrence on these and related matters. Students unable to find their own ways within their catch-all, multiplex environments inevitably become lost. To strengthen their prospects of success in such circumstances, graduate students must learn self-guidance.

Graduate Faculties

Upper and middle academe schools may be differentiated in the light of the certainty and assurance with which the graduate essay requirement is handled. There is minimal uncertainty in top quality schools as to what students must do and how well, and as to appraisal and judgment of student performances. The essay concepts, the qualities which give inquiry and research projects essay warrant, the performance standards for Master's and Doctor's degree candidates, and the evaluative criteria in use are all at least implicitly clear. These matters seldom are subjects of basic faculty disagreements, and students generally understand them.

The problem of degree candidates in top graduate schools is not whether their supervisory committees will concur on and be clear about what they must do and how well. Their uncertainties involve whether their prestigious and sometimes arrogant professors will be available to them for advice and guidance.

Big-name professors become heavily committed as consultants, writers, and speakers. Their teaching tends to become a secondary concern, even an incidental nuisance. They travel much, and some often depart for indefinite periods without notice to or apparent regard for, graduate students working under them.[18] Students wait upon professorial convenience and have their supervisory committees continuously reconstituted. Some candidates also are subject to the hazards of fortuitous professorial clashes, contests of will, jockeying, and quarrels. The majorities of the faculties are only infrequently and peripherally involved in this sort of thing. Nevertheless, some

---

[18] At the other extreme, there are such examples of responsibility as that of an outstanding professor who delayed acceptance of a chair in another university for a year in order to finish work with graduate students. On the matter of faculty faults and perverse pedagogy see Carmichael, *Graduate Education*, pp. 30, 43, 134, 183-84, and 195.

students of real ability have found it difficult and disagreeable to attempt fulfillment of writing requirements in upper academe.[19]

When middle academe schools are considered, the faculty remains the chief source of the needless uncertainties which bewilder and perplex students. But here the kinds of uncertainties and their causes differ.

In middle academe there frequently are contests as to what a thesis or dissertation *is*, and as to what performance standards properly *are*. Faculty disagreements extend from deciding the kinds of projects which warrant theses or dissertations to the appraisal and judgment of student achievements. This kind of uncertainty results from the heterogeneity of the middle academe faculties which makes their arrival at common premises a chore. Personal differences preclude mutual confidence, effective communication, and concurrence on essay requirements. Guidelines that are reliable and definite can obviate this sort of thing.

The graduate councils of middle academe have in these lights an important task of definition and policy formulation. The significance of this task is considerably greater in middle than in upper academe. To the extent that the graduate councils of middle academe fail to define the requirements they set, and to establish clear policies concerning them, they bear heavy responsibility for the conditions of uncertainty generally prevalent in their schools.

Middle academe degree candidates who manage to produce ac-

---

[19] Cf. Berelson, *Graduate Education*, pp. 124-28. On p. 125: "Because the top institutions have more distinguished faculties and apparently turn out better products, it does not necessarily follow that they have better training programs. Are the products better because the training is better, or because the students were better in the first place? . . . . If other institutions give as good training and only need more good students, that is one thing. If their training is inferior as well as their students, that is quite another." The writer is told in this connection of a well-known company which refuses to hire Ph.D.'s from a certain top school if a certain faculty member has served on their committees. Experience has shown that, because he smothers them, many of his students have lost their native creativity. This is serious. The writer also is told of cases where students have been required by their faculty advisors to undertake descriptive counting projects rather than intellectual inquiries as bases for their "dissertations." They are disgusted, embarrassed, and unhappy. All of this suggests that much is to be said for the academic intimacy of the smaller institution or department if it is appropriately staffed and adequately equipped. Beyond certain minimal limits, graduate school quality is not a function of mere size and money. It requires appropriate libraries and faculties competent in and devoted to inquiry and teaching.

ceptable theses and dissertations often find themselves subject to uncertainties on other counts. Their faculties are under pressure to "do research," to write, make speeches, consult, or even recruit students, and are characterized by turnover as the better and more ambitious members move out and, hopefully, up. Their supervisory committees are depleted and reconstituted, often more than once for a given student if he is slow. New committees tend to begin at or near the beginning with students because ways seldom are in effect to make committee achievements cumulative. Like their counterparts of upper academe, candidates in middle academe may be delayed and hurt by uncertainties of faculty availability and committee reconstitution. In contrast to their counterparts of upper academe, therefore, they bear a double burden.

Graduate supervisory committees properly are policy-implementing, not policy-making bodies. Their business does not properly include designation of requirements and setting of standards. These being the proper business of graduate councils and deans, committees should be able to take them as given. The same is true with principal evaluative criteria. When supervisory committees are forced to decide these matters, obfuscations and internal conflicts of interest often impede their work. Committees which bog down in efforts to decide requirements and standards can neither give clear guidance to graduate students nor devote full time and energy to facilitation and evaluation of student brainwork.

In contrast to the high or low quality homogeneity of the faculties of upper and lower academe schools, the faculties of middle academe schools tend to be more or less heterogeneous in source and in quality. For example, departmental faculties in schools of third to sixth quality include declining proportions of graduates from top-quality schools; the proportion of graduates of top-quality schools seldom exceeds even ten to twenty per cent of permanent faculty. Many departments within schools of this group have none. The inferences for graduate students and for those who employ graduate degree recipients are obvious.[20]

---

[20] Berelson, *Graduate Education*, p. 108: "We must also recognize that differences in standards, or at least in the realization of standards, are virtually inevitable in a system of higher education as diverse and massive as ours. When more and more universities move into doctoral training, the range and variation tends to increase." Cf. pp. 107-109.

The members of the faculties of middle academe schools proceed from a variety of premises and points of view. It might be expected of men of learning and science so situated that they would strive for some common set of premises and viewpoints. It might reasonably be expected that they would at least establish common generic conceptions of requirements and standards, as bases for mutual communication if not for guidance of students. This has not been done, certainly not in any general way. Graduate councils and deans perhaps have been too concerned with procedural matters to have supplied the leadership to get substantive matters right. Within the faculties there has been bickering, obfuscating, posing, arrival at impasses, and defensive taking of positions. Occasionally, bitter quarrels erupt and become lasting when participants assert their arrogance or intransigence. The "prima donnaism" is all very genteel, however, and usually only a minority of any faculty or supervisory committee is involved.

What Jacques Barzun has called the "amiable anarchy" appears in many institutions to contain elements too anarchistic and insufficiently amiable.[21] In graduate schools of middle academe, for example, where there is considerable variation in quality of faculty and departments, individual professors may be anarchistic for wrong reasons. Their individualistic arbitrariness may have little to do with their academic freedom as capable scholars. It often has more to do with obfuscation as cover for academic uncertainty and personal insecurity.[22] Thus disagreements lead to quibbling and posing, and eventuate in lack of concurrence as to the conceptual nature, reasons for, and definition of academic requirements. Performance standards are hesitantly suggested, vaguely stated, paid lip-service, and misapplied. Relatively prestigious as they may be, graduate faculties may operate as unamiable anarchies characterized by individual and factional unreasonableness.

Especially in middle and lower academe, the nature of thesis and dissertational essay requirements and the rigor of performance stand-

---

[21] Reference to a top-quality school is obvious. In so-called graduate schools of lowest academe, faculties can be too lax and easy-going to have real scholastic meaning.

[22] Cf. José Ortega y Gasset, *The Revolt of the Masses* (New York: W. W. Norton & Company, Inc., 1932), p. 16. Here Ortega y Gasset describes the successful inroads into intellectual affairs of intellectual pretenders whose unintellectual and anti-intellectual mentalities disqualify them. This is a significant passage.

ards are ill-defined and unclear. Moreover, these vary with supervisory committees and academic politics. Evaluation and judgment of student essay performances may be arbitrary, capricious, or lackadaisical as often as it is careful. Here graduate councils may either have abdicated or not assumed their necessary roles in respect of academic requirements, performance standards, and evaluative criteria. Here graduate supervisory committees are forced to become policy-making as well as policy-implementing bodies. Here candidates for degrees may be made or broken by the chancy business of supervisory committee composition.

The variety of faculty academic backgrounds by universities is not the basic fault in all this. The fault lies in the posing, asserting, and taking of defensive positions which some individuals do to cover insecurities which eventuate from their observations of qualitative variation of faculty members in collegiate backgrounds, scholastic achievements, and academic competence. So long as members of graduate school faculties rest at their impasses, they perpetuate the conditions which produce needless uncertainties, frustration, and discouragement for graduate students. The hard fact is that when faculty members snipe at each other it is students who are shot. It is vital that those at odds join in a quest for reasonableness. This would permit diverse academic bloodlines to join in production of a healthy strain of graduate offspring second to none. A doctoral candidate expressed a common hope when he said: "Until then we must cope."

The needless supervenient uncertainties which beset graduate students in upper academe are indeed difficult, but those which harass graduate students in middle academe are plainly unfair. Here their difficulties are special and basic. They cannot do well what is not made clear to them; and irrelevant obstacles should not be put in their way.

The failure of faculties as groups to determine and concur on basic requirements leaves the door open to inconsistent and contradictory guidance and instructions.[23] Candidates have to be on guard against being deceived by wrongly defined concepts, by acceptance or assignment of inappropriate projects, and by lax application of

---

[23] Cf. Southern Regional Education Board, *The Components of Graduate Education*, pp. 8-9: ". . . the acquisition of an eminent faculty, the provision of facilities and funds to support it, and the attraction of superior students" is not enough. Sound policies "which recognize the characteristics of graduate education . . . are the key element" in it.

standards. The frequency of student difficulties on these counts increases at the lower quality ranks of middle academe. Here student efforts to overcome environmental disadvantages must be doubly sure.

Graduate Students

The immediate source of student difficulties is student ineptitude. The shortcomings of over-privileged, spoonfed students are notorious. Needless uncertainties arise wherever students are inadequately equipped or poorly prepared for graduate study. Graduate students who comprehend neither their academic requirements nor their environments are unready for graduate schooling and soon become lost in its mazes. Those who understand their academic requirements but neglect comprehension of their academic environments are only half ready for graduate study. They, too, are easily confused and perplexed. Lack of understanding is symptomatic of weak methodological training and of faulty faculty advice and instruction. It also is symptomatic of student immaturity and irresponsibility.

Students who attain clarity in these respects can meet high performance standards successfully. They also will obviate many potential frustrations of the kind which misunderstandings and disagreements produce. Their guiding idea could well be that work of good quality will keep supervisory committee members "off *their* hooks." It is the only true key to academic success.

The function of graduate education is to provide training in intellectual work and enhancement of intellectual competence and capacity.[24] Appropriate selection of students for graduate study is a sensitive matter, less than well understood. More or less careful in the institutions of upper academe, and in at least some of those in the third and fourth quality ranks, selection is less and less careful as the quality ranks of lesser institutions are descended. This statement needs modification from the viewpoints of both upper and lesser academe.

---

[24] Cf. *Bulletin of Duke University,* "The Graduate School of Arts and Sciences," XXXV, No. 3-c (January 1961), 7: "A graduate school, ideally, is a community of scholars—apprentice, initiate, and master—engaged in imparting and extending the realm of man's knowledge in the arts and sciences."

In the top schools, the admissions officers have their tasks simplified by two factors. The most highly qualified students apply to them for enrollment, and they apply in numbers larger than can be accommodated.[25] Hence these officers are in strong positions to deny admission to any concerning whom they have doubt. Their counterparts of middle academe, on the other hand, have less choice. Their schools manage to attract only fractions of the best graduate material. Their involvement in competition for increased enrollments has led to dilution of graduate student quality.

The schools of middle academe are pressed by legislatures and other sources of financial support to maintain high student-teacher ratios for "efficiency." Especially in schools ranked at less than third to fourth quality, implementation of the so-called "provision of service principle" has tended to weaken selection. Striving to build and maintain enrollments, schools of the middle and lower quality ranges have diversified and diluted their curricula and reduced standards. They have been accepting some students who, while intelligent, are both intellectually inept and methodologically untrained.[26] Such students get into academic and environmental difficulties wherever standards are maintained.

It is important to consider the bases for graduate student selection. Those now in use include the undergraduate record and some measurement of intelligence such as the Graduate Record Examination or the Miller Analogies Test purport to provide. Here it may be useful to suggest that intelligence alone, important as it may be, is not enough. There are people of the highest I.Q. whose best capabilities are routine. On the other hand, many of more modest I.Q. prove to be excellent abstract and conceptual thinkers. Creative thinkers are not all "A" students, and not all of the latter are creative thinkers. While an I.Q. of 125 reasonably may be taken as a practical minimum for graduate work,[27] another factor may be at least equally important. Not at present adequately taken into account, this factor may be called "mentality." [28] It is the vital ingredient for academic success at the graduate level.

---

[25] Berelson, *Graduate Education*, p. 116.

[26] Berelson, *Graduate Education*, pp. 104 and 108.

[27] Certainly for the doctorate. I.Q.'s of 115-120 may suffice for the Master's degree and for most professional degrees. The ideal graduate student is intellectually curious, forever inquiring.

[28] Southern Regional Education Board, *The Components of Graduate Edu-*

By "mentality" is meant a qualitative factor which is at once an attribute of intellect and more than that. It may be described as a function not only of intellect, but of interests, aptitudes, attitudes, relative size of frames of reference for thought, capacity for organization, interest in independence or dependence, and interest in things of the mind or of the hands.

If a student has intelligence combined with interest in and aptitude for manipulative skills, for routinization and "doing," he appropriately may be guided toward a choice among the curricula of the technological institutes or professional schools. Such a student might have aptitude for and interest in a career, for example, in industrial research. If, on the other hand, a student has requisite intelligence combined with interest in and aptitude for learning and intellectual work, for inquiry, conceptual and empirical analysis, and criticism and if he desires intellectual independence, he appropriately may be guided toward a choice among the basic curricula of the graduate school.

It is easy for a student to get into difficulty in these respects and then discover it hard to find his way. The usual graduate school has none of the straightforwardness of the usual professional school. It couldn't very well have. The typical graduate school is a multiplex catch-all in which the natural differentiation between technical and professional training and graduate education becomes obscure and overlooked. The structural complexities, organizational difficulties, and administrative chores of the graduate school make for over-emphasis of procedures. They make it easy to pay too little attention to such qualitative matters as student mentality. Capacity to learn what is known and to receive training (intelligence) is important; but capacity to use knowledge in original and creative ways (intellect) is vital to success in graduate school.

This contrast suggests a basic differentiation between undergradu-

cation, p. 2: "A graduate student must be equipped with the talent, preparation and aptitude for intensive advanced study." And p. 6: "The problem is one of quality rather than quantity. Graduate education, particularly at the doctorate level, requires superior students, students who have the particular kind of ability, aptitude and training required for advanced study." Cf. Carmichael, *Graduate Education*, p. 144: "One of the most glaring defects in graduate education is its weakness in recruitment of talent. . . . This accounts, in part at least, for the high attrition rate in graduate schools and the distressing gap between the B.A. and the Ph.D." See also pp. 10, 131, 144-45 and *passim*.

ate and graduate schooling.[29] The latter is especially concerned with enhancement of the higher mental capacities. Its concern with reason explains why emphasis in graduate education is on inquiry and research.

Perhaps less than one tenth of any human generation may have true capacity to be educated for intellectual work.[30] Unfortunately, not all such minds are even discovered, let alone admitted to graduate schools. There has been a squeamishness about intellectual selection in high schools and colleges for fear of creating an elite group. Sympathy for backward students combined with false notions of "democracy" has disposed scarce and costly educational resources in favor of those least able to use them effectively. It has obscured the existence of many unusually able students. It certainly has failed to provide many talented students the competence and understanding they need for graduate schooling.

Incompetent graduate students and poor training waste scarce and crucial educational resources. In contrast, competent graduate students who are excellently schooled represent society's highest form of investment for the future.[31] Despite the axiom, the ratio of intellectually qualified to merely intelligent and willing students declines

---

[29] This is not to suggest that undergraduate schooling cannot or ought not be intellectually oriented. It merely recognizes that most of it is not, being concerned with descriptive and technical foundations work and with filling of reservoirs instead of with architecture and lighting of lamps. Cf. Southern Regional Education Board, *The Components of Graduate Education*, pp. ii and 1-9.

[30] Eli Ginzberg, *Human Resources: The Wealth of a Nation* (New York: Simon and Schuster, Inc., 1958), p. 79: "Only a relatively small group in every generation are endowed with high orders of ability to learn to use what they have learned effectively . . ." Graduate schooling is not exploitable for a status symbol, such as "a college education" has been.

[31] Ginzberg, *Human Resources*, p. 79. "While every society must get along with such talent as it has, its accomplishments and even its survival will depend on its developing the maximum number of people with high potential." Cf. Ginzberg's Chap. ii, iv, and vii. See also Theodore W. Schultz, "Investment in Human Capital," *The American Economic Review*, LI, No. 1 (March 1961), 1; and his "Human Capital: A Growing Asset," *Saturday Review*, XLIV, No. 3 (January 21, 1961), 37 ff. Cf. Werner Z. Hirsch's review of Leonard Silk's book, *The Research Revolution* (New York: McGraw-Hill Book Co., Inc., 1961) in the *St. Louis Post Dispatch*, February 1, 1961: ". . . the qualities of the people determine a nation's growth and power. Long term growth depends on the seed beds of American talent, our schools and colleges, the universities and laboratories. Greater imagination needs to be shown to find our most able people while they are still young, develop their abilities, and provide employment, scope and challenge for their talents."

with the quality-scale of graduate schools.[32] Below a certain level, the intellectually gifted disappear in favor of homogeneous low quality.

The quality variation of students within middle academe schools is a source of significant difficulties for both faculties and able students. Poor students slow the pace and lower the quality of instruction and learning. They produce situations which frustrate the able students and try faculty interest and patience. But many otherwise able students simply defeat themselves by failing to act realistically in determining and adjusting to such obvious things as time requirements. Deadlines seem at first so distant that outside activities, love or family affairs, or just procrastination may slow investigations, outlining, and the start of writing. Some students, experiencing sudden humility, fear they don't know enough or where to begin writing. They keep reading and rechecking far beyond the point of diminishing returns.

Master's degree candidates, especially, fail to recognize that they must plan for such time-consuming matters as correcting and rewriting essays, preparing footnotes and bibliography in conformity with style sheet requirements, and typing, editing, and proofing final drafts. Reproduction of detailed charts, tables, graphs, maps, or other illustrations may in some cases have to be repeated several times to make them acceptable. Students sometimes neglect to arrange early enough for an experienced typist or to allow the typist adequate working time. Most students fail to prudently take into account possible unexpected delays such as may be occasioned by their own illness, or by illness within their families or on the part of their typists or committee members.

The most common failing, however, seems to be that of the student who waits until the last moment before the deadline to rush his material breathlessly to his advisor and supervisory committee. The professors involved may be so busy with other last-minute writings —in addition to their regular duties—that they literally have no time

---

[32] This position is based upon observation and discussion. As yet it has no explicit statistical basis; but it suggests an area in which important work might be done on behalf of better graduate education. It should be noted that an appropriate mentality may in many cases offset the apparent disadvantage of relatively lower I.Q. It also should be noted that most assertions of significant academic quality are empty claims, clichés, and obfuscations by collegiate and university spokesmen. The disadvantage this poses for higher learning can only be overcome by ending the practice.

to give him the attention or assistance he may require. Some of these tyros rush their projects to completion on the eve of school vacations, thinking to go off while their dedicated professors work through Thanksgiving, Christmas, or Easter holidays. It is literally true that advisors frequently are not only asked but expected by students to read preliminary drafts of writing on such occasions as Christmas Eve.

Doctoral candidates often write while engaged in off-campus teaching or other employment. They frequently handicap themselves by mailing in their chapters at examination times or at holidays. Professors are apt to meet their campus pressures first, under these conditions, while mailed-in chapters wait. Some candidates understandably attempt personal conferences during holidays, not realizing that professors also need relaxation and may be away. Professors who have been hard-pressed and harried may resent, if they do not deny, advisory appointments at such times. Such behavior on the part of candidates belies maturity requisite for graduate degrees.

Graduate work should neither be attempted nor offered unless it can be of requisite quality. The improving quality and selection of undergraduates soon may yield a rich harvest of intellect at the graduate level. A certain sophistication also will be needed, however, if frustration and discouragement of competent and gifted graduate students are not to formulate a double tragedy of faculty commissions and student omissions. If the script is to be changed, the students may have to rewrite the play.

Summation

Most graduate students confront two sorts of uncertainties in academe. One relates to the nature and quality of their writing requirements. The other relates to the nature and characteristics of their writing environment. Separate treatment of these classes of uncertainties, the first mainly in Part I and the second here, should not be permitted to obscure their close interrelationship. Clarity as to writing requirements on the part of students is a means of reducing, even eliminating, many of their environmental difficulties. Environmental understanding enhances student effectiveness in fulfillment of writing requirements. This reciprocity is impressive and valuable.

Most graduate students begin undertakings to fulfill writing requirements with trepidation. They are hesitant and halting, at least at first; and they stumble and flounder in the throes of their investigative projects. Some try to write before they really have anything to say, and others cannot write what they have learned for fear that it may be inadequate. These difficulties seem in the main to arise because of lack of fundamental preparation for graduate work. Students who have not learned the nature and purposes of graduate education begin it blindly. Disillusionment comes quickly to those whose hopes are dashed because they sought answers where the light was good rather than where their problems were. This chapter has attempted to help graduate students find and explore a problematic region which has had poor illumination. Familiarity with it can provide confidence to come to grips with it. Then trepidation can give way to assurance and poise.

Graduate students can themselves reduce some of the environmental uncertainties which impede them. When they do, they take firm steps toward attainment of excellence.[33] Through reading they can get hold of the general idea of graduate education, its methods and purposes. They can learn the structure and organization of their own graduate schools, and how their faculties conduct the educational processes within the educational apparatus. They can most certainly learn what requirements they must meet and when they must meet them. This information can be used as a basis for early planning and scheduling of their work.

The function and purpose of this chapter have been to provide information and to achieve instruction. The lesson which may be drawn is that a reasonable amount of social and academic sophistication can be a rich source of academic performance dividends. Orientation and understanding can provide competence to avoid or to meet effectively the exigencies of academe. It can help students to adjust enough for smooth sailing without adjusting so much as to be reduced to obedient sycophancy.

The principle of coherence for this book is the challenge it directs to graduate students. They are the crux of their own difficulties and the key to the solution of their problems. They can make better and surer candidates of themselves by learning the nature and implications of intellectual and social qualification for success. Their effective

---

[33] Ginzberg, *Human Resources*, p. 79: "With regard to the individual . . . although power can be transferred from father to son, excellence can never be bestowed. It must be earned. One must work to acquire it."

actions to reduce the needless uncertainties which impose upon them can make graduate studies increasingly attractive, lively, challenging, and adventuresome. This would open the way to making their endeavors increasingly productive of intellectually significant results, and so more rewarding and satisfying. Graduate students can light the lamps of conceptual and environmental clarity to dispel the gloom of vagueness.

The lesson has been given and its corollaries have been stated and implied. The implications of all should be clear. Understanding of these things will be aided by the next chapter. Its task is to show how and why the pathological condition of graduate academe came about.

7

The Present Impasse

> It must bewilder academic visitors from abroad to observe how loosely our educational vocabulary is used in the United States. I sometimes think that all our key terms in education are ambiguous.
>
> HOWARD MUMFORD JONES

> The best way to deal with criticism is not to ignore it or to deny the charges but to eliminate the evils that give rise to it.
>
> PAUL WOODRING

Graduate education is an impressively valuable cultural manifestation and influence. Its purposes and functions are such that the idea of a pathology of graduate education may be shocking. Yet, the idea has been and is being expressed that something is amiss in academe. Where has graduate education gone wrong? Why?

The reasons for error, and the ways in which error has occurred and led to difficulty, can illuminate this matter. These may be most readily perceived and evaluated if selected fundamental factors first are set out in their probable historical sequence.

It may be well to begin by noting that about a century ago pragmatic interests brought about a change of emphasis in American schooling, from ideas and methods for the few, to facts and techniques for the many. This was the time of the "winning of the West," the establishment of free public schools, the inception of the land-grant colleges, and the strengthening of the original contacts with the German universities.

From Germany came the concepts of the doctorate, the seminar, and *Quellenforschung*—source searching.[1] Overemphasized

---

[1] For Gilbert Highet's explanation of and commentary on *Quellenforschung*, see Appendix F.

149

and eventually misconstrued, source searching became fact grubbing and data dredging. In some respects it degenerated into anti-intellectualism. Graduate schools remain infected with the perverted *Quellenforschung* habit. Together with other erroneous ideas it has affected higher learning adversely. Nevertheless, close relations with German universities during the nineteenth century is not the reason for present academic deficiencies.

Proteanization of the Ph.D. was begun early in the present century. Under the aegis of the so-called "provision of service" principle, this process gained impetus after World War I. During the twenties and thirties the Ph.D. degree, no longer limited to the humanities and the moral and basic sciences, became an attribute as well of a "variety of professional and quasi-professional fields." [2]

Proteanization of the writing requirements for graduate degrees followed easily as academe fell into the comfortable but specious and unscientific habit of admitting various kinds of writing under the thesis and dissertation labels. Master's and Doctor's degree candidates submitted reports in growing volume, apparently unaware that they were not submitting theses or dissertations. Disservice was often done to scholarship and scientific competence wherever this occurred.[3] Students were misled where standards were let down and nonintellectual achievements were accepted. The conceptual disinctiveness and significance of the real writing requirements were obliterated when the word dissertation became a status symbol through its use to distinguish a Doctor's writing of whatever kind from a Master's.

Four factors have worked in complementary and supplementary ways to reinforce and combine these processes into a trend. In the first place, loose and ambiguous use of language—a national character-

[2] Berelson, "The Studies of Graduate Education," *The Graduate Journal,* I, 158. Berelson's list includes "agriculture, business, education, home economics, journalism, engineering, librarianship, nursing, social work. As such professions grew, they looked to the university as the home of respectability as well as knowledge . . . and they sought the doctorate both for the substance and for the symbol that they had 'arrived.' In general, this whole process renewed and intensified the earlier argument of purity of standards *versus* provision of service."

[3] Meanwhile, a diversity of concepts and requirements, of standards and criteria appeared among universities, colleges, schools, departments, and even supervisory committees. Cf. symposium on "Problems and Policies of Graduate Education," *The Journal of Higher Education,* XXX, No. 3 (March 1959). Cf. also Thorstein Veblen, *The Higher Learning in America* (New York: B. W. Huebsch, 1918); now in paperback (New York: Sagamore Press, 1957).

istic since the days of railroad building, occupying the land, establishing industry, and digesting millions of immigrants—became a habit of students and faculty. The literary ineptitude of most graduate students and many of the faculty is a commonplace. Perhaps the real fault is the habit of loose and inexact use of language in combination with the national characteristics of casualness and aversion to form and ceremony. In any event, students communicate poorly.[4] Their typical impatience hampers the intellectual exercises of reasoning and writing.

Academic criticism served as a second reinforcing factor. Some of it was clear and sound, but most of it was vague and fruitless. For at least 80 years, graduate schooling has been subject to a stream of criticism which has been in the main ineffectual because it has been both uncoordinated and undirected. It had neither point of attack nor program.[5] It was mainly negative rather than positive. While some of it may have aroused hope in those who viewed with alarm, it stemmed neither basic nor reinforcing tendencies. Instead, it probably contributed to reinforcement by being permissive. Much criticism has been innocuous. It has lashed at the whole "problem of the Ph.D." or at the "problem of graduate study in America," but it seldom has presented either analysis of or basic facts concerning these problems.

The frequency of critical reports during recent decades suggests a "bandwagon" principle at work.[6] Appeals have been made to all concerned, despite the axiom that what is everybody's business is nobody's responsibility. The generations of critics suggest few scholars. Their general approach has been unscientific by any light. Scattered positive suggestions of value have been ignored. There is a ray of

---

[4] Cf. Panel Discussions at Yale, *Graduate Training in Economics*, pp. 11-14.

[5] Trustees of the Carnegie Foundation for the Advancement of Teaching, *Fifty-Third Annual Report*, 1957-1958, p. 20: "The criticisms of graduate education are more numerous than the constructive proposals for reform." Critics mainly have been indignant rather than constructive. It is remarkable how many repetitious reports have been put together on such small foundations.

[6] Carnegie Foundation, *Fifty-Third Annual Report*, p. 25: "For 80 years the graduate schools have been debating the same issues and wrestling with the same problems. The issues have not changed, the problems have not been solved, and the battle lines have remained the same from one generation to the next. It now appears that circumstances will force at least a partial resolution of some of the issues." On the matters at issue and the reasons for failure, see pp. 11-26; and Berelson, "The Studies of Graduate Education," *The Graduate Journal*, I, 160-61 and 165-67.

hope, nevertheless, because those who have known how to work effectively on the basis of sound ideas and clear thinking have produced impressive results. These prove the validity of the concepts and methods employed by the best but avoided by many of the rest.

The nature and position of the graduate school in the United States have been more or less undecided ever since the German concept of the university was appended to the English concept of the college. The concept of graduate work has grown increasingly ambiguous, especially since the post-World War I growth and expansion of the graduate schools.[7] Work of all sorts variously supervised within a scattering of departments has been attached to the graduate school without ever really coming under its control. The nature of the graduate school, its purposes and goals, have been misconstrued. The genre and the mission of this distorted creature of mixed academic breed are unclear.

Finally to be mentioned are the excesses of "scientism" and of "scientific empiricism" which have appeared especially in sociology since the 1920's.[8] Intellectual inquiry has been neglected since "research" has been emphasized. Pragmatism has led to dull empiricism. Concern with data rather than with ideas cannot open the way for anyone to perceive a problem. In some places there is an apparent caveat against intellectual creativity. Scholars and scientists, not clerks and technicians, are the proper products of graduate schools. Technical high schools and colleges are right for training in skills and techniques; but graduate schools should be devoted to education in respect of the liberal intellectual disciplines and their methodology.

The diversion of the graduate school from its true purpose by parvenu interests, and its distortion by scholastic misconceptions and anti-intellectualism, will be further treated in two sections. These follow under the headings of general and specific considerations.

---

[7] Cf. Roy F. Nichols, "The Ambiguous Position of the Graduate-School Dean," and Morris A. Stewart, "The Organization of the Graduate School," *The Journal of Higher Education*, XXX, No. 3 (March 1959), 123 ff. and 136 ff. respectively. Also Berelson, *The Graduate Journal*, I, 155.

[8] An example is provided by the second chapter of John Dollard, *Caste and Class in a Southern Town*, (2d. ed.; New York: Harper and Row, Publishers, Inc., 1949). Otherwise this is a commendable book. Cf. G. A. Lundberg, *Social Research: A Study of Methods of Gathering Data* (New York: Longmans, Green & Co., 1929). This is a treatment of field investigation against which Jacques Barzun warns (above, p. 59). Cf. Lundberg's *Can Science Save Us?* (New York: Longmans, Green & Co., 1947).

General Considerations

The present impasse is the result of a lengthy process of academic arteriosclerosis. As early as 1886, in his Harvard Anniversary address, James Russell Lowell "found it necessary to deplore the new dry rot of learning, the alienation of scholarship from culture and criticism, the narrow pursuit of those facts which are to truth 'as a plaster-cast to the marble statue.' [We have] witnessed since his time an extension of these tendencies to the point of absurdity. . . . [Ours has become] that modern goddess denounced by Ruskin, the goddess of Getting-On." [9] We have been misled into pedantry.

Investigation too often has become an end in itself rather than remaining a means to an end. Forty-three years after President Lowell's criticism, Norman Foerster could write:

> Intent upon erudition of the German type, we do not even take time for reflection. There is truth, as well as caricature, in the saying of John Stuart Mill that "The characteristic of Germany is knowledge without thought; of France, thought without knowledge; of England, neither knowledge nor thought." Knowledge without thought—the amassing of historical data unvitalized by reason and imagination in their deeper manifestations—describes only too well a common mode of American scholarship that passes for real scholarship.[10]

On the close relations between United States and German universities during the late nineteenth and early twentieth centuries, and of the influence of the latter on the former, Foerster wrote:

> Hitherto [1929], the chief debt of American education and scholarship has been to Germany, whence mainly we derived our scientific aim and our scientific method, together with the mechanism of the seminar, the doctoral dissertation, and so forth. With the passage of one hundred years since Everett, Ticknor, and Bancroft took their degrees at Gottingen, during which ten thousand Americans matriculated in German universities, an era in the history of our higher education has definitely closed. . . . It has closed because we have assimilated at last the essential virtues of German scholarship. We have learned, and shall remember, how to get

---

[9] Foerster, *The American Scholar*, p. 46.
[10] Foerster, *The American Scholar*, p. 8.

exact knowledge. Is there nothing else for us to learn? Might we not advisedly turn now to France, where, to be sure, the scientific study of literature has also had a marked influence, but where other traditions of scholarship have offered a resistance wholly wanting with us? French reflection, French lucidity, French finesse, French moderation, the French concern for humane assimilation, the French devotion to general ideas, the French insistence upon taste and style, the French interest in criticism—these qualities, all but absent from our own work, I take to be worthy of imitation. Or we might even turn to England, where again there have been traditions of scholarship capable of resisting and correcting the excesses of scientism, among them a cultural background and a sense of poetic style, together with the sanative powers of common sense and humor—qualities by no means frequent with us.

Wherever we may turn for next inspiration and objectives and method, the fact is that the pattern we have followed is already out of date; that Germany is growing aware that the age of philology and minute historical research is drawing to a close, that, if drudgery remains, the worst of it is over, the important texts are made, the necessary facts are accumulated, and that the time is at hand for a generation that shall justify the labors of their predecessors and give in a higher sense a true account of their gift of reason, to the benefit and use of men. It is conceivable that Germany will learn to do this higher work as well as she did the work of preparation for it. . . . The field is open for America as for other lands. . . . It remains to be seen whether there is also an American as well as a French intelligence.

Is there not more of cant than intelligence in our conventional repetition of such terms as "productive scholarship," "contributions to the sum of knowledge?" [11]

Despite the hope expressed by Foerster, the situation may have worsened since he wrote. No matter when examined—in 1886, 1929, or the 1960's—much graduate schooling is characterized by piddling research and dull empirical scholarship. Of course there are exceptions: many students have won prizes for their written work; much graduate coursework is well handled; and in many places intellectual inquiry is the thing. Still, in general, inquiry has been supplanted by empiricism and "scientism."

Professor David Boroff indicates that more is at fault than graduate students and their scholarship. In the concluding article of a series on American colleges and universities he reported:

---

[11] Foerster, *The American Scholar*, pp. 43-45. Compare the preface to J. B. Black's *The Art of History*, reproduced in Appendix J, and Herbert Butterfield's short introduction to Arthur Koestler's *The Sleepwalkers*.

A professor of sociology in the Midwest offered a modest and revealing rationale for the kind of piddling research that abounds. "You see," he explained, "it provides a function for the guys who are not so talented—you know, those with an IQ of 115 or 120. On their own, they can't do very much. But give them a little area to work in, and then put together what they have done and what others have done, and maybe you'll have something. Sure, there are people like Riesman with powerful minds, but what are you going to do with less gifted people?" [12]

This commentator's remarks suggest both a misconception and a misdirection of graduate schooling. They imply a failure to comprehend either the nature and rationale of graduate education or of qualification for it. They certainly suggest a wrong conception of graduate level teaching. A graduate school is no place for loading of magazines and filling of reservoirs. It is a place for learning the lighting of lamps, a place for the consummation of learning how to learn. In it there must be rigorous emphasis on the methodology of inquiry, analysis, explanation, criticism, synthesis, and proof. The inadequately gifted and inappropriately equipped should not be encouraged.

Some graduate schools are characterized by an exuberant play of ideas, both between faculty and students and among students. At the other extreme graduate schooling is characterized by boredom, the stultification of lifeless empiricism, and rigidities which crush out individualism and mould conformity. Emphasis on fact grubbing rather than on imaginative ideation and intellection tends to obliterate criticism and stimulating debate. It forecloses comprehension of the relationship of facts to ideas, to inquiry, and to proof of solutions or explanations. It can produce only timid careerism and make of graduate students either opportunists or sycophants. It does not help them to become significant as scholars, scientists, or teachers.

Many of the students who attain some semblance of scholarly or scientific competence do so despite the graduate academic system. Many leave it for non-academic careers either upon graduation or

---

[12] David Boroff, "American Colleges: What Their Catalogues Never Tell You," *Harper's Magazine*, CCXX, No. 1319 (April 1960), 39 ff. Why should inadequately and inappropriately gifted students be enrolled in graduate schools? Why should the intellectually and pedagogically inadequate be on their faculties? Cf. David Boroff, *Campus U.S.A.: Portraits of American Colleges in Action* (New York: Harper and Row, Publishers, Inc., 1961).

before. The few who achieve outstanding results do so under the influence of teachers who know and make clear the nature of and relationship between inquiry and research, difference between a problem and a "topic," between an essay and a report. Their students learn what the academic essays are and the nature and significance of the intellectual achievement projects which underlie them. Other faculty seem to deny or ignore the standards of academic performance they set.

After a considerable study of collegiate practices, Professor Boroff had this to say of the effects of professorial narrowness:

> This specialized intellectual efficiency, unfortunately, is picked up by graduate students, a notably timid group. Because of the recent wealth of fellowships and grants, careerism gets off to an early start among graduate students, who are inclined anyway to be opportunists at best and sycophants at worst. . . . When the altar boys receive their Ph.D.'s, they are dispatched to the hinterland with The Word. . . .

> It is well to remember that the graduate student, often subsidized by the university, desperately needs his department's recommendation. This, more than anything else, will determine where he is placed, and his initial placement may well set the tone of his career. Graduate professors, on the other hand, have the assurance of a captive and submissive audience.

> The effect of all this is narrowness, intellectual pallor, professionalization—the very antithesis of the goals of liberal education. C. Wright Mills made this bitter estimate of the younger social scientists: "I have seldom seen one of these young men in a condition of genuine intellectual puzzlement. And I have never seen any passionate curiosity about a great problem, the sort of curiosity that compels the mind to travel anywhere and by any means, to remake itself if necessary, in order to find out. These young men are less restless than methodical; less imaginative than patient. . . . Listening to their conversations, trying to gauge the quality of their curiosity, one finds a deadly limitation of mind." [13]

The unfortunate state of much graduate schooling suggests that many members of graduate faculties either do not know or do not care what they are about. It certainly implies their failure to be cre-

---

[13] Boroff, "American Colleges," *Harper's Magazine*, CCXX, 39. Having concluded a series of articles on individual American colleges, coast to coast, in the December 1959, *Harper's*, Professor Boroff now sums up his findings. This excerpt suggests prudence in the dispensation of subsidies for study.

atively adaptive and original, even to be liberal. The basic reasons for faculty shortcomings may be provided by the ambivalent and indifferent attitudes characteristic of the lay community. Society seems to finance higher education because it must, not because it seeks thereby to fulfill ultimate purposes and attain distant goals. The graduate school has been imperfectly realized because it is imperfectly conceived and understood.

Perhaps the fundamental lack is a consistent and unambiguous purpose for higher learning. Our graduate education is guided by no such general purpose as "manifest destiny" or even natural resource conservation. It reflects no such general conception even as that which underlay the public school and land-grant college movements. The few who have had mind and time for great ideas and long-range programs have been hard put to rally support to see their projects through. Individualistic concern with limited purposes and personal goals has left little room for comprehension of large purposes and distant goals.[14] Education has been provided by communities and pursued by students so that better jobs might be obtained. It is inadmissable to attribute to society the purposes expressed by a few far-sighted men in search of supporters.

University faculties and governing bodies often have been as myopic as students and society. More graduate schools may have been established for interscholastic competition than to fulfill any grand design. The state universities have been subject to political influences and the meddling of outsiders.[15] So have private schools. Pragmatists have been mistrustful of the intellectuals they have not understood.

---

[14] Cf. Ordway Tead, "What Are America's Purposes?" *The Educational Forum*, XXV, No. 3; Part I (March 1961), 317: "We shall need to consider our higher education in terms of a committed personal accountability for aligning ourselves with the wider fulfillment of the purposes we cherish." See also *Goals for Americans, Programs for Action in the Sixties* (Englewood Cliffs, N. J.: Prentice-Hall, Inc., 1960), the report of the President's Commission on National Goals. Is it a cry in the wilderness anticipated by Stuart Chase with his *Goals for Americans: A Budget of our Needs and Resources* (New York: Twentieth Century Fund, 1942)?

[15] Not really independent, self-governing entities responsible to their legislatures, they have been made to serve diverse and contradictory purposes. The best U. S. universities are those which maintain self-government. They reflect a meaningful educational purpose. The well-known private institutions are in this group. It may be well to recognize and consider the implications of the fact that the number of institutions awarding earned doctorates grew four-fold between the 1920's and the 1960's. Cf. note 11, p. 132.

Nevertheless, more general realization of the nature and mission of the university may be at hand. America soon may comprehend the nature and mission of the graduate school. Then the flowering of its finest resource, its liberal brainpower, may eventuate in such a harvest as cannot now be perceived.

Specific Considerations

There are specific reasons for the present problem of the writing requirements in graduate education, as well as general ones. Specific reasons are easier to pin down than the latter, and they are capable of more precise presentation. A dozen of these will suffice. Illustrative examples will not be supplied. The manifestations of the problem are too widespread to warrant risk of inadvertent identification of persons or institutions.

Until the present, provision of graduate educational facilities has exceeded the requirements of graduate students. Outside of upper academe, the supply of students has not been sufficient to go around. This caused a competition for students; and in altogether too many instances there has been more interest in gaining numbers of students than in securing candidates of requisite quality. Poor selection of graduate students undoubtedly has been related to their relatively small numbers. At least until the 1960's, many colleges were unable to attract enough for optimal use of facilities. The rising student-teacher ratios of the present decade, however, provide a basis for hope that selection will improve. In fact, time may replace this difficulty with a different one.

Paul Woodring, editor of the *Saturday Review* Education Supplement, has written: "In the years ahead there will be a superabundance of qualified students and an acute shortage of any kind of faculty members. This reversal requires some drastic changes in policy." [16]

The low student-teacher ratios previously characteristic of many

---

[16] Paul Woodring, "The Future Problems of Higher Education," *College and University Journal*, I, No. 2 (Spring 1962). Woodring asserts, p. 13: "We shall have to give up the notion that every college teacher must be a productive scholar. This view is one we borrowed from the German universities of the 19th century when universities were few, enrollments were small, and professors were rare. . . ."

graduate schools may have supported the delusion that full professor-
ships and accession to graduate faculties symbolized privilege rather
than responsibility. They may also have contributed, strange as it
may seem, to overemployment (i.e., disguised unemployment) of the
faculty. In any event, light teaching loads provided opportunities for
faculty writing and publishing. The present harassing "publish or
perish" formula, together with the competition of universities for
graduate students, financial support, and research funds, have led
faculties to spend more and more time in non-teaching activities.
University faculty articles have become in a way analogous to student
term papers. The grinding out of publishable reports has largely
supplanted the writing of less frequent, but intellectually significant,
essays.[17] Graduate faculties have been diverted from intellectual work
with students by their need to publish, their use for administrative
functions, and their engagement in so-called contract research. The
future growth of graduate student bodies will require better use of
graduate faculties in teaching.

Graduate teaching has been encroached upon by academic committee and administrative assignments, and by such outside interests
as publishing and "consulting." Hence certain shortcomings are attributable to graduate teachers as well as to graduate students. Classroom presentations are too often ill-prepared, even irrelevant. Seminars too often are of the impromptu and improvisational varieties,
and become fruitless "bull sessions" or encourage off-the-cuff faculty
polemics. The good teachers stand out; but students and faculty alike
have been tolerant of poor teaching. Colleagues, department heads,
and deans often are unaware of specific pedagogical deficiencies because curiously it has become a breach of etiquette to observe a
professor's class or seminar without an invitation to do so. The teaching may well be better where classes and seminars are open to all
comers.

Good teachers are in the minority. They too might gain from

---

[17] One notes with alarm that the contents of many of the present "learned
journals" have changed during the last 30 years from a high proportion of
essays to a high proportion of merely descriptive and historical reports of
empirical research. Intellectual inquiry is being abandoned in favor of technical
work. If there is an implicit caveat against intellectual creativity, "print or
perish" may be behind it. If this continues, and the half million faculty of a
decade hence must publish, there will be 50,000 new volumes a year and
10,000 new journals.

skilled observation and criticism, but they have been induced to apply a false conception of academic freedom by those who have reason to fear it.[18] The need for good educational management has been forgotten. Deans and department heads responsible for it have tended to limit themselves to administration of the technical functions of logistical support for the academic enterprise. The military analogue would be a field army which brought up supplies rather than fought battles. Those in the academic life who must "wear two hats" must keep them separate. Too often they have taken the "easy out" by asserting the primacy of the lesser responsibility.

The suggestion has been heard that consideration needs to be given to the criteria by which members of graduate faculties are selected.[19] Traditionally, selection has been on the basis of the inadequate criteria of degrees, rank, seniority, and publications. There has been a lack of concern about the nature and functions of graduate schooling. Graduate teaching calls for adaptable and original thinkers, skilled in inquiry and its methodologies, who are gifted stimulators of intellectual curiosity and effort. It calls for teachers skilled in criticism, able in controversy, and capable of arousing students to achieve all that their intellectual abilities and attained competence permits. Yet in many departments and schools the seniority rule deprives graduate students of better teachers while providing them the poorest.

When guiding students who seek to fulfill the writing requirements for their degrees, graduate professors work outside of classroom, laboratory, and seminar. For this purpose they are assigned to *ad hoc* and *pro tempore* committees. These supervisory committees often are composed of professors whose collegiate backgrounds and intellectual interests and achievements vary. Difficulties are inherent in heterogeneous committees when requirements are only named and not defined, where performance standards are not clarified, and where evaluative criteria are neither given nor suggested. Supervisory committees which lack relevant policy directives must provide their own guidelines. To do so, they must resolve their own internal differences. In this effort, conflicts of opinion often become contests of will. If chairmen are weak or compromising and committee members are obdurate, students suffer. Writing requirement definitions and per-

---

[18] Cf. Woodring, "The Future Problems of Higher Education," *College and University Journal*, I, No. 2, 13.

[19] Newsom, *A University President Speaks Out: On Current Education*, pp. 103 and 105.

formance standards vary with committees. As in the case of teaching, the basic fault may lie in the failure of educational management to supply relevant and appropriate academic leadership.

Graduate faculties which persist in obfuscation provide opportunities for reports and various forms of artistic expression to be submitted under thesis and dissertation labels, and they block the avenues to intellectual significance. Where contract research obtains, graduate students often are directed into technical field investigations in lieu of intellectual inquiry.[20] Confusion as to the nature of the writing requirements has permitted the insinuation of intellectually insignificant activity into graduate "education." Graduate school catalogues which emphasize mechanics rather than content fuel the fires of this running absurdity.

The failure to be clear and consistent about the writing requirements has done more than obscure the concept of independent intellectual work by graduate students. It has permitted the writing requirements themselves to become confused, obscure, and finally distinguished in a false light. This promotes arbitrary variation of the writing requirements. Equally bad, it laid the ground work for their use to differentiate Master's and Doctor's writing. An illustration is required at this point. Even in the "Report of the Four Deans" the thesis not only received brief treatment but it was not given conceptual clarity.[21] The pertinent subsection calls for technical rather than intellectual competence and achievement:

> *The thesis.* This should be a modest *specimen eruditionis.* As such, it should evidence use of techniques of research, ability to organize

---

[20] Especially in colleges of agriculture, for example, the practice is for professors to write up "research projects" as means of securing grants of Department of Agriculture and other funds. Such projects are subdivided into field investigation units for graduate students to carry out. Many professors permit the reports of those who "got their feet wet" to be fancied up, labeled as theses, and submitted as such for degrees. Cf. Cole and Bigelow, *A Manual of Thesis Writing,* p. viii: "Some suggestions as to how the individual student may find a task which promises to yield original results will appear when the choice of thesis-subject comes up for discussion."

[21] See Appendix A, p. 194. A thesis is an essay in explanation of the attainment, and in argument of the proofs, of a solution to a problem. In this report the term thesis subsumes the dissertation despite the fact that the latter is defined as an essay in criticism, clarification, explanation, or refinement of some matter, and therefore is an essay of a different sort than the thesis. The role and responsibility of academic management are indicated in part by the closing argument of the quoted excerpt.

findings, and competence in verbal presentation. Except in most unusual cases, a thesis ought not to extend beyond two hundred and fifty typewritten pages and the subject should be studied and written in one year—a year free of courses, language examinations, qualifying examinations and the like! The subject should be small, compact, and of interest and use. Since, as we said, a thesis should show original, not necessarily creative work, a thesis might handle texts or present an *index verborum* or a translation (provided these are equipped with suitable introductory essays). It goes without saying that the selection of a thesis topic is of elementary importance, and ought to be the joint responsibility of the student, advisor, and department. In this triad we especially accent the role of the department, since many heads can be particularly helpful in querying the extent of a topic and the methods of investigation possible and desirable.

The "Four Deans" aver that "Few theses conform to these prescriptions." Actually, none could. They suggest if anything a report, at best perhaps a treatise. The proposition that the thesis "should evidence use of techniques of research, ability to organize findings" perhaps should be taken to refer to experimental, logical, or mathematical validation of deduced ideas and their proofs, and not merely to acquisition of empirical data. Neither a text nor an *index verborum* nor a translation could be any kind of essay, let alone a thesis or a dissertational essay. With what kind of an "introductory essay" would one of these be "suitably equipped?" Would José Ortega y Gasset's *Mission of the University*, translated and with an introduction by Howard Lee Nostrand, provide a model of such a project for a Master's degree candidate? [22] For a Doctor's degree candidate? This kind of formulation is too vague and loose to provide needed guidance for either students or faculty.

The misleading excerpt just quoted obviously is not in agreement with the views and findings herein presented. Its formulation unfortunately is indifferent and weak. In fairness to the able men who drew up the report, it must be said that their essential concern was with the global problem of "Doctors and Masters—Good and Bad!" Furthermore, this probably hasty paragraph is in sharp contrast to the excellence of the rest of the document.

------

[22] Unfortunately, this valuable essay is out of print. It deserves reprinting: Graduate students and faculties would be well advised to read it. Cf. Max Weber's *The Theory of Social and Economic Organization*, translated by A. M. Henderson and Talcott Parsons: Edited and with an introduction by the latter.

The earlier "Report of the Committee of Fifteen" took the other approach. It wrapped various kinds of projects under the dissertation label—and went on to confuse the thesis and dissertation concepts. Reference is made especially to the first two paragraphs of section C. 2. e: *The Dissertation*.[23] Here, again, a few bad sentences contrast sharply with the excellence of the rest. For instance, a given project cannot well serve as a basis for either a thesis or a dissertation. These essays have different natures and functions. Moreover, neither the thesis nor the dissertation would be based purely on empiricism, as would be reports of discoveries about folk tales. But in other respects than the proteanization of the dissertation, this section is useful. Especially worth consideration is the proposition that "by defining the dissertation as 'an original contribution to knowledge,' pointless research is more often encouraged than discouraged."

Most graduate students receive little realistic instruction as to the nature and significance of their writing requirements. Candidates for graduate degrees typically seem not to know what a thesis or a dissertation really is. Few know how to establish a basis for one. Outside of first class schools, and excepting those working under able mentors, graduate students typically seem to avoid determining what these essays are. This is strange. Their understanding of the thesis and dissertational essay concepts is fundamental to their own choices of thesis problems and dissertational topics.

Growing numbers of graduate students have been assuming erroneously that their advisors should assign them thesis or dissertational projects. This is typical of those who are poorly prepared for

---

[23] Committee of Fifteen, *The Graduate School Today and Tomorrow*, (New York: Fund for the Advancement of Education, 1955), pp. 26-28. Using folk tales as an example, this passage distinguishes between the intellectual work of inquiry and substantiation and the clerical-technical work of tale collection. Darwin reported what he had seen, but his explanations of these things were deduced. It was the intellectual ability of the man which enabled him to present his theory of evolution as a contribution to knowledge. Cf. Alfred Marshall, "The Present Position of Economics," in *Memorials of Alfred Marshall*, ed. A. C. Pigou (London: Macmillan & Co., Ltd., 1925), pp. 167-68. During his inaugural lecture at Cambridge in 1885, Marshall said, "Experience in controversies such as these [re tariff levels and wage rates] brings out the impossibility of learning anything from the facts till they are examined and interpreted by reason; and teaches that the most reckless and treacherous of all theorists is he who professes to let the facts and figures speak for themselves, who keeps in the background the part he has played, perhaps unconsciously, in selecting and grouping them, and in suggesting the argument, *post hoc ergo propter hoc*."

graduate work, and whose interests run to sycophancy. The existence of this assumption probably is attributable to that considerable number of professors who misunderstand the writing requirements. Some smother students or let them "get by" too easily. Some direct students into shallow descriptive projects, often for personal reasons. Too many of the graduate faculties have been pedagogically lazy or indifferent. With some the false *magnum opus* notion is in effect. While intellectual work must be done and minimum standards must be maintained, classics are not required. Nonetheless, superior and distinguished achievements are appreciated. They are the prize-winners.

Availing themselves of opportunities to learn the thesis and dissertational essay concepts on their own is the real basis for students' access to academic freedom—to their *Lernfreiheit*.[24] Yet few students outside of upper academe, and only a minority there, learn on the basis of their own study what a thesis or dissertation is or entails. The pragmatic inclinations and descriptive tendencies of their schooling contribute to this condition. Graduate students who lack sufficient interest to acquire comprehension of their writing requirements, and of the underlying projects of intellectual work which must precede them, embark uncertainly upon their academic voyages and head out into stiff scholastic weather with little navigational competence.

The evidence is clear that many schools and colleges have set their Graduate Record Examination minimum acceptable scores and other fitness indicators too low. It is clear that many schools have not adhered even to their inadequate admission "thresholds." [25] A worse failure than that revealed by maladmission practices, however, has been the encouragement of floundering students who lack requisite abilities and interests to continue graduate schooling. Students incapable of real intellectual work ought to be neither permitted nor encouraged to attempt it. Borderline admissions should

---

[24] *Lernfreiheit* means freedom to learn on the basis of one's own responsibility and self-discipline. It is the student's counterpart of the professor's freedom to teach, his *Lehrfreiheit*. See Hofstadter and Metzger, *The Development of Academic Freedom in the United States*, pp. 383 ff. and *passim*. See also Robert MacIver, *Academic Freedom in Our Time* (New York: Columbia University Press, 1955).

[25] A recent study of a group of scientists revealed that only 3.4% had IQ's under 128. Cf. Ortega y Gasset's view, quoted in note 37, p. 35.

be carefully supervised. Students on trial should be dissuaded from attempting further graduate work as soon as their ineptitude for it becomes clear. They should be carefully guided into appropriate lines of endeavor.

Misguidance of students has been compounded in other ways. Successful fulfillment of writing requirements necessitates knowing how to learn. Students of limited capacity and potentiality generally have not been required to take explicit coursework in methodology as means of qualifying themselves to do advanced intellectual work. Many methodologically weak or incompetent students have been permitted to begin thesis and dissertational essay projects without overcoming their deficiencies in inquiry and reasoning. Small wonder so many have been foundering and quitting. It is wrong to blink at the attrition of graduate students and to ignore and deny the real reasons for it.

A university's reputation usually is based on its graduate school. Its prestige is a function of the scholarly and scientific work and publications of its faculty, and of the number of Ph.D.'s it turns out and what they do. The latter factor may explain the emphasis on "Ph.D. programs" and the small amount of attention given to "Master's programs." There seems to have been too much concern with status for a balanced view. It is true that the Master's degree is not a prerequisite for the Ph.D.; and that one may proceed straight to the latter without taking the former. Nevertheless, the institutions which award doctorates award both degrees.[26] Strong Master's degree programs can and often do provide solid foundations on which sound Doctor's programs can be built. They certainly could be a source of needed scholarly teachers.

These deficiencies and others must be overcome if the national need for trained intellect is to be anywhere nearly met. More than 300,000 graduate students are enrolled in American universities. By 1975 their number will exceed half a million. The present annual output of 75,000 Master's degrees may be doubled in a decade. More than 20,000 doctorates are needed annually but only 10,000 are

---

[26] In 1958 there were in the United States 175 institutions (Berelson's figures) which granted earned doctorates, and 569 which awarded earned Master's degrees. Berelson points out that "the top Master's institutions are different from the top doctoral institutions, and that emphasizes the break between the two degrees." See his *Graduate Education*, p. 94.

produced. This output soon must be tripled. American graduate education faces a monumental challenge for which it is ill-prepared.

Contemporary Academe

Graduate education in the United States either is entering its second century or about to conclude its first. Its age depends upon the point of view. The first doctorates in the United States were awarded at Yale in 1861; but the present system of graduate study had its inception at Johns Hopkins in 1876. Notable men and groups have been criticizing it for at least three-quarters of a century.

Before World War I, main criticism was directed at the quality of scholarship. The doctorate then was awarded only in a few basic fields including the humanities, the moral and social sciences, the physical and natural sciences, and in such "tool areas" as linguistics and mathematics. Departments offering graduate work were relatively few and homogeneous and mainly within the liberal arts and sciences. Graduate student bodies and faculties were comparatively small, and degree requirements more nearly approximated clarity than now. Most doctorates were produced by what are now our top two or three dozen universities.

Since World War I, by contrast, graduate schooling has been widened to include professional, quasi-professional, and applied fields. Graduate schools have become increasingly complex and amorphous; and the number of institutions offering graduate work has increased. As new fields gained access to graduate schooling, appropriate new degrees were invented only in a few notable instances.[27] The Ph.D. became anomalous and the "problem of the Ph.D." became more troublesome. Growing apprehension induced a rising volume of criticism. But the critics trudged repetitiously over the same ground year after year and availed little.

Since the report of the AAUP Committee on Requirements for the Ph.D. Degree, which was chaired by James Rowland Angell (1916-1919), the discontinuous and uncoordinated series of critiques has been characterized by obvious failures of scientific method.

---

[27] For example, see the Harvard University catalogue. See also the Doctor of Social Science program at Syracuse University.

These include: 1) failure to analyze the global problem and to secure basic facts concerning it and its components to interpret; 2) general criticisms and alarms directed to general attention.[28] Meanwhile, an unreasonable and anarchistic individualism became prevalent with respect to purposes and definitions of generic concepts applicable to all.

The problem was not a lack of definitions. It was that ALL defined, increasingly vaguely and to accommodate the parvenus, and that EACH asserted HIS definitions. To repeat an aphorism of Frank Knight's, such a "war of all against all is a prescription for chaos." Tallyrand's suggestive cynicism was that speech was given to men for disguising their thoughts. It does appear that the uncertainties which try the souls and tempers of graduate students result not alone from a lack of appropriate rubrics. They follow as well from the contagious and widespread implementation of the "Humpty-Dumpty principle" of definition:

> "When *I* use a word," Humpty-Dumpty said, in rather a scornful tone, "it means just what I choose it to mean—neither more nor less."
>
> "The question is," said Alice, "whether you *can* make words mean so many different things."
>
> "The question is," said Humpty-Dumpty, "which is to be master—that's all."
>
> Alice was too much puzzled to say anything. . . .[29]

The concluding sentence of this quotation is the significant one. Most quoters stop with the next to the last sentence. What Frank Knight had to say on this matter over forty years ago still holds good, although now he feels somewhat more generously disposed toward "the philistines." On the motives underlying his *Risk, Uncertainty and Profit*, he wrote:

> In the first place, the writer cherishes, in the face of the pragmatic, philistine tendencies of the present age, especially characteristic

---

[28] Berelson, "The Studies of Graduate Education," *The Graduate Journal*, I, 160-61 and 165-67.

[29] Lewis Carroll, *Through The Looking Glass* (New York: Random House, 1946), p. 94. Cf. James, "The Dissertation Requirement," *School and Society*, LXXXVIII, 147-48.

of the thought of our own country, the hope that careful, rigorous thinking in the field of social problems does after all have some significance for human weal and woe. In the second place, he has the feeling that the "practicalism" of the time is a passing phase, even to some extent a pose; that there is a strong undercurrent of discontent with loose and superficial thinking and a real desire, out of sheer intellectual self respect, to reach clearer understanding of the meaning of terms and dogmas which pass current as representing ideas.[30]

The purpose here is not to argue whether the individualistic approach is right or wrong. As it has been implemented it has led to misunderstanding and to uncertainty. Differently implemented, it could lead to improvement and progress. The time is ripe for the academic analogue of a Cecil Rhodes or the Founding Fathers. A great unifying concept of graduate education is needed, a splendid purpose and meaningful goals to enable coordination of action and joint endeavor. Let there be advanced professional and technical training. The fundamental question is: What is graduate education, and what is it to be for?

Graduate work is intellectual work, which can be done in all fields at a requisite level of scholarship. There is a confusion of thought on graduate schooling because of a failure to differentiate forthrightly and clearly between graduate education and professional or vocational training. The difference is generic and important. For one thing, academic freedom applies fully to scholastic learning and pure science. By contrast, the essence of a profession is routinization of performance within the limits set by a specific body of knowledge, required skills, and given terminology, methods, and standards.[31]

The intellectual achievements of upper academe provide light

---

[30] Frank H. Knight, *Risk, Uncertainty and Profit* (Boston: Houghton Mifflin Co., 1921), p. vii.

[31] See Appendix A, p. 190. "The Ph.D. is not a professional degree. No degree could be called professional which sets out to nurture individual discovery and which exalts newness in knowledge." Cf. Committee of Fifteen, *The Graduate School Today and Tomorrow*, p. 12: ". . . the Ph.D. degree, as such, is not a 'teaching degree' . . . it does not certify, and was not intended to certify, teaching ability." On p. 5 of their report the Committee of Fifteen states: "The existing structures and requirements of the present-day Ph.D. programs are, we assume, not sacrosanct; and it is therefore neither malice nor heresy to doubt that the present system will continue to exist unchanged for all time."

for both students and faculty of lesser academe. Berelson refers to the common knowledge "that a doctorate from Harvard or Berkeley or Columbia or Chicago does not mean the same thing as a doctorate from newer and less prestigious institutions." [32] More significant still, the vital questions concerning the recipient of a graduate degree from a school of middle academe may relate not to the name of his school or even department, but to the name of his supervisory committee chairman and major advisor. The implications of this for graduate students are obvious.

Several generations of faculty members have been produced under the handicap of needless uncertainties. The false idea that their students should in turn be subject to similar impediments is in some circles an influential doctrine. Goldsmith's axiom that "Every absurdity has a champion to defend it" may still hold. A better guide is Martin Buber's postulate that "Nothing can be done without awareness," and that "With it, anything is possible."

Differences as to realization of graduate educational standards may be at least temporarily excusable. Differences in standards are not. The idea that performance standards, as for the academic essays, should vary with student and faculty capacities is erroneous. It rests on a perverse view of standards within certain areas of lesser academe. The threshold of acceptability for graduate achievements should be everywhere the same. A common threshold undoubtedly would be exceeded with greater frequency and by wider margins in upper academe than elsewhere. There would be nothing wrong in this. Because graduates of universities tend broadly to compete in a single market, common standards would be an advantage for all. They would provide for stimulated academic competition and lead to general improvement of academic quality.

Alfred North Whitehead believed "that the fate of the intellectual civilization of the world . . . is to no inconsiderable extent in the keeping of our universities. . . . The awful question that confronts American Universities is, what are they doing with their power

---

[32] Berelson, *Graduate Education in the United States*, p. 109. Cf. p. 126, where Berelson found that "recent recipients of the doctorate from the top institutions feel a little less satisfied with the apprentice relation than those from lesser institutions, but at the same time they feel less exploited as research assistants." This is important. The clerical and technical aspects of professorial research projects provide poor training for intellects. However, educational quality is not necessarily a function of school size.

and their duty?" [33] Professor Boroff concluded in this connection
that:

> Higher education is a creature of our society, but it cannot escape
> its obligation to transcend it. We live in a dangerously easeful time.
> There is a lack of roughage in the national diet. . . . In the past,
> our fear of the idea of the superior few pushed us into shoddiness
> and hypocrisy. We are now in position to try the leap for excellence.
> We have the students; we even have the teachers. All we need is the
> will.[34]

Will without leadership and purpose is like steam without
cylinder and piston. This plea for opening the way to better and
more meaningful graduate scholarship calls attention to student
problems of uncertainty. The function of graduate education is enhancement of brainpower. The nation can gain even more from
this than students can.

Summation

In the preface to his *Ideas In America*, Howard
Mumford Jones reminds his readers of Thoreau's aphorism that
the youth begins by assembling materials with which to build a
bridge to the moon, and ends by building a shed in his back yard.[35]
The onus for a similar academic denouement is largely borne by
the graduate schools and those who have produced and supported
them. But it is borne in part by the graduate students.

Graduate students still could learn alone as their predecessors
did. Vitality and initiative are requisite. Thoreau might have a lot
to say about graduate students whose passivity, dependence, and
lack of enterprise hangs them on tenterhooks. He might suggest use
of the library, where all that graduate students need for clarification
is readily accessible.

The academic snake-pit remains a faculty construct into which

---

[33] From Justice Felix Frankfurter's statement at the time of Whitehead's
death, *The New York Times*, January 7, 1948, p. 24. Cf. William P. Tolley,
"Higher Learning in Our Time," *College and University Journal*, I, No. 2
(Spring 1962), 3: "The most critical national asset today is brainpower."

[34] Boroff, "American Colleges," *Harper's Magazine*, CCXX, 40.

[35] Henry David Thoreau, *Journal*, ed. Bradford Torrey (Boston: Houghton
Mifflin Co., 1906) IV, 227: July 14, 1852.

graduate students need not stumble. They have the duty and the opportunity to avoid it. They have the duty and the opportunity to learn what inquiry and research are, how these are interrelated, the nature of their writing requirements, and what the latter entail. They need not be content with building sheds in their back yards. Independent initiative in intellectual learning will place them in position to build their bridges to the moon.

8

The Penultimate Problem
of Graduate Education

There is only one way out of all this: it is, of course, by re-thinking our education.

C. P. SNOW

Nothing will ever be attempted if all possible objections must first be overcome.

SAMUEL JOHNSON

The penultimate problem of contemporary graduate education centers on the writing requirements for Master's and Doctor's degrees. Solution of this key problem could simplify the rest and so reduce their importance and their pressures. It might well eliminate as many dependent problems as it would simplify. In any event, as the second quotation above suggests, the ultimate problem will be to implement the solution.

Reflection on this problem suggests that the reasons for its existence and for its crucial, hinge position, have a common source. These reasons may be less obscure than some appear to think. Two basic ones come readily to mind.

The first of these is that the recent proliferation of graduate school curricula and coursework has been accompanied by a confusion of academic ends and means. The established purposes and goals of graduate education became obscured as the variety of collegiate participation in it increased. The functions and roles of graduate schools became uncertain with the admixture of technical, professional, vocational, and artistic training; and with the introduction of competitive claims by the several new interests. Conse-

172

quently, tests of technical proficiency and artistic creativity became confused with tests of intellectual maturity and competence. This result has been reflected in the frequent appearance of non-essay forms under thesis and dissertation labels.

The second reason is a product of burgeoning graduate student enrollments and rapid expansion of school facilities. These factors have induced emphasis on administration of budgets, building programs, and support services to the disadvantage of management of the academic enterprise of teaching and learning. The rate of growth of many administrative apparatuses has exceeded that of their teaching and research facilities. Substantive academic concerns have been neglected in favor of structural and organizational changes, decentralization of technical responsibilities, and the administration of academic routine. The academic interests of graduate students and their advisors have been overwhelmed by the recent emphasis on administrative problems of physical growth and change.

These two sets of reasons for the nature and significance of the problem centering on the writing requirements indicate the importance of being clear as to the difference in value between the major and subordinate functions of university management. The academic functions which are attributes of the educational role of the university ought not be less prestigious than their supporting administrative services. Yet management of the academic enterprise frequently has lapsed in favor of the lesser interest. Problems of content, learning, and academic qualification have become complex; educational undertakings frequently have a piecemeal appearance of going off in all directions at once. Since graduate education seems to have entered a consolidation phase, following its recent proliferating expansion, perhaps academic management will soon reassert its priority over school administration.

The writing requirements for graduate degrees have been at the root of candidate attrition because they are not clear. They have become the focal point of needless uncertainties which pester candidates from two sides. On the substantive side there are uncertainties about what they are and imply. On the environmental side uncertainties grow from irrelevant and often unanticipated impositions on the student. Just as student problems center here, so do some of those of their faculties. The interests of both appeal for a solution.

It seems a reasonable conclusion that a temporary neglect of

academic management responsibilities lies behind these needless substantive and environmental uncertainties. They are amenable to
solution by sound academic management. To this end they have
been examined along their respective arcs of the academic circle
to the point where the ring is closed. The difficulties many graduate
candidates have because of this root problem now may be summed
up. Although at the expense of some reiteration, it will be helpful to
draw main ideas together as a basis for our final step.

The Writing Component

The needless uncertainties which
plague student attempts to meet writing requirements should be
clearly distinguished from the needful uncertainties which inhere
in such attempts. Before taking up treatment of what is harmful,
therefore, a reminder of what is usefully kept may be in order.
Relevant stress is valuable because it contributes to drive.[1] There
must be some roughage in their academic diet if students are to be
strong. It is the intrusion of irrelevancies which debilitates them.

The needless sort of student uncertainty is that which pesters
candidates from both their requirement and environmental sides.
It arises on the requirement side because of the vagueness of the
writing requirements and their indifferent and inconsistent treatment. It is no help to students that faculty often make no distinction between the terms thesis and dissertation. Distinction between
names can be unimportant, but distinction between the ideas for
which they stand can be crucial. Where faculty members are not
agreed, students are confused by a mixture of inconsistent, incoherent, or even conflicting instructions. This difficulty is underlain
by the intrusion of a complexity of many related factors. Four categories of these may be used to explain the difficulty.

---

[1] See David Mechanic, *Students Under Stress: A Study in the Social Psychology of Adaptation* (New York: Free Press of Glencoe, Inc., 1962). Cf.
Roy Richard Grinker and John Paul Seigel, *Men Under Stress* (Philadelphia:
The Blakiston Company, 1945). For treatment of two other aspects of graduate
student adjustment see Jan Hajda, "Alienation and Integration of Student Intellectuals," *American Sociological Review*, XXVI, No. 5 (October 1961), 758 ff.,
esp. 763-77; and David Gottlieb, "Processes of Socialization in American Graduate Schools," *Social Forces*, XL, No. 2 (December 1961), 124 ff. See also Theodore Caplow and Reece J. McGee, *The Academic Marketplace* (New York:
Science Editions, 1961), *passim*.

In the first place, graduate schools have been experiencing two kinds of unprecedented change and growth concurrently. Proliferation of curricula has been interwoven with growth of enrollment and an academic building boom. The rates of change on both counts have been too fast for digestion of what has been ingested. As a result of these dynamics, graduate schools are characterized by a variety of rationales rather than by a single one, and by an enervating competition between rival functions and purposes. This is what has produced the so-called proteanization of the Ph.D. and of the graduate writing requirements. It has led to emphasis of logistical support administration rather than academic management.[2]

Second, the state of the writing requirements is curious indeed in contrast to the success with which graduate course and laboratory work is handled. One reason has been the failure to take adequately into account the difference in value between the establishment of global writing requirements and specific applications of their concepts. This is like deciding where one is going without knowing where one is. What has been good in the liberal arts college may not fit well elsewhere. Perhaps attempts to extend to professions and vocations the degrees and requirements that are appropriate to the learned academic disciplines have been wrong. The concepts of the Ph.D. and of the writing requirements became increasingly vague as their names were stretched to cover all things. Names which can mean anything fall into indifferent use because they mean little or nothing.

Third, there has been a notable indifference to the distinction between coursework and writing requirements for graduate degrees. Many students receive little realistic preparation during the period of the former for fulfillment of the latter. Methodological study passed from favor with the change from emphasis on learning how to learn to emphasis on learning things. Perhaps the indifferent state of the writing requirements is another support for the adage that what is everybody's business is nobody's business. While coursework is the responsibility of individual professors, with theses and

---

[2] Cf. Harold W. Dodds, *The Academic President: Educator or Caretaker?* (New York: McGraw-Hill Book Co., Inc., 1962); and E. D. Duryea, Jr., "The Organization of the Academic Community," *Improving College and University Teaching*, XI, No. 1 (Winter 1963), 11-12. Also "The College and University President at Work," *The Graduate Journal*, V, No. 2 (Winter 1963), 253-65.

dissertations groups are involved. When students complete course requirements and take up their writing projects, they change worlds. They leave the warm marsupial environments of classroom, laboratory, and teacher for the wide and contentious world of academe.

Finally, graduate education is such that its major involvement is with inquiry and research. The Master's candidate is said to be involved with research training and the Doctor's candidate with research accomplishment. The Ph.D. generally is regarded as a research degree. However, neglect of research training in connection with coursework and seminars often means that research training falls wholly on the thesis or dissertational essay project. This is frequently true, especially at the doctoral level. It imposes the necessity of self-training on candidates at the wrong point and time. Tests indeed may properly serve as learning exercises in addition to being tests; but should *these* tests have to provide *this* kind of learning? If they must, how then can they really perform the testing function for which they were instituted?

Graduate students cannot do well what is not clear to them any more than anyone else can. The failure to be clear about the required essays, including how well they must be done, includes failure to be clear about the relationship between the specified essays and their underlying investigations. This is complicated by the frequent lack of clarity about the relationship between inquiry and research. Inadequate training in methodology is a basic source of such difficulties. For example, the nature of much course testing, even at graduate levels, is associative rather than problem-solving. Even Ivy League students have complained on this score. Where term reports rather than term essays are assigned, students are pointed in the direction of an empirical level of scholarship where intellectual values seldom are perceived.[3] Graduate students often lack sufficient exercise in learned criticism despite its importance as a source of understanding and of additions to knowledge. Excellent examples of learned criticism are available as guides and for interest stimulation in all fields.[4]

---

[3] Here again is a terminological matter that is not really a semantic difficulty. Many excellent teachers use the term "report" but assign problems in such ways that intellectual work is required and essays result.

[4] For especially good criticism, see Kenneth Joseph Arrow, "Little's Critique of Welfare Economics," *The American Economic Review*, XL, No. 5 (December 1951), 923-34.

The Environmental Component

Most graduate students enter academe in anticipation of joining a community of scholars. They expect to do original and creative intellectual work of increasing importance and satisfaction within an atmosphere of academic freedom. Some have their hopes and dreams fulfilled; others have theirs dashed. Many novice and apprentice academicians find neither community of scholars nor opportunities to attempt original intellectual work.[5] Many find themselves on the fringes of a conglomeration of academic interest groups, disputatious factions, and prima donnas.

Instead of an inclusive general "community of scholars," many new entrants to academe find there a more or less incoherent complex composed of both "communities of scholars" and academic "principalities." The workings of academic machinery, hence, are often little less confusing than the workings of academic politics. Some factions refuse even to have "diplomatic relations" with certain others. Students who find their ways into the "communities of scholars" are indeed fortunate. Their prospects are to get on well and succeed no matter how confusing they may find the rest of academe. Students drawn into the "principalities," however, soon find that they are supposed to conform as loyal subjects. In many instances they feel influences and pressures which imply a caveat against originality and creativity. Where academic princes and prima donnas assume privileges and prerogatives they often perform arrogantly. Then arbitrariness contravenes freedom to learn and to achieve.

It is difficult for graduate students to resist being drawn into faculty factional strife and inter-disciplinary disagreements. They must side with their departments or their advisors. They suffer ill effects from particularism whether they are directly involved in it or not. The best course for many students has been to become sub-

---

[5] Cf. Carnegie Foundation, *Fifty-Third Annual Report*, p. 16. See also Leo Marx, "The American Scholar Today," *Commentary*, XXXII, No. 1 (July 1961), 48-53; and Edgar Z. Friedenberg and Julius A. Roth, *Self-Perception in the University: A Study of Successful and Unsuccessful Graduate Students* (Chicago: The University of Chicago Press, 1954), Supplementary Monograph No. 80.

missive sycophants in order to gain the protection and patronage of their academic princes.[6]

Teaching has become a secondary concern of some prestigious faculty who prefer to write and publish or to consult and travel. To them the role of Mentor to graduate candidates attempting to meet writing requirements is incidental, and a nuisance. They seldom are available to students who must wait upon their convenience and pleasure for advice and guidance, which often is hasty and incomplete.[7] There are instances in which it might make sound sense to separate prestigious writers and consultants from teaching and advisory work in frank recognition of the social value of their achievements and of their publicity value to their universities.[8] The subsidization could be less costly than other kinds of subsidies. This suggests no necessary incompatibility of research and writing or consulting activities with teaching and advising. These often are ideally combined in given men and women. Something needs to be done to enhance teaching in the eyes of those best qualified for it and in the eyes of all of academe.

The failure of graduate councils to define clearly and to state performance standards for the writing requirements they have set leaves graduate students and faculty to shift for themselves. Some are well able to do this, and some are not. The purposes and functions of the writing requirements are easily lost to view in such circumstances. Conflicting claims and instructions can as easily be-

---

[6] Graduate students normally have neither the right of appeal nor anyone to whom to appeal. Perhaps they could use an academic analogue of the military Inspector-General. As matters stand, they are forced to accept environmental difficulties, irrational or not. They have to suffer academic and time losses, even frustration and humiliation, in silence. They are in a position neither to correct their betters nor to demand reconstitution of assigned supervisory committees, no matter how ineffectual these may be.

[7] Berelson, *Graduate Education*, p. 125: "Because the top institutions have more distinguished faculties and apparently turn out better products, it does not necessarily follow that they have better training programs. Are the products better because the training is better, or because the students were better in the first place?" Cf. pp. 124-28.

[8] Of course such an arrangement would leave unanswered such questions as: What are universities for? What are graduate faculties for? Why not leave professional research to research institutes? On this matter see Newsom, *A University President Speaks Out: On Current Education*, pp. 105-106. It may be worth considering that the time has come to think about having a *Meisterschaft* degree for those whose achievements in teaching and in research and writing are outstanding. The Italian *Libero Docente* and German *Habilitatzione* provide examples. So does the *Academie Française*.

come the rule. Existing regulations and faculty actions on these matters then can be successfully negated and flouted by individual-istic interpreters acting arbitrarily.[9]

These conditions may be taken to imply a lack of adequate leadership within graduate academe. They contrast more or less sharply with conditions in undergraduate colleges and professional schools. The casual structure and organization of most graduate schools and their dynamic change and growth supply partial reasons.[10] The lack, or at least weakness, of a general purpose for graduate education also is involved. Purposes are indeed there, but instead of one, with appropriate subordinate modifications, there are many. Some highly individualistic and particularistic purposes are asserted. Inconsistency is not necessarily planned. It can appear wherever self-governing people lack the guidance of commonly accepted ideas and values. It will appear where self-governing people are more con-cerned with their "rights" than with their general obligations. Agree-ment on basics may be lacking even within departments and disci-plines; and beyond the level of clichés there often seems to be little recognizable inter-disciplinary agreement. The disadvantages of gradu-ate students in such circumstances can be overwhelming.

Conclusion

Emphasis has been placed in this discussion on the pathology of graduate education as a manifestation of conditions which adversely affect graduate candidate attempts to fulfill writing requirements for their degrees. The presentation becomes quite stark when all that is involved is brought together for close scrutiny. This is a result of the technique, however, and not of any desire to carp

---

[9] The writer has several times heard the assertion, or some variant of it, that: "The important thing is not what the rule says but how we [the speaker really means "I"] interpret it. This is what counts." It is indeed, but adversely. Cf. Jacques Barzun's foreword to Caplow and McGee, *The Academic Marketplace*, p. v: The academic profession's present customs and desires "force upon its mem-bers a tradition of secrecy, ignorance, and self-deception which, though neither deliberate nor perverse, is yet remarkable in a social group wedded to the form of truth."

[10] Cf. Roger P. McCutcheon, "The Conspicuous Persuader," *The Graduate Journal*, IV, No. 2 (Fall 1961), 254-59. Cf. Carmichael, *Graduate Education: A Critique and a Program*, pp. 4-5, 45-51, 54, 57-61, 101-103, 106, 140, 142, 159-60, 179-80, 195.

or cavil. The spirit is constructive and optimistic. Diagnosis is an important part of any cure. It is necessary to see where graduate education is on this matter in order to see what must be done to improve it.

The discussion has a definite point of view, but it presents neither new doctrine nor new usage. Its motivation is not tendentious, being unrelated to the idea of reform.[11] Its basis is the tried and true in graduate education. A doctrine that is sound and valid is implicit in the work of the best professors and in the operations of the best schools. It is available in the relevant literature—in piecemeal form, it is true, but it is there. The attempt has been made to pull such a doctrine together as a basis for generalization of existing good usage, to revitalize it for acceptance as a basis of practice. Selected representative quotations and footnotes have attested the established usage just as others might have done.

Beyond graduate faculties in a number of schools, other groups are expressing growing concern with graduate education. A broad segment of society is having a look at graduate education from the point of view that graduate schools are among the most important of national assets. The faculties will no longer be able to perform in "splendid isolation," indifferent to the interests, views, and assessments of others.[12] The faculty will retain its responsibility for immediate supervision and guidance of graduate students; but accountability for handling of degree requirements may well be demanded. Consideration of what is done and why it is done will become increasingly critical not only within academic communities but by regional and national organizations, and by representatives of industry

---

[11] Reform is not correction of abuses but creation of new usages. Cf. Ortega y Gasset, *Mission of the University*, p. 46: "Reform cannot be limited, even in respect of its main features to correction of abuses. Reform is the creation of new usages. . . . Reformers are aware that it is something *in* usage, and not the breach of it, which needs attention. What matters is usage. A symptom that the usages constituting an institution are sound is the ability to withstand a good dose of abuses without serious harm. But an institution cannot be built of wholesome usage until its precise mission has been determined."

[12] Wide-spread awareness of the necessity to forego abuses for good usage has been commented on by Jacques Barzun, who said: "The nation won't wait for us, and unless we reform our habits we may be by-passed." See *The New York Times*, May 15, 1957, p. 36. Dean Barzun is supported in this contention. Cf. Carnegie Foundation, *Fifty-Third Annual Report*, p. 17: "The alternative is that the changes will occur without their [the graduate schools'] participation . . . and perhaps in directions contrary to their wishes."

and government. The outcome can only be a matter of conjecture at this point.

Graduate schools need to do more than try to resolve the inconsistencies immediately surrounding the writing requirements. They need to screen out unqualified students, and to take more positive action in emphasizing the importance of teaching and counseling acceptable graduate students. They need to give thought to improvement of their management of the academic enterprise as well as to administration of its support functions. A start can be made by clarifying what is meant and intended by degree requirements, especially as these vary by fields of interest.

These means could be employed for improvement of operations and performances within graduate schools. They also could be used to close gaps between performance levels by universities. Decisions should be made only after careful study so that emphases will be correctly placed. For example, more serious study of attrition could be undertaken than has been made, especially as regards the influence of the writing requirements.

There is a need to cut through the cant, disputation, and negativism about the writing requirements to find the appropriate and the possible concerning them. Progress owes much to rebels but not all rebels are progressive. Use of available wisdom can change obstructive strife to constructive growth by providing objective bases for thought and action.

Experience and reflection may reveal that the proliferation of coursework within graduate schools has at least partial justification. The proliferation of means of fulfilling the writing requirements for graduate degrees, however, is another matter. It is an obvious violation of the rule called "Occam's Razor." [13] The historic purpose of graduate education is enhancement of intellectual capital. The function of graduate schools is education for intellectual work. There is no general agreement on any other purpose or function. No such change has as yet emerged from the widening of graduate curricula. Until other purposes and functions shall be agreed, the emphasis

---

[13] Occam's Razor is the philosophic rule that entities should not be multiplied unnecessarily: *"essentia non sunt multiplicanda praeter necessitatem."* On "university" versus "multiversity," see "The College and University President at Work," a summary of the views of Harold W. Dodds in *The Graduate Journal,* V, 253-65 but esp. 264-65. Gen. Charles de Gaulle put the idea differently when he said: "How can you govern a nation which has 246 kinds of cheese?"

must remain on the established means of testing intellectual achievements.

No matter how interesting and otherwise valuable they may be, art forms provide no such appropriate and valid tests of intellectual competence as do the presently specified essay forms. Neither do research reports and other non-essay forms of writing. Excellent treatises provide the single significant exception to the fact that the academic essays remain the best available vehicles for learned explanation of intellectual achievements, and for learned argument of their validity. The appropriate performance standards and relevant evaluative criteria for these are clearly established by sound doctrine and good usage. These lights provide guides to clarity and simplicity which can relieve undue academic burdens and facilitate academic achievements.

The two presently specified essay forms suffice to test intellectual attainments in all fields, at basic and applied levels, as outcomes of both inductive and deductive work. Well used, these tests can contribute to the enhancement of graduate education. The admixture of art and other non-intellectual forms into the intellectual undertaking is mistaken. One must take into account the difference between intellectual and artistic creativity, and that between intellectual and technical creativity. To do this deprives artistic and technical creativity of none of their value. It simply recognizes that tests of artistic and technical achievements are not tests of intellectual achievements—and vice versa. One would not apply tests of "cowishness" to horses. Why should this sort of thing be attempted in academe except as a form of escapism?

Student bewilderment has grown as the alternatives among which they may choose for writing requirement fulfillment have increased. Faculty difficulties have multiplied on this account just as teaching and administrative work-loads have increased with growth of graduate student enrollment and rising student-teacher ratios. The tasks of graduate candidate advisors and supervisory committees are being complicated by attempts to introduce new means of fulfilling writing requirements. Beyond careful definition of these unofficial means, time and precise thought would have to be given to determination of appropriate performance standards and evaluative criteria for each. Until standards and criteria have been decided for each alternative, together with its appropriateness as a test of a certain kind of work, the way is open for individualistic and particularistic arbitrariness to produce unmitigated confusion. The work of supervisory committees could become both difficult and unpleasant.

When the work of collegiate directors of graduate studies is considered, a host of administrative difficulties appears, creatures of ill-considered proliferation which could produce an administrative chamber of horrors. The links which unite artistic and intellectual expression are imperfectly known and understood. Therefore, intermixture of tests of creative achievement along these different lines cannot have any validity. It can lead only to difficult complexities and misunderstandings.

The difference between intellectual and artistic creativity is obvious despite their approximate nature. An essential difference between science and art lies in the distinction between objective verification, demanded by learning and science, and subjective verification in art. The humanities already provide difficulties to spare because of confusion resulting from failure to distinguish between these aspects of creativity and the consequent failure to keep separate their different tests. The social sciences also are deeply involved in this difficulty. Meanwhile, the confused state of thought and opinion in the world of the graphic, plastic, audio, and literary arts implies the virtual impossibility of setting meaningful performance standards for painting, sculpture, musical or dramatic compositions, or for novels or poetry. The determination of relevant evaluative criteria for these areas would be at once more basic and more difficult. These observations raise no question as to values of various schools of thought. The problem is one of general values which could be applied effectively and meaningfully in academic situations.

There is neither need nor desire to curse the darkness. The faculty need not play the role of an academic Dr. Frankenstein by creating an academic monster. The rule of Occam's Razor need not be violated and none of the difficulties alluded to need appear. Existing difficulties can be reduced. Constructive proposals do not come readily to mind, but it may be helpful to decide the purposes graduate education is to serve and the functions it is to perform. Both curricula and performance tests could be made relevant to these. So could degrees. While the prevailing systems of graduate educaton are under study, practices of students and their advisors can be readily clarified. This could relieve the larger study of much difficult complexity. Graduate students and graduate faculties have available courses of action which could significantly reduce irrelevant uncertainties under which they labor. They might begin by recognizing the artistic and intellectual duality of some minds, and then by realizing that injustice is not done to the former capacity by honing and testing the latter competence for a graduate degree.

The graduate faculty has placed itself under obligation to complete its inquiry into the difficulties students experience in attempting to fulfill degree requirements. It could begin by fair examination and appraisal of its own actions and their results. It could isolate and eliminate many of its shortcomings by overcoming self-indulgence. Graduate students are equally under obligation to overcome their faults. The ways in which they can learn to stand on their own feet in scholarly and social maturity have been explained.

A graduate school is presumed to provide some semblance of a community of scholars as a working milieu. The goal of an academic community should be to provide an environment conducive to learning. Instead, the academic environment often is only a product of learning endeavors. The graduate school is esteemed as the most important element within a university. Its characteristics should include rationality and reasonableness. These could facilitate concurrence on the nature and rationale of graduate education even in its diversity. The competence is there, but the task needs clarification and leadership if it is to be performed well. Here is work for graduate councils and deans with support from collegiate deans and departments.

Inter-student and inter-scholastic comparisons call for concurrence on degree requirements and for common performance standards for them. Concurrence is needed among, as well as within, institutional faculties because their graduates compete in a national market. The national associations of the scholarly disciplines and basic sciences, like many of the professional associations, could adopt relevant requirements and performance standards. These might be reported to the universities for thought and discussion; and they could be collated, say, by the Association of Graduate Schools, the Council of Graduate Schools, or even a foundation such as the Fund for The Advancement of Education, or the Carnegie Foundation for the Advancement of Teaching.[14] Working through committees

---

[14] The AGS has access to the men and funds and facilities needed for such

on definitions, standards, and criteria, the selected organization could produce a most valuable report and statement of recommended policy.

Taken as a guide to best available thought, such a report need in no sense impinge on academic freedom. On the contrary, it would represent academic freedom at its best. As a condition of self-government, responsibility is as necessary to an association as to its membership. Widely scattered members having varied training, diverse interests, and divergent views cannot carry through a common effort in a common cause without effective coordination.[15] In any event, since most learned associations have neither legislative, executive, nor judicial functions, but are in effect only clearing houses, they can impinge neither on academic freedom nor on the initiative of member institutions.

If any program is to have assurance of success, banners must be raised and performance stimulated and sustained on the firing line. Thought must be given within graduate schools and academic departments to implementation of policies and attainment of goals. Appropriate directives could simplify the work and increase the effectiveness of supervisory committees. They would enable students to go ahead and advisors to overcome much of the wasteful academic backing and filling which now hinders them. Most important, such directives could eliminate most of the existing uncertainties which now hinder attempts to meet degree writing requirements.

The vital work of meaningful leadership will not be easy, especially at first. Protests and obfuscation will have to be overcome. But they can be, as the productive results become cumulative and increasingly helpful. In support of good usage it seems an acceptable axiom that the one thing both requisite and sufficient if a graduate student or faculty member is to live to the full of his powers is that his "life be the true, authentic fulfillment of its powers, and not some

---

an undertaking. On the need for a central effort, see Carmichael, *Graduate Education*, pp. 48-56 and 121-23. Cf. Berelson, *Graduate Education*, pp. 123-24 and 254. On the CGS, which was founded in Chicago in March 1962, see Gustave O. Arlt, "The Council of Graduate Schools: Its Origin and Program," *Higher Education*, XIX, No. 2 (December 1962), 4-8.

[15] It is important to guard against the anarchism of personal arbitrariness. A successful democratic policy demands from democrats the observance of certain rules for its effective implementation. On the over-emphasis of liberty, see Negley, *The Organization of Knowledge*, pp. 85-86.

falsification of this inexorable destiny, imposed on it by our stubborn and arbitrary preferences." [16]

There is a still larger necessity to which Whitehead called attention. He wrote:

> In the condition of modern life the rule is absolute; the race which does not value trained intelligence is doomed. Not all your heroism, not all your social charm, not all your wit, not all your victories on land or at sea, can move back the finger of fate. Tomorrow science will have moved forward yet one more step, and there will be no appeal from the judgment which will be pronounced on the un-educated.[17]

The course of academic history need not hang precariously in the balance. It can be crucially influenced by individuals even when acting alone. Groups and movements can help enormously, but much rests on the ability and willingness of individual students and individual teachers.

---

[16] Ortega y Gasset, *Mission of the University*, p. 47. Cf. Alfred North White-head, *The Aims of Education and Other Essays* (New York: The Macmillan Co., 1929). In *Book of the Judge* [*Buch des Richters*, Ger. ed. by H. Gottsched (Jena: Diedrich, 1905)], p. 172, Sören Kierkegaard said: "He whose task it is to produce a corrective idea, has only to study, precisely and deeply, the rotten parts of the existing order—and then, in the most partial way possible, to stress the opposite of it."

[17] Quoted by Reece McGee, "The State University: A Prolegomenon," p. 236. This article is the second of a symposium of twelve under the title of "Forum," all of which have greater or less bearing on this idea, *The Graduate Journal*, II, No. 2 (Fall 1959). Cf. Carmichael, *Graduate Education*, pp. 29-30.

PART THREE

Appendices

Report of Committee
on Policies
in Graduate Education[1]

Doctors and Masters—Good and Bad!

We face a starkly pressing demand for Ph.D.'s on all sorts of fronts—for college teachers, scientists, government experts, business consultants, and for no end of other purposes. What are we in the graduate schools going to do about tightening up our programs and requirements for this critical degree, which now seems to offer nearly as many services as the A.B. itself? Current pressure forces us to examine our myth-enveloped Ph.D. with candor. What we see makes us look away with shock: for compare our Ph.D. programs with the professional programs in law, medicine, or business. We must ruefully conclude that the Ph.D. is tortuously slow and riddled with needless uncertainties; that it is frequently inefficient and trau-matically disagreeable to the bewildered and frustrated candidate. The basic flaw is: we have never cleanly *defined* this protean degree.

The Uncertainties

When a college graduate considers going to law school or business school, or even to medical school, he at least knows beforehand *how long a time* such training will take if he does decent work. Not so at all for a Ph.D. One may say, in

---

[1] *Journal of Proceedings and Addresses . . . Ninth Annual Conference of the Association of Graduate Schools* (1957). Reprinted by permission of the AGS, Copyright 1957.

reply, that law and business and medicine are *professional* programs and thus can be easily defined, but that the Ph.D. is essentially an individual matter between student and master; that it is therefore filled with unpredictable elements, and that, in short, it is *non-professional* and therefore cannot be laid out so neatly in terms of years. We agree. The Ph.D. is not a professional degree. No degree could be called professional which sets out to nurture individual discovery and which exalts newness in knowledge. Nor would we know at all clearly for *what* profession we were training our candidates for the Ph.D. For teaching? Or business? Or the Foreign Service? Or a consultant for *Life* Magazine? The Ph.D. is bound to defy exact definition in terms of time. But yet need the time-factor be so very imprecise? Generally the Ph.D. takes at least four years to get; more often it takes six or seven, and not infrequently ten to fifteen. Financial need, to be sure, often comes into the picture. But all the same we know that too many programs have taken too many years simply because faculty members and the graduate office have failed to give hard-headed advice at the right time, have shied away from making their students *work hard enough*, and have generally thought a well-bred air of amateurishness more gentlemanly and becoming than down-to-earth efficiency. If we put our heads to the matter, certainly we ought to be able to say to a good student: "With a leeway of not more than one year, it will take you so and so long to take the Ph.D."

Uncertainty about the time required leads in turn to another kind of uncertainty—financial uncertainty. Doubt and confusion on this score have a host of disastrous effects. Many superior men, facing unknowns here, abandon thoughts about working for a Ph.D. and realistically go off to law or the like. In the light of our pressing need for college teachers, nothing could be more undesirable. Other men, bolder or more sanguine, enter a graduate school of arts and sciences but are finally compelled for financial reasons to leave before taking their degree. Now that something like forty per cent of our men are married, this is becoming increasingly more common. They leave with good and serious intentions of returning when they have the money. One good reason gives way to another to prevent the man's ever finishing his work and all too often the files of the dean's office become a last repository for uncompleted thesis projects.

Then consider the uncertainties about what might be called the end-use of the product. In the world of the Ph.D. there is no licensing, no state examinations, and often no fairly sure concept of what a man is to do with the degree or any fairly precise expectation of this or that salary. This, of course, is a realm in which the universities can do little directly. Yet it involves important matters—fundamentally related to the application of the training—about which we should be militantly aware.

Suppose that a superior man is sufficiently fired and sufficiently determined to try for a Ph.D. despite his uncertainty about time and money and final outcome. What surety does he have about the kind of training he will meet? What kind of program is usually mapped out for him, and how wisely and thoughtfully has this been designed to suit his individual needs, talents and aspirations? Here too much is obscure and too often the assignment of routine courses replaces careful faculty consideration. Too much is mechanical; too little is personal. It is easier to tell a man to take the traditional courses—unexciting, shallow, and often repetitious survey courses—than to conclude that this particular man could well be allowed to do much of this work on his own—reading and listening and talking where he can profit most. The frequent result is depressing indeed, for we see many a man *less* mature, *less* self-poised, and *less* confident after two years in a graduate school than he was as an inspirited college senior!

Our achievement far too frequently turns out to be the very reverse of what we wanted: the second-year man under our system of traditional courses, examinations and grades emerges a puzzled fellow indeed, rapidly losing any feeling of his own progress or coming to mistrust the yardstick by which progress is measured.

When at the middle or end of his second year the student looks ahead, all is equally dark. What are the general examinations like, what are they meant to cover, and what do they aim at? How long should he try to prepare for these ill-defined and sprawling areas? And once that Scylla is somehow desperately skirted, what of the Charybdis of the thesis? So many questions arise here that it is no wonder that only one solution seems at all sure; make the thesis a long one, cram it with learned footnotes and keep your own feelings and taste out of it.

The Poor Results

Most of the uncertainties just adumbrated can be removed. Reluctance to give up the *status quo* or the desire, having been hazed yourself, to go and do likewise, have permitted these uncertainties to be kept alive. Still, we might tolerate them if we could proudly point to the results of the system—or lack of system. Far too often we cannot.

First of all, too many men emerge from the ordeal spiritually dried up. A queer kind of virtue indeed is under test here. The desire for finding out what had not before been known, the imaginative urge to reinterpret—these the tired and weary student has gradually lost. He has been wrung dry, and, knowingly or not, he often finishes his thesis with the firm resolve to have no more to do with "scholarship." The drive—almost the poetic drive—which first excited him and sent him on from college to graduate school is now run out.

So much for his feelings, but what of his abilities? What has the traditional training done for him as a potential investigator? The emerging Ph.D. is not what we mean by an *educated* man, a man who combines wide-ranging learning with an attitude of simplicity and vividness, and who commingles good taste with an excited curiosity. Rather, he likely has become a sort of expert plumber in the card catalogues or other areas and neither as teacher nor scholar will he throw off this inhibiting heritage. As a teacher, he may well lack that vivid excitement before fact or expression which is the basis of real communication. As a scholar, he may lack the means which a rigorous training in disciplines and techniques ought to have given him. If he *knows* that he does not possess the necessary tools with which a piece of work ought to be tackled, and that his training in form was so deficient that he cannot effectively put forward a valuable contribution, he will invent one or another reason for avoiding further efforts in scholarship. Or worse, if he does not recognize his own deficiencies, students and libraries hereafter pay the price. But the Ph.D. assures him that he *can* investigate and *can* write and *can* lecture with success. It is the presence of this "make-believe" element in our common concept of the Ph.D. that we must root out, and in its place we must put rigor and realism so that he can, in fact, do these things successfully.

We reaffirm what we take to have been the original idea and intent of the Ph.D.; namely, to train men to do advanced work of an original nature, without either maiming them spiritually or assuming that they are Methuselahs. Such training should obviously include a wide grasp of what is already known—we ought not, however, to require ALL knowledge—and it should equally include strict introduction to methods and tools.

The degree is not, we said, a professional degree. Rather, it implies a high *technical* ability—and, we hope, taste and skill in the art of written and oral communication. The result should be *original* work, especially in the sense of having the work reported with individuality. We cannot require a man to be creative. To avoid further generalities an outline of a specific plan is presented.

Time. Except in most unusual cases (e.g. in the middle-Eastern studies, where new languages must be gotten up before one may go very far), the whole program should take no more than *three* years of residence. In the first two years a man should take what courses he needs, and should have all the freedom from prescribed courses for his own individual work that his previous training will allow. At the end of his second year he should take his general examinations. At the end of his third year, he should have completed his thesis.

Admission. More precise recommendations for work in the three years will follow, but first it is obvious from the brief outline just presented that admission policies must be tightened up if a three-year plan is to be workable. Beyond tightening up the standards in the field in which the man proposes to work, we would especially ask that the language requirements now on our books be fully implemented and that a candidate be required to show that he can *write respectable English.* As for the first, we all know how much time in graduate work is given over to preparing for the foreign language examinations—time that should have been spent in high school or in college—and we know, too, how handicapped a student is who cannot read German. He should know German *while* taking seminars, and not just before he takes the degree. As for ability to write good English, we need no demonstration of the frequent lapses here. And yet no one would question the paramount importance of a man's ability effectively to put forth his findings.

Accordingly, we propose that before registration in the *first* year a man should take an examination in one foreign language and in the writing of connected English prose. If he fails in either or both, he must make up this deficiency by the beginning of the second term of the first year. The examination in the second foreign language may be taken at the start of either the first or second term of the first year or of the first term of the second year. In any case, if a man has not passed both foreign language examinations by the end of the second year's residence he should be put on probation or dropped. This whole matter does not so much call for deadlines and a calendar during the first two years as for increased emphasis on ability in the native and foreign languages as an admission requirement.

Advising and the first year. The best interest of both the student and the school demand that a member of the faculty deal fully and thoughtfully with the *individual* student. We need not stress the heterogeneous backgrounds of our graduate students. The adviser, meeting with the first-year man *before* registration and after the results of the foreign language examinations are known, ought to find out what survey courses a man really needs to take to fill in gaps, ought to see that he takes needed courses in techniques, and ought to see whether the man may properly be excused from courses so as to participate in the best kind of instruction—self-instruction.

The first year. Two courses should be mandatory: a first-term "pro-seminar" in which the student would be introduced to basic methods of investigation and standard books of reference and, not least, taught how to write a scholarly paper; and a second-term "seminar" which would involve extensive reading and writing. If these two courses seem restricting, the plea for them rests on the greater liberation which would follow. We are all in favor of pushing students out of the nest as soon as they appear ready for a life of their own.

The second year. Here again we should make one course mandatory—a seminar which we hope might lead a man smoothly and directly to a thesis topic.

Qualifying or general examinations. Here we should search not for a vague acquaintanceship but for *mastery.* Consequently, these should not test students on a *whole* field (Plato to William James or the like) but on selected periods or subjects. A department should let its students know ahead of time just what it considers necessary for a demonstration of competence. Depth, not breadth, is the aim here.

The thesis. This should be a modest *specimen eruditionis.* As such, it should evidence use of techniques of research, ability to organize findings, and competence in verbal presentation. Except in most unusual cases, a thesis ought not to extend beyond two hundred and fifty typewritten pages and the subject should be studied and written in one year—a year free of courses, language examination, qualifying examination and the like! The subject should be small, compact, and of interest and use. Since, as we said, a thesis should show original, not necessarily creative work, a thesis might handle texts or present an *index verborum* or a translation (provided these are equipped with suitable introductory essays). It goes without saying that the selection of a thesis topic is of elementary importance, and ought to be the joint responsibility of student, adviser, and department. In this triad we especially accent the role of the department, since many heads can be particularly helpful in querying the extent of a topic and the methods of investigation possible and desirable.

Few theses conform to these prescriptions. Generally their fantastic bulk not only prolongs graduate years but too often inculcates bad lessons. The idea of discrimination in citing references, or the thought that there is something good about a vivid and graceful English style too frequently go down to defeat before mere undigested mass. It is not by such ways that a man will learn to write either a book or an article of merit and interest. And as for the subjects themselves, one pauses to decide what to complain of first. Many a topic is breathtakingly vast in scope; others can only be carried out by two or three living scholars; still others must be pursued, if they are to be properly pursued, only in distant places.

A sample chapter of the thesis should be handed in to the director soon after the subject has been decided upon and his criticism should be sharp and pungent, ranging from methodology and organization to style. Lastly, the final oral examination should include a serious and prolonged *défense* of the thesis, and not just a brief résumé of its contents by the writer with assists from the director. Hence members of cognate departments should be asked to read the thesis and to seriously participate in a searching examination.

The A.M.

The situation with regard to the A.M. is almost as disturbing as that of the Ph.D. but for quite different reasons. The Ph.D. is a "new" degree, and has never been clearly defined because as it grew apace, time was not taken to ask what it was and what it should do. The A.M., on the other hand, is a venerable degree and for centuries it was quite clearly understood, until gradually the German-born degree began its encroachments.

At present, requirements for the A.M. vary sharply over the country and as the requirements vary, so does the respect paid the degree. If the A.M. were of universal dignity and good standing and not viewed here and there as a mere "consolation degree" for an unobtainable Ph.D., as just a "quick degree" or as representing a superficial performance, this ancient degree could bring us succor in the decade ahead. If the A.M. were considered as worthy in its way as the Ph.D. in its—each reflecting different amounts of the same thing and not performances different in quality—we might fill our demand for college teachers with men holding the A.M. A grim alternative awaits us—the cheapened, debased Ph.D. or else some new degree, untested and competitive.

The nub of the problem, then, is to get rid of "good" and "bad" A.M.'s and to set up generally a "rehabilitated" degree which will have such worth in its own right that a man entering graduate school will consider the possibility of working toward the A.M. as the first step to the Ph.D. At this point we should add that, if an institution concludes that it cannot, with its limited resources, embark upon the rehabilitated A.M. program, then at least it should refrain from harming the degree by issuing cheap ones.

Our proposal is this: the program should take one and a half years. The first year should be exactly like that of the candidate for the Ph.D., since the difference between the degrees should pivot on amount and not on quality. In the third term (the first of the second year), each candidate should take a course directly concerned with the teaching of his subject. This course should be taught only by members of the student's department, and would generally take up typical problems and various methods of approach suitable to the particular field. In this same term the student would write an essay of seventy-five to one hundred twenty-five pages, preferably stemming from his seminar of the second term, which need not be the original contribution demanded of the Ph.D. Finally, the student's subject should be named on the master's diploma.

If we do not take some steps toward defining and tightening the Ph.D. program, and toward rehabilitating the A.M., we shall gradually lose the power to get our own houses in order. For doctors and masters will be called for in the next decade with a resistless intensity. If we continue to allow—nay encourage—men to remain in graduate schools for eight or ten years while amiably working toward the nebulous Ph.D., we shall fail to meet the demand for trained minds. If we permit a large number of A.M.'s to represent nothing more than "consolation prizes," we shall do worse. Others will step in to supply the market, and to predict what kind of degrees will then emerge calls for no prophet.[2]

> *Committee on Policies*
> *in Graduate Education*
>
> J. BARZUN
> J. P. ELDER
> A. R. GORDON
> M. E. HOBBS, *Chairman*

---

[2] This report was discussed at the conference but was not adopted by the Association. For the discussion which followed the report, see *Journal of Proceedings and Addresses . . . Ninth Annual Conference of the Association of Graduate Schools* (1957), pp. 41 ff.

The Graduate Student:
A Profile[1]

Theodore Solotaroff

Now that college education is becoming a commonplace in American life, the graduate student seems to have pre-empted what novelty and prestige remain in being a student. In some ways he resembles that young intellectual hero of pre-World War II days, the boy who was working his way through college. Like him, the graduate student—particularly the Ph.D. candidate—is viewed by many people, including the more scholarly undergraduates, as a man of opportunities and purpose. He spends his days and nights on the frontiers of nuclear physics, or of learning theory, or of logical positivism. Sacrificing the opportunity to earn a good living for the sake of continuing his education, he works in a community of scholars and lives in the stimulating graduate student enclave, where young people are cheerfully poor together and one keeps up with the Joneses by reading Samuel Beckett. If the student is married, as he usually is, it is to a woman who shares in his purpose as she shares in his sacrifices; in some respects, she is a modern version of the American female pioneer—a young woman of enterprise and pluck, who types her husband's term papers while her infant naps, her cake bakes, and her laundry goes through the community washing machine. Or, advanced woman that she also is, she may be off taking a seminar of

---

[1] *Commentary*, XXXII, No. 4 (December 1961), 482-90. Reprinted by permission from *Commentary*, copyright 1961. Theodore Solotaroff, an associate editor of *Commentary*, writes frequently in its pages on literary and cultural matters.

her own, while her husband rocks the bassinet with one hand and turns the pages of a Russian grammar with the other.

These images have been circulating ever since the veterans of World War II returned to "revolutionize" university life. One principal change that did occur was in the displacement of the formerly staid and monastic atmosphere of graduate school by a more robust intellectual, domestic, and egalitarian spirit, as large numbers of bright and irreverent ex-GI's—many of them the first members of their families to go to college at all—went on to work for advanced degrees while raising families in converted service barracks.

The new social pattern of graduate student life continued to prevail after the veterans had left campus. Increasing numbers of students now took advanced work as a matter of course,[2] either to improve their chances in an increasingly crowded and specialized job market or to prepare for careers in the academy itself. For the gifted children of families on the social or economic margins of the society, graduate school became one of the best ways to move up, and the names of the top departments became familiar and magical, like the names of the medical schools. Meanwhile the campus continued to be a domicile of early marriage and parenthood. Thus, when one of the national weeklies took its readers into university seminars and student housing, they would find an alert-looking cross-section of American facial types preparing to meet the challenges to the free world, and serious young couples gazing thoughtfully into the future at the end of an evening. Furthermore, the new intellectual spirit that the veterans had produced was presumably being sustained by the much-discussed influx of writers, artists, and other non-academic types who were finding their way to university careers, and by the more open relationship generally between the academy and the society.

Recently the image of the graduate student's favorable situation —a seemingly normal life-style joined to an aura of heightened possibilities—has received a good deal of support from a leading sociologist, Bernard Berelson. In his book, *Graduate Education in the United States,* he concludes that the students themselves believe both their academic and private lives to be gratifying. Who should know better?

---

[2] According to Bernard Berelson's *Graduate Education in the United States* (1960) there were some 105,700 graduate students in 1940 and over 250,000 during the 1950's, nearly half of whom were doctoral candidates.

Questioning his sample of recent Ph.D.'s, Berelson found that "on the whole they were quite satisfied with their social life as graduate students," that most of them had completed their degrees out of "academic" rather than "practical" motives, that the five or six years or more spent earning the degree was not too long, that their dissertations were worth the time and labor they had put into them, and so forth. In sum, 35 per cent of the group reported they were "very satisfied" with their experience generally, and 53 per cent said they were "satisfied." Of the handful of malcontents—about one out of ten—Berelson judged that their grievances were probably related to their dissatisfaction with the academic posts they had been given for their labors.

Now the popular attitudes I have been caricaturing do not penetrate very deeply into the actualities that seem to me to characterize the world of the graduate student today; and like Lewis A. Coser, who reviewed Berelson's book in COMMENTARY (March 1961), I have a distinct sense of unreality when Berelson describes and evaluates this world largely by means of the responses of people who have successfully completed their graduate work. This is rather like describing how Americans feel about military service on the basis of what the members of a veterans' organization might say about life in the army. In both cases there is a vested interest in expressing satisfaction and a summary sense of personal history. At the veterans' club it takes the form, "I went in a boy, I came out a man"; at the faculty club, it is likely to be phrased, "As an undergraduate I was a dewy-eyed impressionist, but when I took my doctorate I had a disciplined mind."

At the same time my own years in graduate school [3] lead me to

<hr>

[3] Most of the following is based on an awareness of what life is like in three graduate schools usually listed among the top five in the country. What I have to say is perhaps less true of the less prestigious and high-pressured schools, though many of these schools are curently expanding in size and ambition, and their models are likely to be the more famous universities. Also the kind of graduate student I have in mind is someone in the humanities or social sciences, rather than in the natural sciences, which tends to be a world of its own, though not very different in respect to the student's relation to his work and to his private life from what I shall describe. It should, finally, be noted that I shall be describing only one type of student, though one whose progress has, I believe, a good deal of general reference. For an excellent typology of contemporary graduate students, as well as a remarkably sensitive treatment of their problems, see Edgar Z. Friedenberg and Julius A. Roth, *Self-Perception in the University*. Supplementary Educational Monographs, No. 80 (University of Chicago Press, 1954).

believe that the dissatisfaction which Coser (a professor of sociology at Brandeis) finds among his students and the "strong vote of approval" which Berelson's all-rightniks give to the institution are not irreconcilable. Rather, these opposing reactions often represent stages in a subtle process by which even the fiercely critical students slowly and ambiguously sign on with the system in order to fight their way through it. For all the talk about the revolution in university life, about its new role as a creative center in the society, this painful conforming to academic attitudes and scholarly methods, with resulting gains and losses, still characterizes, it seems to me, graduate education in America; and underlying the process, is often the quiet and deep desperation of the student's private life.

To understand the experience of graduate school, it is useful to begin with the contrasts ordinarily encountered between undergraduate and graduate training. For the sake of the argument, let's take a bright, if somewhat wayward, student in a good liberal arts college; after two desultory years of general education he is still undecided about his vocation, and in his junior year drifts into an honors program. What he will probably find is that there is no longer any "horsing around": work is piled on, the standards are rigorous and professional. For a while he resents the tougher demands made on him, but in time begins to respond to the challenges—to the note of seriousness in his class lectures and discussions, and to the illuminations of his instructors, who are likely to be top men, dedicated to their program and unwilling to suffer fools gladly. Under their influence, the student begins training himself to read, to write, and to think. As part of a strict but rational program, taught by men with a stake in teaching, he finds himself engaged in his work, and sees that most of his fellow-students are similarly engaged. A strong sense of community almost inevitably develops. Faculty supervision is apt to become more benign and informal as the student demonstrates his seriousness, and friendships often follow, especially with the younger teachers in the program. Under the direction of one of these young teachers the student starts reading for his honors essay, having been led to a subject that really interests him—let's say, "The Modern City as Viewed by Dickens and Marx." During his final months of intensive reading and writing, he begins to feel at home in the library and more comfortable with scholarly method. His stubborn prejudice for contemporaneity dissolves, as he finds himself living in the Victorian London of his imagination as excitingly and perceptively as in his courses and in his conversations on campus. The campus has by now become a very satisfying place to be. The charm of research and of the past, together with a sense of vocation settle upon the student. After receiving his B.A. he moves on to a famous university to do graduate work, bearing with him his fantasy of becoming an erudite teacher and writer.

On the face of it, the graduate school might be expected to be similar enough to the honors program our student has just left. His new group of M.A. candidates is presumably a select one; his program is demanding but again rational; his teachers are members of the graduate school faculty of a top-ranking institution, men of long experience and high standing in their fields. But the student, from the first day on, feels himself living in a radically changed atmosphere: any resemblances to his past situation seem mainly coincidental.

Undergraduate education is still largely "liberal education"; it provides, at its best, a curriculum and instruction proper to the training of the free man, that is, the man capable of thinking independently and critically about himself and the world; further, by its program of general and specialized education, it envisages the intellectual development of the whole man. Graduate education likes to say that its main purpose is the "training of teachers and scholars," but in practice, the "teaching function," as it is called, gets lost in the "research function." The most satisfying vision of the graduate school is full production of functioning scholars. Indeed, were graduate schools to take seriously their own announced purpose, and prepare teachers fit for their own undergraduate colleges, they would be very different institutions.

Thus, while the undergraduate in a good college has the sense of being directed toward realizing his best intellectual possibilities, the graduate student finds himself part of an impersonal and often rigid orientation. The department's techniques, values, and needs of research are quickly placed between the student and his passion for the larger reaches of the subject matter. Other than that, he is left to fend for himself.[4] The student who was interested in Dickens *and*

---

[4] Or as the late Dean Woodbridge of Columbia is reported by Berelson to have once put the matter: "interest in the students (rather than the subjects) is the great temptation which tries the graduate school and the great obstacle to its success."

Marx *and* the modern city finds himself forced to choose one of the three and prepare himself to study Dickens or Marx or the modern city by the methods which conform to his department's canons of acceptable research.

The men who formulate these canons, and teach the three-year program of graduate courses, are likely to be the senior men of the department. Most of their professional attitudes naturally tend to have settled on the fixed base of their special academic interests, their annual offering of the same courses to more or less unresisting students, and their role in the department hierarchy. In general, as Paul Lazarsfeld and Wagner Thielens, Jr. have suggested in *The Academic Mind* (1958), these older men are the conservative members of the department, inclined to exercise "a dampening effect on the innovating spirit" of their junior colleagues and certainly of their students. Members of the academic elite, they maintain the traditions and values summed up in the phrase "respectable research." The ideal of the advancement of scholarship, inherited originally from the German universities, still sets for them their standard of prestige and their purpose as educators. In practice, this can mean little more than working the treadmill of "scholarly opinion" in their specialty, and training students—when they think of the matter of graduate education at all—to do likewise. Now and then, one of them happens to be a wise and civilizing figure, even a powerful and provocative thinker or a rebel who has won his unconventional way—often through his prestige outside the academy. But the spirit of most graduate departments remains reductive and restrictive, and our entering student soon begins to feel that the large, benign world of his undergraduate honors program has given way to a system which in effect operates directly against the open and inward attitude toward learning that he had been encouraged to cultivate.

One way and another, he discovers that his attainments as an undergraduate are discounted. The courses he is now required to take may even seem designed for the express purpose of disabusing him of any pretensions toward creativity or sophistication; they work also to disabuse him of his enthusiasm and confidence. A key course, often titled, "Principles and Methods of Research," will immediately lay upon his spirit the wet blanket of pious procedures and apparatus. Otherwise, the atmosphere is perfunctory and amorphous: the famous scholar he has come to study under turns out to be a supernaturally remote figure whose lectures are drawn from his books; the course that looked so fascinating in the bulletin he pored over all summer turns out to be taught by a cranky old man, who has been treading the same shallow waters for thirty years, or by a very intense young scholar, who conducts impressive monologues in a strange new jargon. Gone is the relaxed and inspiriting communication that our student once had with his undergraduate teachers; he moves, now, in a world where such relations seem to him more like those between the townspeople and the officials in *The Castle*.

His first semester is likely to drag itself out in a succession of gray realizations. He may, at first, attribute his initial sinking feeling to being uprooted and lonely, but he soon perceives that some other students are as apathetic and resentful as he. With a shock, he sees himself in a mechanical process by which some fifty students are being run through the assembly line of an M.A. program. Classes seem divided—about evenly—between those who madly take notes during the hour and then hustle back to the library, and those who doodle or look vacantly out the window and then wander off into one of the coffee shops. He himself alternates between feeling intimidated and feeling contemptuous. Sometimes he envies the "stacks rats"—those fellow students who seem to have a consuming passion for bibliography and the language of "the learned journals." He becomes dull and disconsolate, wearing a path from his desk in one of the graduate reading rooms to his classes and back to his desk again. He begins to wonder if he should drop out.

But his situation does improve by the second semester. With a somewhat freer selection and with a knowledge of the faculty, he can line up one or two engaging courses. He discovers a few fellow students who manage to be intellectually independent and yet efficient in the ways of the department, and he takes heart. His social life picks up as he runs into some of the less stuffy manners and morals that exist on the margins of the university community. He goes to parties, meets girls, enters a circle of friends. He is more at home—and less hobbled to his role as a graduate student. But his relation to this role is likely to remain no less problematic. He still feels intellectually curbed. He comes upon a vital and provocative teacher but notices that, even so, there is little passion or controversy in the classroom discussions, and that a brilliant lecturer can speak for weeks without being asked a question. He himself is, to be sure, better able to imitate the attitudes and jargon that prevail in his field, but wonders what purpose they serve to anyone outside the academy. Now and then he pauses in the stacks of the library to thumb through a Ph.D. dissertation and thinks that some day he will have to write one. Reading the dreary learned journals in his field, he thinks that some day he will be forced to write for them—his career will depend on it.

Many students who are working for a Ph.D. give up at least once along the way. Often as not, the break comes at the end of the M.A. year. Some of the men go into the army; some journey out into the world to see what the other possibilities are, often in the belief that they will find there a healthy dose of "reality." What the ex-student usually discovers is that the universities these days have no priority on dullness or conformity. After the regimentation of the army or the corporation or the public agency, the venality of publishing or advertising, the intellectual inertia of teaching in a secondary school or a fourth-rate college, the graduate school can begin to loom in one's mind again as a place of meaningful effort. Such phrases as the "academic community," "intellectual honesty," "a meaningful way of life," begin to drift through the ex-student's mind and eventually he may surprise himself in the act of writing away for bulletins and enthusiastically making plans to go beyond his Master's, to get his Ph.D.

Let us then pick up our student who after a few years has decided to go back to graduate school again. And let us give him the additional typicality of having acquired a wife and a child or two.

Certain things now work to help him adjust. Having been once through the graduate school mill, he has few illusions to trip over. He is better able to accept the hard, gray facts of the Ph.D. program as part of the hard, gray facts of life, having seen that imagination or independence or intellectual ambition count even less outside the academy. The less extreme examples of academic triviality leave him indifferent—or cynical—rather than rebellious. Also, the responsibilities of marriage and parenthood make him less self-indulgent, more determined. The amorphousness, the uncertainty, of the first year of graduate work is replaced by a more definite set of norms—the alternatives, in line with the need to specialize, are fewer; and the department's standards of competence are more strictly imposed. Among the better students there is a more uniformly accepting spirit, a more committed academic stance.[5] Our student now sees before him a straight and narrow path and with whatever self-irony prepares to climb it. The major demand for accommodation, however, will come from outside his classes—from the daily struggle to meet the requirements for the Ph.D. as quickly and as successfully as possible, for behind the married student's academic situation usually lies the much more intense pressures of his private life.

The graduate student is typically self-supporting (unlike the student in a professional school like law or medicine who—as Berelson points out—generally receives financial assistance from his family). Unless he has a fellowship, he will have to devote half his time to some sort of job—usually either research or teaching. Most such positions that I am aware of range from $1,500 to $3,000 a year, which is also the customary range of fellowships in the humanities and social sciences. With the help of the GI Bill and later the Korean War Veterans Bill, some students could manage, but otherwise the economics that govern the world of the married student community are grim.

At the state universities the student loses a smaller proportion of his stipend in tuition but also finds that his job opportunities are more or less restricted to campus and to its exploitative wage scale. The main purpose of graduate student teaching is not to offer training and experience but simply to cut costs. Where there is a large freshman population, as at the state universities, the graduate student is used to provide instruction at one-half to one-third the cost. Similarly, smaller schools in a university area such as Chicago are able to hire a graduate student to teach four courses at a salary of $2,400 a year. Thus the usual teaching stipend will pay the graduate student only about $50 a week for nine months and leave him without any resources during the summer. At the private city-based universities such as Harvard, Columbia, and Chicago the student may find more lucrative part-time teaching at the other schools in the area (or may simply be free to teach more courses at the slave-labor rates), but this advan-

---

[5] Thus Friedenberg and Roth find that in their group of successful graduate students in the social sciences at the University of Chicago, "there is a remarkable correspondence between the officially stated purposes of the University" and those of the group, "between the consciously held attitudes and those deemed by the division to be appropriate." The authors find also that "only one of the nine individuals whose perceptions of the scholarly life were unique was declared by his department counselor to be successful. . . ."

tage is undercut by higher tuition costs and living expenses. Consequently, whether he has a teaching or research job or a fellowship,
he is likely to end up at the same financial impasse.

The student can, of course, live on his $50 a week for several
years; he can even support a wife and have another child and drive
a used-up car. But a root-canal, a siege of flu, a burnt-out clutch, can
precipitate a crisis and drive the student further into debt, and a
major financial set-back can mean leaving school for a year. The
expense of spirit is severe. The young couple's eager will to "make do"
fades into the daily sense of slogging through a mire of difficulties.
The "compact" or "cute" little flat in married student housing becomes a cramped, tense, depressing scene. Savings run out, and in
time the look of the veteran graduate student family shows—the
male, drawn, tense, frayed at the cuffs; his wife, lean and a bit haggard
in her uniform of blue jeans; and even the children looking the worse
for wear.

Aside from financial problems, other pressures of the student's
situation multiply as he advances through successive stages of course
work, qualifying examinations, thesis. During the first two or three
years his teaching or research job can be fitted into a more or less
manageable schedule, depending on how skillful he is in cutting
corners at each end. Also the rhythm of the academic semester helps
to carry him along, and the vacations between give him a chance to
regroup his forces and settle down with his family for a stretch of
relatively normal living. Then, too, he is apt to find that his teaching
or research job offers a welcome release from the regimen of his
courses.

Once he finishes his course requirements, however, or concurrently begins to prepare for his examinations or "prelims," he loses
the support of his clear, limited program; and has to provide his own
momentum in order to get over vast amounts of material. Now he
pushes himself harder, partly in response to the demands of the
examination which will comprehend most, if not all, of his general
field, and partly in response to the accumulated tensions of his private
life—the increasingly pressing need to do well or at least to get done.
He holes up much more in the library, and at home is at it farther
into the night. His working day can run to sixteen hours and carry
over into entire weekends and vacations. The closer the examination
date, the more he resists the contending claims of his job and his
home life. A batch of student themes or tests now get pushed aside

until the last moment; his teaching itself is done more *ad lib,* in varying degrees of cynicism and recklessness. And as the concentration,
nervousness, and fatigue of his days undermine his powers of patience
and consideration, his marriage tends to suffer in more marked ways.
His wife's needs become a distraction, to be dealt with as summarily
as possible; communication between them declines—so too, likely as
not, does sexual interest. The children get on his nerves altogether.
During these months before "prelims," if not earlier, the special
desperation of the married graduate student has set in.

After six months, perhaps, he takes his examinations and—if he
has been sufficiently systematic and sufficiently ruthless in his prepara-
tions—passes them. The siege is over, a few weeks follow of relaxation,
of straightening out the private dislocations and disorders, of looking
briefly at what had been swept under the rug. He paints the flat and
takes walks with the children. Meanwhile, the financial problems,
the little deprivations of mean, cramped living, go on. He sees how
the other students are already looking for dissertation topics, and
begins to grow restless. Thus, if he chooses to stay on campus and
write his dissertation, the climb to the top of the last, roughest
mountain begins.

All this is not to say that the world of the graduate student is
one long unrelieved ordeal. There are the particularly deep friendships
that develop—the close ties between students dependent on each
other's ideas and irony to keep the channels of personal intellectual
communication open. Then, too, there are the close ties between
couples who need each other for ballast and cheer as well as for baby-
sitting, and who have little to protect or begrudge. There is the
concert, the lecture, the foreign film series that give university life its
pleasant cultural style. There are the livelier graduate student parties
in which couples can come alive again and let go. There come periods
of satisfaction when the course has been completed, the qualifying
exam passed, the dissertation chapter approved, or simply when the
student's work is going well and he accepts his own efforts and the
impersonal discipline of the system and the whole vast, intricate web
of tradition and endeavor with which a great university transcends its
academic vices and follies and keeps the spirit of learning alive. The
graduate student has his moments of illumination, of achievement,
and of peace, and I have no wish to gainsay them, for they can be
very intense.

At the risk of repeating myself, what I do wish to say is that the daily existence which goes on in the cramped quarters of the graduate student enclave, is neither cosy nor simple, and that it exerts a powerful influence on the student's relation to his work. At best, it provides a steady push from behind to make him climb the long trail upward to the degree. At worst, it may drive him right out of graduate school once and for all; or, as often happens, it may drive him to leave the campus before he has completed his dissertation, in order to teach at a smaller school. Here he can double his income as a regular faculty member and provide a better life for his family. This he does at the hazard of trying to write a dissertation, as it were, by mail and at a more intermittent pace—which in the long run can create graver problems than pushing on to the end.

In terms of his intellectual development, the peculiar circumstances of the graduate student's private life foster the process by which even the intellectually ambitious and independent student eventually fits himself into the mold of the efficient, unobjectionable young scholar. The daily price that not only he but his wife (and children) are paying for him to remain in school impels him to steer a prudential course. The man who is struggling to keep his head above water is not likely to try diving for pearls. The student may even come to prefer the routine but manageable course to the challenging but difficult one; the low-pressured, humane, sensible professor to the brilliant but unreliable man; the trivial but safe dissertation topic to the adventurous and problematic one.[6] He learns to go along with the acceptable style of scholarly thinking, in which "originality" means mainly finding a problem, or segment of one, that is still to be explored, "pertinence" means mainly the amount of fresh factual documentation that can be accumulated, and "soundness" means mainly working within the existing body of "scholarly opinion." Moreover, he begins to find satisfaction in the close, skeptical examination of evidence, in the thoroughness of research, in accumulating a great deal of knowledge about a particular question. He develops a respect for factuality and for careful arguments that

---

[6] One reason that the interdisciplinary programs such as "American Studies" or "History of Ideas" have not attracted the students they should is that they are felt to involve risks, both in obtaining a degree and a satisfactory position afterward. It is doubtful whether these risks are, in fact, any greater than those involved in the conventional Ph.D., but with all of the compulsion to view the doctoral program as a straight and narrow and prudential path, the student even becomes suspicious of the opportunities for breadth and freedom that are available.

remain within clearly defined terms. He discovers that in many cases it is both easier and more satisfying to do the research and ride with the evidence than it is to spin a position out of a few hunches. He realizes that competent scholarship does temper the mind, that to suspend value judgments can contribute to understanding, that small discoveries have their own excitement. In short, he reaches the stage where he is able to write an acceptable dissertation, possibly even a valuable one.

Some dissertations are done in one frantic year, the majority in two or three, some stretch out over ten. But the pattern is usually much the same: a prolonged period of submerged anxiety followed by a growing momentum of nervous energy, as the student begins to see glimpses of the summit of the mountain. The typical intellectual quality of the experience itself is perhaps best suggested by the description which an urbane professor once gave to a class: "First you find a little desk in the stacks where most of the books you will need are shelved. Then, one by one, you take down a book, read it, and transfer its contents in cryptic, quotable form to little white cards. After you have gone through all the books, you take the cards and put them in an order. Then, one by one, you transfer their information to your manuscript. When you are all finished, the manuscript is bound, and one day a librarian carries it back to your place in the stacks and puts it on the shelf." Of course, not all dissertations are done this way but few escape the common fate of being mainly a complicated, exhausting, and expensive form of exercise. For one thing, it is increasingly difficult to find a meaningful research problem which the legions of doctoral students and scholars combing the field each year in search of the same thing have managed to overlook. Besides, the more comprehensive and illuminating the thesis, the more prolonged and uncertain the research and writing will be. The wise dissertation adviser tells the student to get his degree and then worry about doing a definitive piece of work, and if he is as desperate to get done as he usually is, the student tells himself the same.

William James said that by the time a man is thirty his character has set like plaster. However rebellious he may have been at the outset, the man who emerges from graduate school at about that age has inevitably moved in the direction of accepting the scholarly image. Exploited by a research or teaching job, subjected to the dislocations of his inner and family life, disarmed by the genteel authoritarianism of the academic will, he has become habituated to the feeling that the deeper questions of personal purpose are not worth asking and that the risks of intellectual freedom, passion, and nonconformity are not worth taking. The intellectual virtues which he has learned to emulate are pretty much those that Leo Marx, recently in these pages, associated with modern documentary scholarship— "precise, neutral, and impersonal." [7] He has become more narrow, diligent, and cautious in his ideas, more respectable in his style of thinking and writing, more politic in his behavior. He worries more about being "sound" than being stimulating; he finds it more natural to adopt a middle position rather than an extreme one, an analytic line of inquiry rather than an evaluative one, an academically fashionable stance rather than a personal one. He is likely to be more in touch with "scholarly opinion" about his subject than with his own feelings, intuitions, and sense of relevance, and thus to find himself having as much difficulty thinking and writing about history or literature or politics or society in direct, open, non-technical terms as he once had in disciplining his personal demands on his field to the methods and vocabulary of research. The gain in his ability to contribute to the learned journals can involve the loss of the intellectual energy or confidence to communicate beyond them. Five or six years is a long time. The graduate student who once cynically put on the mask of the conventional scholar, planning in his heart to remove it as soon as he has his degree, finds often enough that his face—as George Orwell remarked in another connection—has grown to fit it. Even—judging by Berelson's Ph.D.'s—to grin through it. By then our graduate student, perforce, will have joined the community of scholars. Whether he will still possess a capacity for breadth, inwardness, and risk-taking, a grasp of the time and the culture to which he belongs, whether he will be fit for the intellectual community without which (as Leo Marx wrote at the end of the essay I have cited) "the culture dies"—all of this is another question. One that lies outside the scope of the present discussion, as they say in graduate school.

---

[7] "The American Scholar Today" (July 1961).

The Cult of
"Research" and "Creativity"[1]

Jacques Barzun

If anyone attending a university today happens to mention to someone outside that he is engaged in research, the chances are that the immediate reaction will be "How wonderful!" or at least "How interesting!" Then possibly he may be asked what the research is about.

By now this familiar dialogue no doubt sounds perfectly natural; but a little reflection will suggest that it is, on the contrary, quite unnatural. Fifty, or even thirty years ago, the idea that doing research is in itself a wonderful or interesting thing was not the commonplace it has now become, nor would the question "Research into what?" have then come as an afterthought or been overlooked altogether.

To put it differently, the bare word "research" has in the last two decades become the symbol of an activity at once mysterious and sacred. And the popularization of the idea and of the practice has been accompanied by a universal confidence in the value of the results.

History contains no parallel to this extraordinary state of affairs —unless it be the medieval attitude toward pilgrimages. In those

---

[1] *Harper's Magazine*, CCXXI, No. 1325 (October 1960), 69-74. Reprinted by permission. Copyright Jacques Barzun, 1960. This article grew out of a speech that Jacques Barzun gave in 1959 at the University of California. Mr. Barzun is Dean of Faculties and Provost of Columbia University, as well as a distinguished critic and historian.

times, I imagine, one who was impelled to save his soul by going to a distant shrine was seldom dissuaded. He would take off his shoes, pick up a stick, and go off with everyone's blessing—just as today he abandons his occupation, picks up a box of index cards, and is on his way with shining eyes, or a research grant, or both, amid general admiration. The very way in which we use the phrase "*do* research" implies that it is the act, not the goal, that matters; and although few think of research as a pilgrimage for saving their souls, modern society does believe there is salvation in it.

Research, one concludes, is no longer a neutral term descriptive of an activity that should be gauged exclusively by its fruits. Rather it has become a badge of honor, an excuse for the flight from teaching —and a sign that despite all our lip service to liberal, enlightening, and philosophical learning, we find individual and general security only in the trappings of specialization. And this wholesale mania for research as a self-justifying activity, without regard to its need or its object, has produced a corresponding folly in our culture-at-large— the no less deplorable cult of creativity. Creativity, which has come to be equated with happiness, is seen as the counterpart and comple- ment of research, the complete article as against the fragmentary, the source of private pleasure as against the mere industry that is required for earning one's daily bread. Together, these two oddly related pur- poses, research and creativity, encourage or excuse the repeated act of omission that is having an insidiously weakening effect on our entire intellectual life: the unwillingness to judge.

For it is obvious to all that the righteousness of research is no longer confined to the academic world. Business respects the magic name fully as much. Let me quote from a recent newspaper advertise- ment which is headed like a news story: "Credit for Kent's Sales Leadership Goes to Research." In the body of the article we learn that "For many years, Lorillard research scientists have been experi- menting in order to create a cigarette of such excellent taste quality that it would appeal to all smokers, yet with a lower tar and nicotine content than all other leading brands. In 1957, the years of research were crowned by the development of the new Kent."

The drama that emerges from this report is, of course, patterned after what we have come to accept as the story of all scientific en- deavors: an heroic struggle with nature yielding at last the secret and the power.

But advertisers are not the only imitators of the scientific researchers. Corporations and public bodies carry on paperwork called research and help sustain the prestige to which the activity has risen. Research may be simply a search through documents; it may be tabulating answers to questionnaires; it may be interviewing strangers and combining their replies; it may be mailing out three different styles of flyers and meditating on the reasons why one "drew" better than the rest.

Students in all branches of learning outside the physical sciences have also caught the spirit of titanic battle with the unknown, so that what used to be called Scholarship (formerly regarded as a quiet and self-indulgent occupation) is now Research, and it is deemed heroic and self-dedicated. In short, "finding out" defines research, regardless of the manner and occasion. The word has been so worn down by common use that people in doubt about a spelling tell you that they "did a little research in the dictionary."

Corruption of Teaching

This confusion of ideas and purposes would be merely laughable if the endless praise of research had not deeply corrupted certain of our indispensable institutions. Perhaps the most important of these is the educational system. We have all become familiar with the frivolous make-believe indulged in by our lower schools under the pretense that children of ten can "do research," in such forms as collecting travel folders and pasting them attractively in "research reports" about foreign lands.

But one may fail to see how harmful the mania for research has become in the centers of higher learning, where it now produces symptoms of some gravity. I refer to the invidious system of academic promotion, the perversion of the undergraduate curriculum, and (most recent) the professional teacher's contempt of teaching. These three are related to one another and to a rather vicious habit, which used to be absent from scholarship when the phrase "a gentleman and a scholar" still had meaning. The habit I have in mind is self-praise. Today, it is no longer forbidden to parade oneself as "a research scholar" and to look down on those fallen creatures who "do not publish"; it is no longer improper for university departments to boast of their greatness, due to So-and-so and So-and-so, mighty "pro-ducers" in the sight of men. A golden glow is diffused over an entire academic community from the individual halos earned by research. When one of these halos is extinguished by retirement or death or—worst of all blows—by removal to another institution, there is no peace of mind until a replacement is found.

I should not have said "found," but *bought*, for the way to build or recoup "strength" in the world of learning is to seduce a great scholar from his university and his teaching. He is offered a larger salary, the promise of immunity from students and other burdens, and the facilities of research, which means defraying the expense of travel, documents, and helpers.

Why does research bring so much prestige in our century and why is it—unlike the pilgrimage—a collective rather than an individual merit? The most likely answer is that we associate research with social benefits—progress, increased production, new means of defense, better ways of coping with poverty, disease, and other common ills. In a democratic age, no greater good is recognized than that bestowed upon society, and society has learned to connect its comforts and happy surprises—from penicillin to supermarkets—with the frequently obscure or remote enterprise of research.

This being so, one begins to understand not only the prestige but also the self-praise of the researcher. As a member of an inquisitive and demanding society of equals, he feels compelled to justify his existence and his work. He can find no surer way than to point to his chosen occupation. Even if his subject is pure humanistic scholarship, he is "in research" and can find admirers. Though only the little money of university advancement will reward his labors, this, coupled with the satisfactions of prestige, suffices to keep the system going and to multiply the products of research.

Meanwhile, certain unpleasant side effects are noticeable. The requirement that every young college teacher shall "produce" is arousing discontent in young teachers and in their students, while tempting some in each group to a premature cynicism. "Neglect your teaching and you will rise; attend to it and you will be fired." Teaching continues to be honored on all pious occasions, such as commencement. In reality it is considered a fool's way of mismanaging a career.

It is not as if the system required one to be a great scholar, or a good scholar, or even a scholar at all: it only requires that one *produce research*, which being translated means publish papers. Their contents should be in a certain form and they should be documented and if possible accurate—that is all. Thought, relevance to the interests of any other human being, engaging exposition or lucidity of prose are not mentioned among the specifications. The papers are merely asked for as evidence of professional discipline justifying one's existence—and promotion. And at the same time, "research" can be given as an excuse for neglecting the interests of students or of the university. The modern teacher flees to the library and cries "research" as the medieval thief fled to the church and cried "sanctuary!" Thereafter both are untouchable by law or society.

To equate scholarship with publication might be reasonable if the impulse to publish were spontaneous. If one *is* moved by curiosity and skilled in the act of discovery, then it is both generous and modest to tell one's peers what one has learned, for their edification and their criticism. But when filling a block of print is done at regular intervals under tacit compulsion, and a judicious silence greets each successive teasing of the obvious or the trivial, the idea of scholarship itself is compromised. Indeed, the cynicism and discontent of the young are justified, and the observer of the academic scene is at last brought to think that there may be something wrong with a system in which Lord Acton could never have become an assistant professor.

Nor is this the worst effect of the potent principle. In the undergraduate college, which cannot afford to have anything but active, full-time teachers, the devouring ideal reappears in the form of the Honors program, which requires juniors and seniors to "do research" in the form of an "important paper" or a "senior thesis." Those who take and those who teach this part of the curriculum are esteemed the happy few. To prepare or supervise a dubious imitation of scholarship is considered "real work," whereas to teach or learn the fundamentals of great subjects is accounted an inferior task.

In the overriding determination to share in the prestige of research it often happens that freshman-sophomore courses are taught as if every member of the class were to become a professional scholar in the subject. This malpractice is not considered incompatible with the designation: liberal arts college.

Looking upon these antics in a comic spirit, one is led to ask what whimsical or mad forces have been at work. The natural and legitimate bent of great talents toward specialization cannot explain this universal passion for taking the pose of the researcher, aloof from the world and its cares, incubating the new knowledge which shall make us free. Visibly, a more common influence has entered the academy within the last twenty years and turned all the heads there.

An Influx of Money

That influence is undoubtedly money, which has come in sudden abundance from three sources—the foundations, business, and government. Though with different aims, these institutions have all put a premium on research. The foundations thought they could not discharge their obligation to society if they did not insist on the production of *new* knowledge. Their grants have gone chiefly to projects which otherwise could not have been undertaken or even conceived. Business at first offered its subsidies solely for studies of recognized commercial interest. But by now it too has begun to relish what is entirely novel. And government has divided its funds, largely for scientific purposes, between fundamental and immediate research.

This distinction, desirable in itself, scarcely matters when compared with the transformation of university life. Under the threefold influence, academic men have been lifted out of the even tenor of their ways and made aware of tempting new prizes. The award of a grant is tantamount to a patent of nobility, coupled with a higher standard of living. In short, the influx of private and public funds for new enterprises has turned the university inside out like an umbrella in a storm, taking the holder by surprise and letting him see much that his former shelter hid from view.

By another twist of fortune's wheel, the great subsidies have academicized the non-academic world which provides the funds. This was inevitable. The results of the research enterprises necessarily take the form of papers and reports, which have taught businessmen, civil servants, and foundation officials the tone and language of the academy. Yet this unexpected conquest of the world by the professors, and the insidious corruption of their conscience and judgment by the world, would not have been so rapid and complete if research at large had not been generally equated with *scientific* research.

In nearly everyone's mind, physical science has been the model that inspired and gave reassurance. Scientific research is unquestionably useful; scientific research is solid and certain; scientific research is never a waste. If the results of experimentation are negative, so much is gained for other workers; if the facts ascertained are at the moment unconnected with any line of thought, they will nevertheless play their role at a later time. For science is gradually compiling the great dictionary of nature, in which ultimately we can read our fate.

The humanities and so-called social sciences have drawn on these points a literal analogy with science and relied upon it as if it were self-evident. Newness, certainty, applicability are their confident expectations from all the projects in educational research, opinion research, psychological and behavioral research, as well as from certain studies in literature and art, which range from measuring physical elements in paintings to counting images and themes in poems and novels. Almost alone, history has so far adhered to its traditional descriptive role.

All this is taken as a matter of course, not to say as a sign of modern enlightenment. And yet within the last few years a kind of unease has overtaken the most able and thoughtful workers in this great mill which grinds ceaselessly day and night. The disquiet was voiced by a distinguished American scientist addressing the Fourth International Congress of Biochemistry:

"A unified and consistent vision of nature has become impossible in our day, at any rate for working scientists. Ironically enough, the only universal scientists left are the publishers of scientific books and the writers of science fiction. Each science protects itself from its neighbors by a cordon of slogans and catchwords; and fashion dictates whether this year we are featuring enzymes or proteins or nucleic acids, and whether we wear the molecules long or short. New journals are born every day by Caesarean section performed by skillful publishers; and as new disciplines are formed, so are new and mutually unintelligible languages; a Tower of Babel made of paper."

To Be a Poet

It does not take much imagination to respond to this somewhat disenchanted view of the scientific adventure. But since at present no obvious steps suggest themselves for checking its momentum and reversing its tendency, what does the newborn discontent produce in the culture at large? Every strong feeling generates an act or a gesture to express it, and the new stance that I detect as the first sign of skepticism about the cult of research is its complement, the cult of creativity.

What "creative" means in common usage is hardly clear—it seems to correspond to the idea of fullness, to the completion of effort, a synthesis of parts, while it also conveys, like "research," the notion of something new and unexpectedly good. Some months ago, an article appeared in *Coronet* on "The Greatest Problem in Marriage"—the word "problem" there betrays the scientific outlook—and we could read how a couple had achieved the desired solution: "If they look out and see it is raining and decide to stay home and have fun reading, they have creativity, the highest state of good marriage adjustment."

Perhaps we are meant to infer that in popular speech creativity has come to mean knowing enough to stay out of the rain, but the word covers other purposes—so many as to become a virtual synonym for happiness. What emerges is that creativity in the meaning of happiness suggests to the modern American the making of something expressive of his whole being—something intimate and joyful and which does not have to be justified by its utility to others.

It was inevitable that a quality so rare in our time should be immediately annexed by those who want to show that their workaday occupations are also capable of being transfigured. We find, for instance, that the behavioral scientists use the word creative to dignify the small innovations needed in business. They accordingly study what in one recent report, emanating from Ann Arbor, is called "Creativity and Conformity: a problem for organizations." We are never told why conformity turns out to be the opposite of creation. But we note that academic committees in general are fond of applying to themselves the epithet "creative." In the proposals for a Ph.D. program in economics at a respectable university, one finds under General Objectives this typical statement: "The program should be imaginative. It should stimulate creative, imaginative scholarship among participating students and faculty. Although traditional approaches can serve as its guides, we should be prepared to innovate."

The yearning here is not hard to understand. The desire is to have brilliant men make great discoveries and thereby produce an atmosphere of high intellectual joy in the department of economics. One sympathizes with the repeated call for imagination as the source of this creativity and suddenly one perceives what all these people— from the advertiser to the business manager and from the stay-at-home couple to the professor of economics—really want. They want the blessedness of feeling like poets. Nor would they refuse to be known as poets, as artists, if at the same time they could share the credit and prestige of researchers, of scientists.

We may say, then, that the professional man in our day, whether in academic life or outside, is hypnotized by two figures of commanding prestige—the scientific investigator and the maker of works of art. Being neither, he wants to be both. To say this without qualification would suggest more disapproval than I intend. Many academicians, businessmen, and free-lance experts of all kinds are perfectly sincere in their attachment to the ideals of science and of art. They often understand the ways and appreciate the masterpieces of each. What is more, artists and men of science themselves frequently lay claim to the virtues of their counterparts. I have heard Nobel prize-winners in physics boast that their work is "creative" in the same sense as that of the poet, painter, or musician. And I have heard poets, painters, and musicians declare that their productions are born only after the most rigorous research into fundamental laws.

But while I can recognize and can partly reproduce in myself the feelings that lead to such utterances, I confess to a still stronger feeling of impatience at what strikes me as childish boasts. Just as I see no reason why doing research should make one self-righteous and imbue others with a sense of awe-struck gratitude, so I see no reason why artists and scientists should all remind themselves of Leonardo da Vinci. The very popularity of that great man seems to me suspect: he is not so much admired for what he was as for what too many people think they are near to being.

My general reason for objecting to the joint cult of research and creativity is that like most cults it is not sober, and soberness—it seems to me—is the very definition of the competent professional. Lack of sobriety is the great corrupter. Once again, I point to the situation in the academy, where so much of our intellectual life is reflected.

Thanks to the cult of creativity, most colleges and universities now offer courses in creative writing. Students enjoy them, if only because the name has something liberating about it. But what is the result? Another opportunity for avoiding the discipline of words and —through words—the responsibilities of feeling and thought. You may object that since the work is to be "creative," it should indeed express any thoughts and feelings dear to the individual and in whatever form he chooses. Granted. The only question is whether that self-expression should be made easy, should be solicited and encouraged, instead of being forged and tempered by the application of resistance and criticism. The motives at work that are appealed to in "creativity" do not strike me as resembling those that have presided over the birth of genuine creations. Here is what an instructor in one such course says in the campus paper about these motives: "If you want to write, write! Only practice will bring excellence. Write for your own pleasure; then, having written, try and see if some editor won't pay you for it. The chances are he won't, but you're only out a few cents' postage, some paper, and a number of hours spent in doing something you wanted to do anyway. It's cheaper than drinking beer, and who knows? You might hit the jackpot anyway."

Fun and Cash

From this program, one enterprise at least may be seen for what it is—a pastime, of which the by-product might conceivably be cash. As such, it is entirely acceptable. But to give it the name of creation is *not* acceptable. For with the one word creative we destroy the whole effort presumably made by the departments of English, fine arts, music, and history in trying to explain to their students what it was that Milton and Mozart and Gibbon and Michelangelo miraculously performed with the common materials available to all men. That is properly creation. Creation is rare, sometimes difficult to do and always difficult to understand. And it follows that the inexpert aping of ordinary professional work, whether commercial or highbrow, bears no relation to the thing we dignify by comparing it with the act of a god.

In the writing classes, then, creativity means, on the student's part, evasion of standards of performance; and on the instructor's part, abdication of judgment. If the student were truly creative, no one would be capable of judging him, and certainly no one would like or approve what he did. If, contrariwise, the instructor keeps his hands off some ordinary or perverse production, he is shirking his duty. He seems to imply that existing standards must be waived when someone says, "Lo! I am about to create!" or again he implies that there is value and merit in repeating forms and ideas already well worn. To put this more generally, creativity cannot be a goal in education, for it means that formal instruction is pointless.

By the same token, creation is the opposite of research. This does not mean that research is necessarily pedestrian or lacking in opportunities to display ingenuity and original views. But ingenuity is a common talent that we should not confuse with genius; and original views in research—like what we mistakenly call imagination—should be strictly subordinated to the evidence of facts. None of what is the proper business of the scholar, teacher, researcher, or student is creative.

Am I then arguing about a word? I do not think so; but if I am, then I say the consequences of using that word are so grave as to justify the argument. For what I clearly see in the use of the word creativity is a device by which we give ourselves easy satisfactions while avoiding necessary judgments. That the faculty of judgment is at stake can be shown from a simple enumeration:

——Creative may mean the neglect of technical competence—witness a great deal of so-called new writing, new painting, and new art generally.

——Creative may falsely dignify certain ordinary virtues—quickness of mind, sense of order and relevance and skill in using words—all of which can be resumed under intelligence and intellectual training.

——Creative may suggest modern, fresh, or unshackled by convention or tradition. In that sense it can be used to justify waste of time, as when students analyze contemporary writers and attribute to them as innovations literary devices that are found in Homer and Virgil.

——Creative may also stand for a conscious or unconscious denial of the tremendous range of human ability. If a child in kindergarten is called creative for the finger-painting he produces, the distance between him and Rembrandt has somehow been shortened. Through a likening of potential and actual, a kind of democratic equality has been restored.

And with this thought we are back at the position research occupies in our culture, and especially our academic culture. For we found that a good deal of research—too much of it—merely filled a ritual need. The products are used to satisfy requirements rather than one's curiosity or that of other men. And it is a sense of the futility of these products that leads scholars, teachers, and researchers to sit up suddenly and call themselves creative.

Here, then, are the two halves of one great act of omission we are all more or less guilty of: the unwillingness to judge that springs from our desire to maintain the democratic tone of life. If small talents are creative, then since everybody has them, everybody has a

Leonardo-like mind. If research is to publish papers and nothing more, then we are all worthy and all safe—in the name of creativity. Thou shalt not judge my research, and I swear I will not judge thine. Unfortunately, as a result of this agreement, we may come to think too little of ourselves. So we restore our spirits by murmuring, "Creative!" To cry, "Hands off! Creativity is going on!" is the right of every man, just as doing research which none will question is the duty of every academic man. And to make every man both academic and creative is the manifest goal of evolution.

But what else, someone is sure to ask, are we to do? As to any general, collective answer, I have none. But a particular, individual one seems to me obviously to follow from everything I have said: Let each man who is persuaded of the futilities I have tried to describe, rouse himself from his waking dream of magic by research and glory by creativity and let him get to work—plain, solid, sober work. There is plenty to do—teaching, not only some specialty, but the three R's. In his specialty, let him organize and consolidate knowledge; reflect and deduce principles. When opportunity permits or spontaneous curiosity dictates, then one may add his small bit of fact that is needed and that fits onto what we know, or yet again one may worthily keep the public informed of these advances, thus preventing the existence of an unbridgeable gap between learned and laity.

If even a few should do this faithfully, quietly, and with good judgment, they will earn the thanks of their contemporaries and posterity alike. And when a creative man, properly so-called, comes into our midst, perhaps our work will have prepared us for accepting his. We shall then not be made uncomfortable and hostile by his short cuts or other unprofessional ways, nor shall we hamper him in *his* work, because we shall know the distance that separates us and the need for every degree of excellence. And that too will be counted to our credit, as no amount of mechanical research and assumed creativity could possibly do.

The Mythology
of Educational Research:
"The Methods Approach"[1]

Fred N. Kerlinger

The mythology of educational research is a body of legends and beliefs purporting to be the rationale, purpose, and methods of educational research. It has an essentially mystical character which seems to be rooted in the past. To question the mythology amounts to heresy.

The foundations of the mythology are: a general ignorance among educators of science and scientific research; an overwhelming preoccupation with practicality; and a negative and sometimes anti-intellectual attitude toward science and research. Educational research often has been criticized for its triviality, superficiality, and scientific naïvete. It has been said that these deficiencies are due to education being a young discipline, to the lack of theoretical development, and to general lack of sufficient attention to the canons of science.[2] These points have truth. But more important, perhaps, are the mythology and the knowledge, training, attitudes, and values of people doing, supporting (or not supporting), and consuming educational research—the educators themselves.

The mythology of educational research includes a number of interesting individual myths: methods, statistics, measurement, prac-

---

[1] *School and Society*, LXXXVIII, No. 2171 (March 26, 1960), 149-51. Reprinted by permission from *School and Society*, copyright 1960. Mr. Kerlinger is a faculty member of the School of Education, New York University.

[2] *Cf.*, B. O. Smith, in W. S. Monroe, editor, "Encyclopedia of Educational Research" (New York: Macmillan, 1950), pp. 1145-1152.

ticality,[3] "educational research is special and different," action research, etc. The concern of the present essay is the methods myth, one of the more influential of the myths in distorting the research thinking of educators and students of education.

The methods myth seems to be very prevalent in the research thinking of American educators. The teaching of educational research in university schools of education, for example, seems to concentrate largely on "methods of research." Indeed, what is perhaps the most-used text in educational research courses is entitled "Methods of Research." [4] The methods approach is rather narrowly pragmatic. If you want to investigate an educational problem, you must do some research on it. In order to do the research, you need a method. So find a method, the "right" method. Concomitantly, the way to train students in research is to teach them "methods of research."

An example may help to clarify the point being made. Perhaps the most naïve form the methods approach takes is the idea that if you want information on an educational subject, then use the "survey" and/or mail questionnaire. It is difficult to tell which of these is the more hackneyed and misused. Both are usually done poorly. This is *not* to say that the school survey has no useful function. It is an important part of the educational enterprise. But to confuse a school survey—which is basically clerical work of a higher order—with a scientific study of the relations among certain variables is another matter. For example, we might do a survey to determine the success of a new system of school consolidation. This is perfectly legitimate and necessary. But to call such an investigation research, much less scientific research, is misleading. Such a study can be scientific. Needless to say, however, the great difficulties in the way of scientifically studying anything as complex as a drastic change in educational administrative practice and its effects on educational outcomes are hardly appreciated.

A basic aspect of the methods approach is the general idea that gathering data constitutes research. This is closely related to the notion that science is fundamentally concerned with gathering, classifying, and storing facts. It is a confusion of the taxonomic func-

---

[3] The practicality myth has been discussed elsewhere. See the writer's article, "Practicality and Educational Research," *School Review*, 67:281-291, Autumn, 1959. Other myths will be discussed in future articles.

[4] C. V. Good and D. E. Scates, "Methods of Research" (New York: Appleton-Century-Crofts, 1954).

tion of science with science itself. In addition, it is a static view of science and research which emphasizes fact-gathering and which reinforces the methods approach, since it leads to a search for the best "methods" for gathering facts.

Part of scientific research activity unquestionably consists of gathering and classifying facts. But a more advanced and fruitful notion of research is a dynamic one which conceives it as an ongoing scientific activity in which hypothetical and theoretical propositions are tested systematically, not necessarily and primarily to yield knowledge (although this is, of course, important), but to help refine and formulate theories and to yield further hypotheses for further testing. Few educators seem to have this conception of research. The notion which seems to be held is that the purpose of research is to increase knowledge so that education, particularly school practices, can be somehow improved. This is not necessarily a wrong notion; it is, rather, an incomplete and too narrow one. What it succeeds in doing is to choke off higher-level, theoretically oriented investigations in education.[5] It also distracts attention from the most important part of scientific activity—theory-building and testing—and focuses attention on a less important part of science— so-called methods of research. Thus, education becomes saddled with a methods orientation, and the attention of students of education tends to be distracted from research problems and the theories behind them.

The argument on the other side of the question seems to be that education is not ready for theories, that many more facts are needed, and that the facts gathered must be pertinent to the solution of practical educational problems. But no area of investigation is ever "ready" for theory; facts by themselves are meaningless; and facts gathered only for practical ends tend to throttle scientific activity. Cohen put it nicely:

------

[5] An interesting example of this tendency is the explanatory material for research proposals put out by the U. S. Office of Education, Department of Health, Education, and Welfare, in connection with Public Law 531 on cooperative research projects. Under the heading, "Criteria for the Evaluation of Proposals for Research Under P. L. 531," 13 criteria are given, not one of which says anything directly about basic research or theory in educational research. The first of these is significant: "1. The proposed research, survey, or demonstration is concerned with the development of new knowledge directly applicable to the educational process or with new applications of existing knowledge to the problems in education."

. . . There is, however, no genuine progress in scientific insight through . . . accumulating empirical facts without hypotheses or anticipation of nature. Without some guiding idea we do not know what facts to gather. Without something to prove, we cannot determine what is relevant and what is irrelevant.[6]

Education needs both data and fact-gathering *and* the systematic testing of theoretical and hypothetical propositions in a rigorous fashion. But an emphasis on methods leads persuasively to a stereotype of educational research as mere data-gathering, since methods are devised to gather data. This mode of thinking makes it difficult, if not impossible, for the educational scientist to work in a theoretical framework.[7] The scientific purposes of theory, prediction, and control are lost with such a viewpoint, and it is probably just these features of science which are the most fruitful stimulants of scientific curiosity and scientific research.

What implications does the methods myth have for educational research? Because of space limitations, only two of these will be discussed. Perhaps most obvious is the effect on graduate curricula. Evidently few schools of education require systematic and thorough study of research design, statistics and statistical inference, and measurement. Courses offered in these fields tend to be practical and "consumer-oriented." They are designed supposedly to help students understand ("consume") rather than to do. When a course in research is offered, it tends to stress the various so-called methods "appropriate to educational research"—the normative-survey, the causal comparative method, the case study, the correlation method, and so on.[8] Little or no stress is put on design of research springing from the adequate statement of a problem or problems, statistical

[6] M. R. Cohen, "A Preface to Logic" (New York: Meridian Books, 1956), p. 148.

[7] It is interesting and distressing to note that the large foundations interested in educational problems are channeling huge sums of money into research with rather narrowly conceived practical ends. Unfortunately, little of this support seems to go to theoretically oriented investigations. Apparently one must show that the results of one's research will help make a better educational world, especially according to the foundation's definition of a better educational world.

[8] Good and Scates, *op. cit.* Significantly, the earlier edition of this work carried a whole chapter called "The Classification of Research Methods" in which attempts to categorize educational research were summarized. This chapter is one of the best pieces of evidence of the tendency I am discussing—the tendency to think directly and basically in methods terms. See C. V. Good, A. S. Barr, and D. E. Scates, "The Methodology of Educational Research" (New York: Appleton-Century-Crofts, 1936), Chap. V.

inference and probabilistic thinking are de-emphasized, and the many recent, significant developments in social scientific and other branches of research—multivariate analysis, such as the analysis of variance and factor analysis, the mathematics of sets, matrices, and probability, and the several important developments in measurement —either are ignored or dismissed in a few words.

Judging from the products of doctoral students of education and the understanding of educators of science and scientific research, courses in educational research have been failures. They neither have trained students to do research and to use statistics and measurement, nor have they given students much understanding of these matters. It is not claimed that the methods approach is the cause of the much-bemoaned incompetence of doctoral students of education in handling thesis problems. It is, rather, a symptom of the deeper disease of educational thinking, outlined earlier as the foundations of the mythology, which can be epitomized in three words: ignorance, practicality, anti-intellectualism.

The immediate point is that doctorates are conferred upon methods-oriented doctoral students, some of whom will be the future educational leaders who have to train the next generation of students. The argument often is used that schools of education are and should be basically concerned with turning out practitioners and not "theoreticians" and researchers. But whether this should be so, while pertinent, is not the real issue. The hard fact is that the professors of the next generation are selected from the doctoral students of this generation. If the training now is no better, or even worse, than it was in the past, then we can expect nothing more than a perpetuation of the mythology with, perhaps, a few more, newer, and possibly more defensive rationalizations than have been used in the past. Along with this is the equally devastating thought that the present attitudes of doctoral students tend to become the future attitudes of educators in general. Thus, the relatively narrow methods-centered and even covert anti-intellectual attitudes of present doctoral students—due to their training, the social milieu in which they train, and the mythology—become the attitudes of most educators.

A second implication or consequence of the methods approach in educational research thinking is the cultural lag attendant upon such a conception of research. Educational research is perhaps 10-20 years behind other related fields of research. Psychological research, for instance, has well incorporated into itself the multivariate thinking of Fisher, Thurstone, and others. More important, a large proportion of psychological research is science-oriented and not methods-oriented. The same is more or less true of sociology and sociological research. But not so in education. The school of education which insists that its doctoral students learn to understand science and to use modern scientific analytic tools seems to be rare. The emphasis, instead, is on the vague vagaries of methods which, in the last analysis, help the education doctoral student—or, for that matter, any investigator in education—very little. On the contrary, they seem to be successful only in confusing the student. They confuse him, as hinted earlier, because they lead him to believe that research problems can be solved mainly with their aid. And, generally speaking, this is not so. The graduate student of education needs to learn, among other things, the nature of science and how the scientist thinks and works, modern multivariate approaches *and their rationale*, and modern modes of analysis of data. There are other indispensable ingredients, naturally. For instance, the student also needs to understand modern measurement conceptions, such as the recent advances in thinking on the validity problem.[9] But a good start could be made by simply dropping out of the curriculum of the graduate education school the whole methods approach as it has been preached for decades and by substituting rigorous courses in research design and scientific thinking.

Lest too negative an impression be left with the reader, it should be noted that there are visible chinks in the educational research armor. Occasional excellent studies always have been published—but they have been too occasional. In the last four or five years, however, there has been an increasing upsurge of significant and well-designed and executed studies.[10] It probably is still true

---

[9] E.g., see E. E. Cureton, in E. F. Lindquist, editor, "Educational Measurement" (Washington, D. C.: American Council on Education, 1951), pp. 621-694.

[10] Four good examples of this upsurge are: N. Gross, W. S. Mason, and A. W. McEachern, "Explorations in Role Analysis: Studies of the School Superintendency Role" (New York: Wiley, 1958); E. B. Page, "Teacher Comments and Student Performance: A Seventy-Four Classroom Experiment in School Motivation," *Journal of Educational Psychology*, 49: 173-181, Aug., 1958; D. G. Ryans, "The Investigation of Teacher Characteristics," *Educational Record*, 34: 370-396, Oct., 1953 (general report on a series of studies); I. Sarnoff, *et al.*, "A Cross-Cultural Study of Anxiety Among American and English School Children," *Journal of Educational Psychology*, 49: 129-136, June, 1958.

that many or most doctoral theses continue to be poor. But if the present trend toward broader theoretical and methodological thinking continues, educational research will be revolutionized. And it is the business of schools of education to hasten and not to hinder this revolution. Above all, it is the business of schools of education not to create and perpetuate mythologies, but to destroy them.

How to Produce an Idea[1]

Helen Rowan

The six-year-old child who succeeds in repairing his broken tricycle bell has a creative experience, New York University psychologist Morris I. Stein is fond of pointing out, but no one would claim that the repaired bell constitutes a "creative product" in the generally accepted meaning of the term.

It is possible, in other words, to differentiate roughly between individual creativity and social creativity. If you have an idea, it may be creative in comparison to all the other ideas you have ever had, which certainly represents individual creativity. Or it may be creative in comparison to all the ideas everyone has ever had; this represents social creativity of the highest order.

In short, the basic difference may be one of degree rather than kind. The highly creative person may be so because of the kind of problem he sets for himself and the quality of his response to it. But his creative process is not necessarily very different from what everyone goes through, or at least can go through.

It is necessary to bear this in mind because of the aura of mystery which has surrounded the creative process—a mystery which has been augmented rather than dissipated by the numerous ac-

---

[1] *Think Magazine*, XXVIII, No. 10 (Nov.-Dec. 1962), 13-15. Reprinted by permission from *Think Magazine*, copyright 1962 by International Business Machines Corporation. Helen Rowan has spent a good deal of time reporting the work of social scientists who are investigating creativity. She is a free-lance writer, whose home is San Francisco.

counts left by the geniuses of history. Almost to a man—ancient or modern, writers, artists, musicians, scientists—they have gladly committed to paper accounts of how they did what they did and how they felt while they were doing it. The trouble with this kind of evidence, fascinating as it is, is that it is impressionistic, imprecise and incomplete. Furthermore, one aspect has tended to overshadow all others in the public mind; this has to do with the role of "inspiration" in the creative process.

It is true that most highly creative individuals, even those as different in temperament and field as Samuel Coleridge and Bertrand Russell, do report flashes of insight, of sudden "knowing." But when these bursts of inspiration are seen in the context of the entire process of which they are a part, they take on different significance.

The Four Stages

To most people who have studied the problem, it seems apparent that the creative process occurs in four (or five, as some would have it) stages. Others say that what knowledge we have of the various stages is of little help because it is sheerly descriptive.

But for whatever it is worth, many participants and observers have described the stages of the creative experience in the following terms:

> Preparation.
> Incubation.
> Illumination.
> Verification.

Some break the preparatory stage into two parts, saying that in a sense one's entire life—the gaining of experience, education, the mastery of a medium, whether it be pigments or words or mathematical symbols—is preparation for the act of creating. Then next (or first) comes the stage of intensive preparation: The individual works, consciously and hard, on whatever problem he is trying to solve. This preparation involves enormous effort and eventually, in many cases, great frustration, with accompanying tension and anxiety.

The Creator Withdraws

Then the creator often withdraws from the problem, perhaps for a very short time, perhaps for a long period. There is no certain knowledge of what occurs during this period. Some psychologists believe that the subconscious is at work. Others believe that the period of incubation frees the individual of previous fixations, and that he is then able to see the problem with new eyes when he returns to it. Others would add to this hypothesis the idea that during the withdrawal period the creator is receiving helpful cues from his environment and experience.

Whatever it is that happens, next comes the moment everyone yearns for: the burst of insight, an experience of the "Aha" or "Eureka!" type that we all have had in some degree. But when considered in the light of all that has gone before, it loses some of its mystery. Remember that the individual has already established an outside criterion against which he may check his idea or insight; he has been desperately looking for something; he sees it, recognizes it, and cries, "Eureka!" (To give a homely example that has nothing to do with creativity, set yourself the task of finding a redheaded man who is speaking German and wearing green socks. When you see him, you, too, will have an "Aha" experience.)

Following the illumination comes the period of verification or completion. In this time the individual applies all his skills and craft and intelligence to make solid the original insight and finish the creation.

A distinctive characteristic of highly creative individuals seems to be their ability to maintain an exceedingly delicate balance between the most intense effort, on the one hand, and suspension of conscious effort on the other. Even though few would go as far as Edison did in saying that genius is only one per cent inspiration, the other 99 per cent being perspiration, all genuinely creative people do show that "transcendent capacity for taking trouble" that Carlyle said made genius. But other kinds of traits seem to be just as essential to their creativity. Many observers have mentioned the attitude of playfulness highly creative individuals reveal—the ability to get both enjoyment and amusement from juggling ideas or paints or words or whatever. They also show a certain kind of restraint:

They are not driven to pursue their purposes implacably and directly at all times, nor to force a solution arbitrarily. They seem to trust themselves to recognize the right solution when it emerges, and have enough confidence to wait for it.

No How-to-do-it Books

The "how-to-do-it handbook of creativity" has never been written and probably never could—or should —be. Nevertheless, it seems possible that all of us might increase somewhat the degree of creativity we show in our daily lives by making deliberate attempts to develop the kinds of attitudes, habits, and modes of operation that mark highly creative individuals. There is pretty general agreement that conscious effort alone cannot produce a creative achievement. But conscious effort may put us in a position where creative achievement is more likely.

Excerpt on "Quellenforschung"[1]

Gilbert Highet

The false parallel with science caused many more errors and exaggerations in classical study. One odd one was the habit of _Quellenforschung_, the search for sources, which began as a legitimate inquiry into the material used by a poet, historian, or philosopher, and was pushed to the absurd point at which it was assumed that everything in a poem, even such a poem as the _Aeneid_, was derived from earlier writers. It is a typical scientific assumption that everything can be explained by synthesis, _but it omits the essential artistic fact of creation_ [clause not italicized in original].

The scientific approach, as well as the expansion of knowledge, has also been responsible for the fragmentation of classical study. For several decades the majority of scholars have preferred writing small studies about single authors, of separate aspects of single authors, or tiny areas of social and literary history, of topics obscure and peripheral and unexplored. Meanwhile, _much remains to be done on the great central subjects_ [not italicized in original]. There has been a widespread belief, not without foundation, that scholars actually chose to write on subjects which were safe because so few people knew anything about them. In Germany the custom was invented of awarding doctoral degrees only to students who had produced a piece of "original research." Because of the close relation

---

[1] Gilbert Highet, _The Classical Tradition_ (New York: Oxford University Press, 1953), pp. 499-500. Cf. pp. 470-71. Reprinted by permission of the publisher. Copyright 1953.

between American and German universities in the latter part of the nineteenth century, the habit spread to the United States where it now rages unchecked. Hundreds of Ph.D. candidates every year produce dissertations on subjects which often interest neither themselves nor anyone else; and which the doctors seldom re-explore in the light of their later, more mature knowledge. The defense usually offered for this practice is that each of the dissertations is like a single brick, which helps to build the great edifice of scholarship. The image is true enough so far as it goes; but the terrain is getting more and more littered with scattered heaps of bricks which are manufactured and tipped out without any plan whatever, unless it be to cover every inch of exposed ground. As they accumulate, the task of scholarship becomes not less but more difficult. And meanwhile, those looking in from outside see no cathedral arising, and very few builders have appeared. For brickmaking does not produce architects.

It is, then, the fundamental fault of modern classical scholarship that it has cultivated research more than interpretation, that it has been more interested in the acquisition than in the dissemination of knowledge, that it has denied or disdained the relevance of its work in the contemporary world, and that it has encouraged the public neglect of which it now complains. The scholar has a responsibility to society—not less, but greater, than that of the labourer and the business man. His first duty is to know the truth, and his second is to make it known.

Model Doctor's
and Master's Theses

The following lists are not exhaustive of what the several disciplines and sciences offer, but selected reading from them can clarify the idea of the thesis essay. Publication of some has improved their accessibility and enhanced their value as models while giving them a finish beyond the standard for degree candidates. The unpublished essays are available through inter-library loan. Model Master's theses are difficult to locate because of the scant consideration given them since the growth of emphasis on the Ph.D. Access to the good ones would be useful.

Model Doctor's Theses

Chamberlin, Edward Hastings. *The Theory of Monopolistic Competition.* ("Harvard Economic Studies," Vol. XXXVIII.) 7th ed.; Cambridge: Harvard University Press, 1956. (Degree, Harvard University.)

Dashiell, J. F. *The Philosophical Status of Values.* New York: Columbia University Press, 1913. (Degree, Columbia University.)

Gordon, Lincoln. *The Public Corporation in Great Britain.* London: Oxford University Press, 1938. (Degree, Oxford University.)

Gottheil, F. M. "The Economic Predictions of Karl Marx." Unpublished doctoral thesis, Duke University, 1959. (Degree, Duke University.)

Kenen, Peter B. *British Monetary Policy and the Balance of Payments 1951-1957.* ("Harvard Economic Studies," Vol. CXVI.)

nomic Studies," Vol. XXXI.) 2d ed. revised. Cambridge: Harvard University Press, 1948. (Degree, Harvard University.)

Boorstin, Daniel J. *The Mysterious Science of the Law.* Cambridge: Harvard University Press, 1941. (Degree, Yale University.)

Chang, Pei-kang. *Agriculture and Industrialization.* ("Harvard Economic Studies," Vol. LXXXV.) Cambridge: Harvard University Press, 1949. (Degree, Harvard University.)

Dollard, John. *Caste and Class in a Southern Town.* New Haven: Yale University Press, 1937. (Degree, University of Chicago.)

Fraiberg, Louis. *Psychoanalysis and American Literary Criticism.* Detroit: Wayne State University Press, 1960. (Degree, University of Michigan.)

Frank, Joseph. *The Levellers: A History of the Writings of Three Seventeenth-Century Social Democrats: John Lilburne, Richard Overton, William Walwyn.* Cambridge: Harvard University Press, 1955. (Degree, Harvard University.)

Hansen, Alvin H. *Cycles of Prosperity and Depression in the United States, Great Britain and Germany: A Study of Monthly Data 1902-1908.* ("University of Wisconsin Studies in the Social Sciences and History," No. 5.) Madison, Wis., 1921. (Degree, University of Wisconsin.)

Iulo, William. "Inter-company Variations in Electric Utility Unit Costs." Unpublished doctoral dissertation, Department of Economics, University of Wisconsin, 1957. (Degree, University of Wisconsin.)

Johnston, Henry W., Jr. *Philosophy and Argument.* State College: The Pennsylvania State University Press, 1959. (Degree, Harvard University.)

Knight, Frank H. *Risk, Uncertainty and Profit.* Boston: Houghton Mifflin Company, 1921. (Degree, Cornell University.)

Knorr, Klaus E. *British Colonial Theories, 1570-1850.* Toronto; University of Toronto Press, 1944. (Degree, University of Chicago.)

Mantoux, Paul Joseph. *The Industrial Revolution in the Eighteenth Century: An Outline of the Beginnings of the Modern Factory System in England.* New York: Harcourt, Brace & World, 1927. (Degree, University of Paris.)

Martin, David Dale. *Mergers and the Clayton Act.* Berkeley and Los Angeles: The University of California Press, 1959. (Degree, University of California at Los Angeles.)

O'Connor, William Van. *Sense and Sensibility in Modern Poetry.*

Chicago: University of Chicago Press, 1949. (Degree, Columbia University.)

Oleson, Tryggvi J. *The Witenagemot in the Reign of Edward the Confessor.* Oxford: The University Press, 1955. (Degree, University of Toronto, Ontario, Can.)

Petegorsky, David W. *Left-Wing Democracy in the English Civil War: A Study of the Social Philosophy of Gerrard Winstanley.* London: Victor Gollancz, Ltd., 1940. (Degree, University of London.)

Pope, Liston. *Millhands and Preachers: A Study of Gastonia.* London: H. Milford, Oxford University Press, 1942. (Degree, Yale University.)

Poteat, William Hardman. "Pascal's Conception of Man and Modern Sensibility." Unpublished Doctor's Essay, Graduate School of Arts and Sciences, Duke University, 1950. (Degree, Duke University.)

Ray, Delmas D. *Accounting and Business Fluctuations.* Gainesville, Fla.: University of Florida Press, 1960. (Degree, University of Florida.)

Robertson, D. B. *The Religious Foundations of Leveller Democracy.* New York: King's Crown Press, Columbia University, 1951. (Degree, Columbia University.)

de Roover, Raymond. *Money, Banking and Credit in Medieval Bruges.* Cambridge, Mass.: The Medieval Society of America, 1948. Published in "greatly revised form." (Degree, University of Chicago.)

Salter, L. A. *A Critical Review of Research in Land Economics.* Minneapolis: University of Minnesota Press, 1948. (Degree, University of Minnesota.)

Saulnier, Raymond J. *Contemporary Monetary Theory.* New York: Columbia University Press, 1938. (Degree, Columbia University.)

Schoeffler, Sidney. *The Failures of Economics: A Diagnostic Study.* Cambridge: Harvard University Press, 1955. (Degree, New School for Social Research.)

Sievers, Allen Morris. *Has Market Capitalism Collapsed? A Critique of Karl Polanyi's New Economics.* New York: Columbia University Press, 1949. (Degree, Columbia University.)

Viner, Jacob. *Canada's Balance of International Indebtedness, 1900-1913: An Inductive Study in the Theory of International Trade.*

Cambridge: Harvard University Press, 1924. (Degree, Harvard University.)

Wiener, Norbert. *The Fourier Integral and Certain of Its Applications.* Cambridge, Eng.: The University Press, 1933. (Degree, Harvard University.)

Model Master's Dissertations

Covey, Charles Dean, "Some Considerations Affecting Producer Equality in the Florida Flue-Cured Tobacco Program." Unpublished Master's essay, Department of Agricultural Economics, University of Florida, 1959. (Degree, University of Florida.)

Dewey, Donald J. "Federal Wage Policy in the Classified Civil Service." Unpublished Master's essay, Department of Economics, The State University of Iowa, 1947. (Degree, The State University of Iowa.)

Kraus, C. Norman. *Dispensationalism in America: Its Rise and Development.* Richmond, Va.: John Knox Press, 1958. (Degree, Princeton University.)

Reynolds, Lloyd G. *The British Immigrant: His Social and Economic Adjustment in Canada.* ("McGill Social Research Series," No. 2.) Toronto: Oxford University Press, 1935). (Degree, McGill University.)

Prize Winning Dissertations

A readily accessible source of model doctoral dissertations has been provided by the Ford Foundation which has announced publication by Prentice-Hall, Inc., of award-winning dissertations in its annual Doctoral Dissertation Competition. Information about these competitions may be obtained from the Ford Foundation, Program in Economic Development and Administration, 477 Madison Ave., New York 22.

Twenty prize-winning dissertations in the fields of business administration and in the social sciences and other fields relevant to the study of business problems are in print. They are available to students, teachers, and educational libraries at $1.00 per volume prepaid on mention of academic affiliation. They are available to the general public at $4.50 per volume. Available titles are:

1961-1962 Award Winners:

Alexander Barges, *The Effect of Capital Structure on the Cost of Capital*

Charles P. Bonini, *Simulation of Information and Decision Systems in the Firm*

James M. Ferguson, *The Advertising Structure in the Daily Newspaper Industry*

Gordon M. Kaufman, *Statistical Decision and Related Techniques in Oil and Gas Exploration*

H. Martin Weingartner, *Mathematical Programming and the Analysis of Capital Budgeting Problems*

1960-1961 Award Winners:

Geoffrey P. E. Clarkson, *Portfolio Selection: A Simulation of Trust Investment*

George William Summers, *Financing and Initial Operations of New Firms*

Donald E. Farrar, *The Investment Decision Under Uncertainty: Portfolio Selection*

Richard S. Hatch, *An Evaluation of a Forced-Choice Differential Accuracy Approach to the Measurement of Supervisory Empathy*

David Meiselman, *The Term Structure of Interest Rates*

1959-1960 Award Winners:

Leon V. Hirsch, *Marketing in an Underdeveloped Economy: The North Indian Sugar Industry*

Fred M. Tonge, *A Heuristic Program for Assembly Line Balancing*

Bernard H. Baum, *Decentralization of Authority in a Bureaucracy*

Bedros Peter Pashigian, *The Distribution of Automobiles, An Economic Analysis of the Franchise System*

Martin Patchen, *The Choice of Wage Comparisons*

1958-1959 Award Winners:

Kalman J. Cohen, *Computer Models of the Shoe, Leather, Hide Sequence*

Bob R. Holdren, *The Structure of a Retail Market and the Market Behavior of Retail Units*

Frank Proschan, *Polya-Type Distributions in Renewal Theory, With an Application to an Inventory Problem*

Andrew C. Stedry, *Budget Control and Cost Behavior*

Victor H. Vroom, *Some Personality Determinants of the Effects of Participation*

Model Thesis Prospectuses

Leonard P. Ayres, *Turning
Points in Business Cycles*[1]

Business cycles result from the fact that all industrial nations
produce their durable goods in waves or surges of output instead of
manufacturing them in steady flows varying little in volume from
month to month and year to year. By contrast they manufacture
their nondurable goods . . . in comparatively steady volumes of
production. . . .

Durable goods . . . are long-lasting goods, and the ones we
have can almost always be made to do service for a few additional
years if that seems desirable. In fact we do postpone replacing them
in all the depression periods, and we busily renew and increase them
in times of prosperity. . . .

This book is the account of a study undertaken in the attempt
to find out why the expanding production of durable goods turns
downward at the top of prosperity and begins to contract, and why
it stops shrinking at the bottom of depression and turns upward
and begins to expand once more. Clearly these turning points result
from decisive changes in the amounts of money being spent for the
purchase of durable goods. . . . The changes in volumes of purchasing of durable goods are largely changes made by business enterprises, but why are they made, and are they made from choice or
necessity? . . . .

An important part of the present study is the extension back-

[1] New York: The Macmillan Company, 1939, preface. Reprinted by permission.

244

ward over many decades of a series of data reflecting changes in the volume of purchases of new corporate securities by investors. . . .

These new data make it possible to show that there has been in this country during the past 75 years a long series of wide, wave-like, fluctuations in the volume of new funds going into business enterprises from the subscriptions of investors buying new issues of corporate securities. . . .

With almost complete regularity during the long period studied, the downturns of the security prices at the tops of bull markets, and their upturns from the bottoms of bear markets, have followed upturns and downturns in the levels of short-term interest rates. . . .

Throughout this book the evidence has supported the central thesis that turning points in business cycles normally result from changes in the volumes of inflows of new funds into business enterprises. In most cases these changes are internally generated by the interactions between and among the reserve ratios of banks, the levels of interest rates, the trends of security prices, and the alternating expansions and contractions in the volume of new security issues. This means that our business cycles have generally been caused by operations of our banking laws and regulations, our business procedures, and the processes of our security markets.

Sometimes the forces that have brought about the turning points in business cycles have been externally generated by such developments as the outbreaks or the conclusions of wars, or by business developments in other countries. Nevertheless, an analysis of the evidence over the long period under review leads definitely to the conclusion that turning points in business cycles, whether resulting from forces internally generated or from external forces, are brought about in almost all cases by increases or decreases of the inflows of new money into business enterprises.

Data are available in the business cycles of the past 40 years for studies of the changes in the volumes of production of non-durable or consumers goods. They show that in almost all the cases the upturns and downturns of the volumes of new security issues in the business cycles came before those in the production of consumers goods. The finding is important because it shows that the consumer purchasing power theories of business cycles cannot be valid explanations. Those theories underlie the policies of pump-priming, and of bonuses for veterans and for farmers in so far as those payments have been made as parts of the recovery program.

The same theories are parts of the philosophies of such schemes as the Townsend Plan. . . .[2]

Peter B. Kenen, *British Monetary Policy and the Balance of Payments 1951-1957.*[3]

This essay began as a study of the United Kingdom's balance-of-payments difficulties in 1945-1955. But it soon came to focus on the government's attitude and response to the balance-of-payments crisis, rather than the causes and implications of the adverse external position. I have tried to survey Britain's domestic economic policies, especially her monetary policies, in the light of her balance-of-payments position.

I contend that Britain's attempts to maintain external balance have worked a revolution in Bank of England policy. In the nineteenth and early twentieth centuries, the Bank guarded Britain's gold reserves by manipulating short-term interest rates to vary net British overseas investment. In the 1950's the foreign-exchange position was still of primary concern, but the ways of controlling it had necessarily changed. Stabilization policies had to regulate the balance of payments on current account, not the rate of international investment, to preserve the value of sterling. They had to operate upon the level of domestic spending by affecting the volume and price of credit available to British business rather than upon conditions in the discount market.

This essay appraises the Bank's recent efforts to control the supply of credit. I conclude, somewhat reluctantly, that its orthodox monetary policies played a relatively small part in the redress of payments disequilibrium, that the most effective weapons in the government's arsenal were the most heterodox. Increased purchase

---

[2] While this book was written a decade and a half after publication by Wesley C. Mitchell of his *Business Cycles and Employment* (New York: National Bureau of Economic Research, 1923), for the advantage of today's graduate student and in fairness to Mr. Ayres it should be pointed out that he wrote before the so-called Keynesian Revolution had taken place and before National Income Accounting had become established.

[3] Cambridge: Harvard University Press, 1960, preface. Reprinted by permission.

taxes and selective credit controls did more to correct the balance of payments in 1956 than did the attack upon the credit base.

Toward the end of this study, I propose ways in which the Bank of England can better control the credit base. I reject the common prescription—that the Bank should sell long-term securities to fund the floating debt—because this remedy is inconsistent with the Bank's collateral responsibilities in the capital markets.

Model Dissertational Prospectuses

J. B. Black, *The Art of History: A Study of Four Great Historians of the Eighteenth Century*[1]

This book does not profess to be a discussion of eighteenth century historiography in general; its object is specific, viz., to examine sympathetically and critically, the ideas entertained by Voltaire, Hume, Robertson, and Gibbon, with respect to the theory and practice of the historical art. At the same time, an attempt has been made in the *Introduction* to throw into relief the chief differences between the ideals of this literary-philosophical school and those which prevail among historians today; and perhaps a word is necessary concerning the standpoint from which the argument has been conducted. The assumption on which it rests, and indeed the motive behind the entire essay, is that the intimate union between literature, philosophy, and history, so amply demonstrated in the writings of Voltaire and his "school," is not merely an ideal of the eighteenth century but one which bears validity for all time. Or, more explicitly, history devoid of philosophic and literary interest, which concerns itself only with the establishment of the fact, however scientifically handled, has always seemed to the writer to be blind of an eye and lame of gait: a study, in short, of contracting horizons and diminishing cultural value. In the eighteenth century, history was written, not only by "scientists" but by humanists, who brought to it the fruits of ripe wisdom; and it would not be an exaggeration to say that under their aegis it became a

---

[1] New York: F. S. Crofts & Co., 1926, preface. Reprinted by permission.

complete and satisfying culture in itself. Is it permissible to believe that when the humanist has come into his own once more we shall see the subject, freed from excessive subserviency to "science," rise again to the commanding position it held in the days of Voltaire and Gibbon—the indispensable passport of every educated person, and a social force of first magnitude? Such, at any rate, is the belief underlying the following studies.

Lionel Robbins, *An Essay on the Nature and Significance of Economic Science*[2]

The purpose of this essay is twofold. In the first place, it seeks to arrive at precise notions concerning the subject-matter of Economic Science and the nature of the generalizations of which Economic Science consists. Secondly it attempts to explain the limitations and the significance of these generalizations, both as a guide to the interpretation of reality and as a basis for political practice. At the present day, as a result of the theoretical developments of the last sixty years, there is no longer any ground for serious differences of opinion on these matters, once the issues are clearly stated. Yet, for lack of such statement, confusion still persists in many quarters, and false ideas are prevalent with regard to the preoccupations of the economist and the nature and the extent of his competence. As a result, the reputation of economics suffers, and full advantage is not taken of the knowledge it confers. This essay is an attempt to remedy this deficiency—to make clear what it is that economists discuss and what may legitimately be expected as a result of their discussions. Thus on the one hand it may be regarded as a commentary on the methods and assumptions of pure theory: on the other hand, as a series of prolegomena to work in Applied Economics.

The object of the essay necessitates the taking of broad views. But my aim throughout has been to keep as close to earth as possible. I have eschewed philosophical refinements as falling outside the province in which I have any claim to professional competence; and I have based my propositions on the actual practice of the best

---

[2] 2d ed., revised and extended. London: Macmillan and Co., Ltd., 1949, preface to the first ed. Reprinted by permission.

modern works on the subject. In a study of this sort, written by an
economist for fellow-economists, it seemed better to try to drive home
the argument by continual reference to accepted solutions of particular problems, than to elaborate, out of the void, a theory of what
Economics should become. At the same time, I have tried to be brief.
My object has been to suggest a point of view rather than to treat
the subject in all its details. To do this it seemed desirable to be
concise even at the expense of sacrificing much material which I had
originally collected. I hope, however, at a later stage to publish a work
on general Economic Theory in which the principles here laid down
are further illustrated and amplified.

For the views which I have advanced, I make no claim whatever
to originality. I venture to hope that in one or two instances I have
succeeded in giving expository force to certain principles not always
clearly stated. But, in the main, my object has been to state, as simply
as I could, propositions which are the common property of most
modern economists.

Daniel J. Boorstin, *The Mysterious Science of the Law*[3]

This book is addressed to the lawyer, to the student of history,
and to people generally concerned with the problem of method in
the social sciences. For the lawyer, it is designed to suggest how he,
in common with the rest of the community, employs the ideas and
assumptions of his day about the whole of human experience; for
the student of history it is meant to give evidence that the lawyer's
work, whether or not the lawyer is aware of it, is in the main stream
of the history of thought; for the student of method in the social
sciences, it is meant to contribute to an understanding of the place
of reason and rationalization in the study of institutions. For all these
readers this book attempts to indicate how the ostensibly impartial
processes of reason are employed by the student of society to support
whatever social values he accepts.

I have taken as a microcosm for this problem a classic—perhaps
the most important single book—in the history of the common law.

---

[3] Cambridge: Harvard University Press, 1941, preface. Reprinted by permission.

By making a detailed study of Sir William Blackstone's *Commentar-ies on the Laws of England,* I have approached the general problem of the function of reason which faces the student of institutions in every age. For this work employed the assumptions prevalent in its day about science, religion, philosophy, history, art, and reason, to give the legal system and the values embodied in it an appearance of rationality and acceptability. Because a principal task of the lawyer in all periods is to find a rationale for institutions, the study of the law provides a convenient laboratory in which to study the use of reason in the explanation of social phenomena.

To deal adequately with the process of rationalization of any age one should, of course, have an encyclopaedic knowledge of the life and thought of that age. Lacking that knowledge, I have thought it better to attempt this task with the materials at my command, and with the expectation of just criticism from learned specialists, than to impose an inappropriate and perhaps misleading limitation on the problem I am considering. In several of the following chapters, there-fore, I hope that the relationships I have pointed out between legal thought and thought about things other than the law, and my description of the use of these ideas in the process of rationalization, will be suggestive rather than simply expository. I have hoped at least to suggest the all-inclusiveness of the intellectual vocabulary of the lawyer, the implications of his uses of these ideas, and something of the intricacy of the workings of the human mind in turning logic to its moral purposes.

Norman Foerster, *Toward Stand-ards: A Study of the Present Critical Movement in American Letters*[4]

Now in criticism there are, broadly speaking, three possible points of view. . . . the personal estimate, the historical estimate, and the real estimate. . . .

It happens that today [1930] all of these estimates are prominent. The personal estimate is that of the impressionists. . . . The his-

---

[4] New York: Farrar & Rinehart, 1930, preface, pp. xi-xiii. Reprinted by permission.

torical estimate is that of the historians of literature. . . . The real estimate is that of their chief opponents, the humanists. . . . Whereas the criterion of the impressionists is relative to the individual creator or critic, and that of the historians is relative to the age and nation, the criterion of the humanists is relative to nothing less than mankind.

The object of this book is to outline the claims set forth by these three groups of critics and thus to throw some light upon the conflicts in which they are engaged. I have tried to find the fundamental issues. I have tried to invite deliberation rather than prejudice. I have tried to assist the reader to take a stand based on conviction.

Writing Style and
Style-Sheet Conventions

Writers of theses and dissertations are instructed by their respective graduate schools to comply with certain directives as to the form, layout, mechanics of typographical conventions, paper, and binding of their essays. Such directives are found in graduate school catalogues, but they are spelled out in handbooks for student guidance. Schools which have their own style manuals require compliance with them. Others require compliance with some designated manual in print. A selected list of these is furnished below.

Style is both a technical and an art term. In the latter sense, it is a way of writing, of expressing ideas. Candidates may be closely directed as to the physical and mechanical aspects of style-sheet conventions, but they receive little realistic instruction in writing as such. Graduate schools tend to begin by assuming that graduate students can write and that their supervisors can judge writing, and end by insisting that grammar and spelling be correct and that "the essay must be of publishable quality." This designates a performance standard and implies certain evaluative criteria. However, it provides no instruction in how essays should be written.

The dichotomy of style as art of expression and as technique of presentation provides a basis for an exhibition of guides to writing and mechanics in separate categories. Between them there is a linking category of guides to research procedures and writing preparation. Before listing these, a statement about writing style is in order.

The thesis and dissertational essays, like the shorter scholarly essays, were presented as products of the reasoning power of the mind. They are based on achievements in brainwork as outcomes of scholarly and scientific investigations. Their tone is more or less formal, their structure and organization are logical, and their writing should be crisp and sure. This does not mean that it should be dull. Precise writing can be lively writing. A sprightly style is a worthy achievement which can be attained through practice in writing term essays. Such style requires the full and firm control of substance which gives the deceptive appearance of ease.

To become a successful essayist, one may begin by learning about the essay as a literary form and about its discoursory style. This can be done by reading such books as R. D. O'Leary's *The Essay*, Benjamin A. Heydrick's *The Types of the Essay*, and Edward S. Noyes' *Readings in the Modern Essay*. The works of such skilled essayists as Emerson and Howard Mumford Jones then might be read. Other excellent examples on a wide range of subjects will be found in the volumes of the *World Perspectives* series, published by Harper and Row, and in the "Adventures of the Mind" series of *The Saturday Evening Post*. Good examples also appear in the learned journals of every field.

Skill as an essayist can enable candidates for graduate degrees to use their specialized knowledge flexibly and imaginatively. As intellectual exercises in argument, essays communicate and substantiate intellectual accomplishments in inquiry. On this point Jacques Barzun declares: "A chief virtue of an intellectual work is its articulate precision in the establishment and substantiation of an arguable view." Such skillful expression requires competence in substance and method. It also needs the enhancement of good writing style. This is a matter of practice in the elements of style once they have been learned. A short list of guides to effective writing follows.

Guides to Effective Writing

William Strunk, Jr. and E. B. White, *The Elements of Style* (New York: The Macmillan Company, 1959).

Stuart Chase, *The Tyranny of Words* (New York: Harcourt, Brace & World, 1938).

Henry Watson Fowler, *A Dictionary of Modern English Usage* (London: Oxford University Press, 1950).

Glenn Legett, C. David Mead, and William Charvat, *Handbook for*

Writers (3rd ed.; Englewood Cliffs, N. J.: Prentice-Hall, Inc., 1960).

Eric Partridge, *The Concise Usage and Abusage* (New York: Philosophical Library, 1954).

Eric Partridge, *Adventuring Among Words* (New York: Oxford University Press, 1961).

Arthur H. Cole and Karl W. Bigelow, A *Manual of Thesis Writing for Graduates and Undergraduates* (New York: John Wiley & Sons, 1960).

Allan Nevins, *Master's Essays in History: A Manual of Instruction and Suggestion* (New York: Columbia University Press, 1933). Out of print.

Theodore Menline Bernstein, *Watch Your Language:* A lively informal guide to better writing, emanating from the News Room of the *New York Times* (Great Neck, L. I.: Channel Press, 1958).

Daniel Fogarty, S. J., *Roots for a New Rhetoric* (New York: Bureau of Publications, Teachers College, Columbia University, 1959).

Guides to Research and Writing

John Foster, Jr., *Science Writer's Guide* (New York: Columbia University Press, 1963).

Robert R. Rathbone and James B. Stone, A *Writer's Guide for Engineers and Scientists* (Englewood Cliffs, N. J.: Prentice-Hall, Inc., 1962).

Robert Ferber and P. J. Verdoorn, *Research Methods in Economics and Business* (New York: The Macmillan Company, 1962).

Walter J. Gensler and Kenereth D. Gensler, *Writing Guide for Chemists* (New York: McGraw-Hill Book Co., Inc., 1961).

Donald F. Bond, compiler, A *Reference Guide to English Studies* (Chicago: The University of Chicago Press, 1951).

Griffith Thompson Pugh, *Guide to Research Writing* (Boston: Houghton Mifflin Co., 1955).

Donald H. Menzel, Howard Mumford Jones, and Lyle A. Boyd, *Writing A Technical Paper* (New York: McGraw-Hill Book Co., Inc., 1961).

Fritz Machlup, *The Production and Distribution of Knowledge in the United States* (Princeton, N. J.: Princeton University Press, 1962).

Clarence Gohdes, *Bibliographical Guide to the Study of the Literature of the U. S. A.* (2nd. ed., rev. & enl.; Durham, N. C.: Duke
University Press, 1963). Esp. chap. i-vii, pp. 1-18.

Guides to Form and Style Conventions

William Riley Parker, compiler, *The MLA Style Sheet* (rev. ed.;
New York: The Modern Language Association, 1962).
Kate L. Turabian, *A Manual for Writers of Term Papers, Theses and
Dissertations* (Chicago: The University of Chicago Press, 1962).
Marjorie E. Skillin, *Words Into Type, A Guide in the Preparation of
Manuscripts* (New York: Appleton-Century-Crofts, 1948).
Lucyle Hook and Mary Virginia Gaver, *The Research Paper* (3rd ed.;
Englewood Cliffs, N.J.: Prentice-Hall, Inc., 1962).

Style-sheet conventions provide acceptable ways of handling
certain forms of expression and details of format and typography.
From a technical point of view, three propositions need to be taken
into account: (1) There is a considerable, often confusing, diversity
of style conventions; (2) a great many problems of style cannot be
reduced to rules even if a uniform convention and style could be
agreed upon; and (3) the single absolute style rule is that writers
must be consistent in whatever practice they adopt. The basic question to be decided is that of relevancy and appropriateness. If school
or assigned style manuals do not cover certain problems of expression,
it remains for the writing candidate and his supervisory committee
to reach agreement in these respects. Besides appropriateness and
relevancy, the rule to follow in matters not covered in a style sheet
is that of fitness. If the candidate and his committee cannot reach
agreement by eradicating doubt as to fitness, it is appropriate for the
candidate to secure a graduate school ruling on the matter.

The principal style-sheet conventions have been brought together
in several good manuals. Each of these differs somewhat from the
others, but the better ones do excellent jobs of collecting and collating
the principal conventions of scholarly writing into consistent, coherent style systems. If a student cannot find what he needs in one,
he may in another. Study of these manuals can be concurrent with
study of writing style and its practice in term essays. Good writing
style and a good style sheet are marks of scholarly maturity and
competence.

Index

A

AAUP Committee on Requirements for the Ph.D. Degree, 166-67

Academe:
admissions in upper, middle, and lower, compared, 142
lower, 132, 135n
middle, 132 (*See also* Middle academe)
graduate councils of, 137
quality ranking of, 132-36
and growth, 133-34
and student quality, 134-35, 144-45, 145n
upper, 132 (*See also* Upper academe)
upper and middle, differentiated, 136

Achievement, original intellectual, 4

Achievement, intellectual, 108, 108n

Administrative shortcomings, 160, 173, 175

Admissions, 88, 89, 89n, 141-44, 158, 164-65
bases for, 142-45
minimum I.Q. for, 142, 142n
upper, middle, and lower academe compared, 142

Advisor, 73, 74-75, 79, 81, 121, 137n, 145-46, 177

Aiken, Henry D., 24n

Almack, John C., 62-63

Alternatives to essay, 6, 7, 13-14, 23n, 26n, 75, 150, 159, 161, 161n, 182-83

Ambiguity of terms, 7-8

Anderson, H. H., 101

Approach to given idea, thesis v. dissertation, 36-37

Archimedes, 27n

Argumentation, 28, 38, 69-70, 72, 100 (*See also* Validation)

Aristotle, 47n

Arnold, John, 48n

Art form in lieu of essay, 6, 7, 13-14, 150, 161, 161n, 182-83

Assignment of topics, 74-75, 75n, 163-64

Association of Graduate Schools, 90n, 126-28, 181

Assumptions, 32, 32n (*See also* Premises)

Attitude of graduate student, 118

Atwood, Sanford S., 88, 90n, 104n

B

Barzun, Jacques, 25n, 52n, 57, 59, 126n, 139, 179n

Beach, Leonard B., 95n

Bent, Henry E., 89

Berelson, Bernard, 103, 103n, 127n, 132n, 133n, 134n, 135n, 137n, 138n, 150n, 169n, 178n

Bibliographies:
graduate education, 118n, 119, 119n
methodologies of particular fields, 59
scientific investigation, 58-59

Bibliography in lieu of essay, 61

Bigelow, Karl W., 20, 20n, 64, 64n, 90-91, 91n, 161n

Birkhoff, George David, 39, 105n